In Memory of SOCS Ty Woods (ret.)
(KIA 11 September 2012 in Benghazi, Libya),
who told me the secret to BUD/S:

"Just get the fuck after it, don't be a pussy, and you'll be fine."

Breaking BUD/S: How Regular Guys Can Become Navy
SEALs
by Mark Owens and DH Xavier

Chapter 1

An Introduction to BUD/S.

"Well it ain't no chainsaw-bearing clown, so what do I got to fear?"

- The Lost Trailers

Eating The Elephant.

How do you eat an elephant? Elephants are huge. Your mouth - despite what your high school teachers said - is small. You eat it one bite at a time.

You want to be a Navy SEAL, we call ourselves Team Guys. You want to be paid to jump out of airplanes in the middle of the night, to sneak behind enemy lines and snatch bad guys out of their beds, to be elite and be silent and be deadly. You want to test yourself against one of the hardest selection and training programs in the world and prove to yourself there's nothing you cannot do.

This is no small order, as you likely know. It takes a special level of dedication and focus to make it, but it isn't impossible. If you can pass the basic SEAL Challenge physical requirements, you can physically become a SEAL.

SEAL Challenge Requirements:
500 yd. swim (breast stroke or CSS): 12:30
10 minute rest
Pushups (2min): 42
Situps (2min): 50
Pullups (unlimited time): 6
10 minute rest

1.5 mi. Run: 11:00

If you can meet or beat these scores, you have what it takes to be a Team Guy. Let that sink in. Better scores indicating better fitness might make it easier on you mentally, but if you can meet or beat these scores, you have everything you need to become one of the world's elite Special Operations Forces (SOF). You don't need to have an XBOX or Playstation to get your action fix: you can get it at work every day.

There should be an alarm going off in your head right now telling you something's wrong here. If that's all there is to it, then why do so few make it? Why do so many dedicated men fail to become Team Guys, despite their "burning desires" or "extreme dedication?" Why do thousands of men give up on their "dream" every year?

They're not eating that elephant one bite at a time.

Unlike every other book about Basic Underwater Demolition/ SEAL Training (BUD/S) in general, this book is going to show you how thousands of normal guys before you have successfully navigated BUD/S and gone on to become Navy SEALs. By the time you finish this book, you will be more prepared for BUD/S than any other candidate out there. You'll know the best way to keep up on soft-sand runs, you'll know the best techniques for Log PT, you'll know what to focus on during Pool Comp, and you'll be better prepared for Hell Week.

You'll have the best set of tools possible to complete BUD/S. This won't make it easy by any means and the book won't do it for you. There are no cheat codes at BUD/S - you still have to do everything yourself. You might still Drop On Request (DOR) and quit. But knowledge is a weapon, and if you know what to expect and how people have done things before, you have a psychological edge and will be able to keep your head in the game.

And it IS a game. BUD/S is a long, terrible, miserable game that you won't want to play most of the time. But if you want to be a SEAL, you'll play the game to the end. And at the end you get your Trident. I'll show you how.

Why a SEAL?

Pudgy, Cheetoe-eating, window-licking 12-year-old videogamers and Airsoft commandos cloud the internet with claims of what Special Operations (SpecOps) forces are the best/ most elite. Watch a video on YouTube about any SpecOps force and a dozen wannabes will post comments below claiming that SEALs are better than the Rangers, which are better than PJs, which are more elite than SWCC, who aren't fit to wipe their asses with Green Berets, who are better than everyone except Marine Force Recon, who all wish they were SAS. Those conversations make every single operator gag and want to kill people. Those conversations are absurd and only take place among people who don't know a thing about the subject. In fact, if I find out you take part in one of those online flame-wars after reading this book, I will come to your house in the middle of the night and kill you. I'm kidding. I think.

So here's the requisite discussion of differing mission sets, responsibilities, etc. The goal here is not only to set the record straight, but also to make sure you're pursuing the right unit to do what you want to do.

SEALs. Navy SEALs (SEa, Air, Land) are commandos with a maritime capability. We call ourselves Team Guys. The basic mission sets of the SEAL Teams are Direct Action (DA) and Special Reconnaissance (SR). DAs are target assaults, like the one that killed Osama bin Laden, with the ultimate goal to capture or kill targeted personnel. SRs vary in length, but involve getting eyes on an unwitting target in order to gather intel, designate targets for air assets, or take a sniper shot. If you want a bad guy snatched out of his bed and brought in for interrogation, you call the SEAL Teams.

Navy Special Warfare Combat Crewmen (SWCC). Navy SWCC are small craft specialists. They pilot a number of maritime insertion platforms used by SEALs. While the large number of BUD/S dropouts in the SWCC ranks has inspired the occasional Team Guy to insist SWCC stands for "SEAL Wannabe, Couldn't Cut it," the Special Boat Units are an integral part of the Naval Special Warfare (NSW) squadron and SWCC Operators fulfill a large number of versatile roles in the NSW Community.

Navy Explosive Ordnance Disposal (EOD). Navy EOD techs do a broad array of jobs related to explosives. After completing their own extensive training, some EOD techs are attached to SEAL platoons. They complete the entirety of the platoon's pre-deployment workup alongside the SEALs and use their expertise in IED (Improvised Explosive Device) detection and disarmament to save SEAL operators from booby traps and land mines. Only a small portion of Navy EOD techs are attached to SEAL platoons, but those few are very much considered brothers in arms.

Army Rangers. Army Rangers are a well-trained light infantry unit. They don't do much low-visibility work, but they get a lot of combat. They're not out-of-the box operators, but they're both violent and well-organized.

Army Special Forces (aka "SF" or "Green Berets"). SF guys exist to train indigenous forces to fight in proxy. Their tactical teams are called Operation Detachment Alphas (ODAs). Their speciality is guerilla warfare and counter-insurgency. They are extremely well-suited to being in remote areas without external support. They thrive on austerity and live in the grey.

Marine Force Recon. Force Recon guys are the closest relatives to SEALs under SOCOM. Their training is different in a number of ways, but they're the only other SOF force with universally-amphibious capabilities.

Marine Special Operations Battalion (MSOB). MSOB (often

called MARSOC) guys are the Marine Corps' answer to SF ODAs, but with a universal maritime capability similar to Force Recon guys.

Air Force Combat Control Teams (CCT). CCTs are Air Force Joint Tactical Air Controllers (JTACs). Their specialty is controlling aircraft and munitions. When units drop bombs from jets or launch missiles from helicopters, it's a JTAC who controls the aircraft from the ground. All SEAL platoons have their own organic JTACs. CCTs are spread out over the combat theatre to teams (ODAs, SEAL Platoons, MSOB teams, etc) who need additional JTAC capabilities.

Air Force Pararescue (aka "PJs"). PJs are specialist paramedics. When a helicopter goes down, PJs are part of the recovery package because they are the most practiced medics in all of SOCOM.

Are The Teams For You?

There is a pivotal moment all Team Guys have had: the possibility - the realization that being a SEAL wasn't a fantasy, like being an All-Star baseball player, but a very real option. It's an exciting realization accompanied by a quickening heartbeat. Perhaps you've already had it. Perhaps you're reading this book in search of it.

When I was young my father was in the service and I lived on dozens of Navy and Marine Corps bases. Like most Kindergarten boys, my friends wanted to be commandos, to be Navy SEALs or ninjas. Not me: I wanted to be a neurosurgeon, a veterinarian, or a lawyer. It alternated every few weeks depending on what I was reading or what TV shows I'd been watching. I was very mature and incredibly boring - but I reveled in my realism. I knew none of my friends would grow up to be what they wanted to be; I knew I very well could realize my dreams. Anyone can be a doctor or a lawyer. There aren't really ninjas, at least not professional ones, and almost nobody could be a Navy SEAL. My friends were silly.

I stuck to my realistic rotation of boring jobs (not realizing they were boring) throughout grade school, high school, and the first part of college. I started taking classes that would open the doors to my low-hanging dreams. I took Biology in case I wanted to be a doctor or veterinarian; I studied Philosophy and English in case my destiny lay in a legal career. A funny thing happened though:

as I took steps toward these careers I met countless people who'd given up on their dreams of being ninjas in favor of law school or medicine. They were encroaching on my world of the easily obtained, mediocre, professional life. It was about this time, as I moved closer and closer to these jobs, that I realized I was bored. And I was uninspired. I realized I wasn't pursuing my goals for me anymore. I was just following a plan I'd laid out years before. That's a bad reason to do anything.

Life without inspiration is lonely and boring. So I threw it all out. I threw the bathwater out; the baby went, too.

Square one: if I could do anything, what would I do? What excited me? What would be new every day? What would I do if I didn't have to worry about money? Sitting at a desk in a suit was repulsive to me - what was the complete opposite? What had I automatically written off without even thinking about?

I'm uncoordinated and only passably athletic. I am a "geek" or a "nerd." This cannot be denied. I'd never really been in a fight - though I'd been beat up a few times because of my previously-referenced "nerdiness." I'd also never been camping, hunting, or fishing. I'd never shot a gun or been scuba diving. I didn't know how to sharpen a knife, change the oil in my car, or navigate without a GPS. I had sufficient skills to support myself, but felt trapped by my limited practical skills - when the zombie apocalypse came, I would be completely and utterly fucked. I was an unlikely candidate to become a SEAL.

How could I complete myself as a man while fulfilling my desire to do something extraordinary? It didn't take long for me to stumble on the idea of special operations. If I do something, I do it completely, so I chose the unit with the hardest training, the best missions, and the organizational values that spoke to me. I was drawn to the ideal of the silent professional: the combination of elite capabilities and profound humility pulled strings deep inside me.

I realized the SEAL Teams would be the ideal place to exercise the meticulous attention to detail I learned from my academic undertakings. The Teams would give me a sense of purpose, a fraternity of like-minded perfectionists, and a feeling of honor I couldn't find anywhere else. The process would make me a better, more complete, more confident man than I could ever make myself. And this could be my occupation.

But how realistic was this, really? Video games, movies, and books aside: could I even make it happen? There are very few things that piss me off like self-delusion, so I needed to be sure that:

(1) This was actually what I wanted to do. That I wasn't infatuated with the idea and out of touch with reality.

(2) I could actually be a Navy SEAL. If so few people make it, what made me think I could do what so many could not?

I can tell you the answer to the second question is that you can become a SEAL. I did, and you're probably more qualified than I was. The retired Master Chief SEAL who runs the mentorship program at BUD/S told my class that "lesser men than you have completed this program." Remember that. For those who want it enough, becoming a Team Guy as realistic and obtainable as going to law school or medical school. It's just different.

But nobody can answer the first question for you. Being a SEAL is fantastic option for some people, a terrible option for others. There isn't really any way to know which category you're in without knowledge. You'll find a reading list at the end of this book. Shipping out without having read all the books on the "Required" list is nothing short of negligent; shipping without having read at least some of the "Recommended" books is dumb. If you're serious about becoming a Team Guy, you'll want as much information as you can possibly get your hands on. You'll be skimming forum threads on defunct website forums for a scrap of new information. You'll watch every video on YouTube that even remotely refers to the Teams - probably you'll accidentally watch a lot of SEAL-themed AirSoft or paintball videos made by 12-year-old wankers who haven't yet given up on being ninjas. Pity them because you're taking the first steps to living your dreams (and theirs, too) and their AirSoft video is likely the closest they're ever going to come.

Yes, each book you read is one step closer to being a SEAL. Start here and keep going. The power of action, the momentum of inspiration, these things are on your side already. Develop this mindset now and in a few chapters I'll show you how it will get you through Hell Week and beyond.

In all your reading you'll find that the video games only capture a very few moments of life in the SEAL Teams. They can't capture the suck of a 8-km insert with full kit and 75-lb rucksack. They can't capture the joy of lying perfectly motionless during a sniper stalk, shitting in your pants and being eaten alive by mosquitos and fire ants you can't slap away for fear of detection. They can't come close to communicating the misery of being rained and sleeted on the entirety of a 3-day Special Reconnaissance (SR) mission, of soaking wet socks, of leaking bivy sacks, of having your face so frozen you're incapable of speech.

If you were to take a picture of any of these moments, you would think it was bad ass. And it is, but it's also more miserable than you've ever been in your life. A normal day in our lives would make a grown man cry. We embrace the suck even after BUD/S is over. We go in where people least expect us, in violent weather, through swamps and thorns. None of us enjoy the misery. If you think this sounds like fun, you don't understand what you're getting into. You don't have to like the pain to be a Team Guy, I don't know a single SEAL who wants to wade through a swamp of thorns. You just have to do it.

But it's not all gloom. You'll spend weeks upon weeks doing nothing but shooting. You'll spend a month jumping out of planes. You'll go camping in the mountains of Nevada with top quality gear you didn't pay a dime for. And you'll feel like you're cheating, like you're pulling one over on the system, because you're making money doing things you'd be willing to pay for. Even in the middle of the most painful exercises there are these amazing, focused, vivid, almost transcendent moments where you look up and think "My God, this is the coolest thing I've ever done." These moments of awe are far beyond the cool effects of a video game or the action sequences of a movie; they are well worth the price of admission.

So read and watch everything you can. Understand your undertaking.

Educate yourself.

Know thy enemy.

Then, step back and examine your options. Be painfully honest with yourself about what you're getting into. Do you want the reality or just the fantasy? Don't let the hollywood glamour sway you. Be sure you're ready to commit to the real thing. Acknowledge that the path will be hard and painful. Ask yourself if you're willing to see it through, regardless of how you feel in the moment. If you've been honest with yourself and you still want to be a SEAL, then the rest is easy.

Lock that commitment in your mind and throw away the key. This will separate you from the quitters and those who never even got to BUD/S. You are committed to becoming a SEAL and you are not allowed to re-examine your commitment or desire. This is the difference between men who become SEALs and boys who "went to BUD/S once."

If you quit between this moment and your SQT graduation, you will not have done it because you rationally "realized" you didn't want to be a SEAL. You will have done it because you were weak. You will have done it because you couldn't take it. You will have wasted your time and damaged your honor because you broke this simple rule. You simply cannot make a rational decision that "the program just isn't for me" while you're in it. If reconsidering isn't an option, you won't be able to choose it. Instead, when you inevitably ask yourself "why am I even doing this?" you'll have no choice but to answer, "because this is what I'm doing right now." It seems simple, but if you allow yourself to re-examine your commitment, you will quit. Guaranteed.

So, don't quit.

If you get your Trident and don't want to be a SEAL, you can quit then. Not before.

The Pipeline: A 30,000-foot View.

Before we get into specific evolutions, phases, tips, and the real reason you bought this book, we need to make sure everyone's on the same page. If you've read every book on SEAL training this will be mostly review, but there's valuable information here that isn't specifically covered in other books.

Training is a long process, taking anywhere from a year to 18 months to complete (not taking into account any extra-BUD/S you earn yourself by getting rolled).

First, you've got to prepare yourself physically, mentally, and administratively to join the Navy.

For guys who are enlisting, this process often starts by joining the DEP (Delayed-Entry Program), where you have the opportunity to work with a local SEAL/SWCC Mentor. Your Mentor should be able to provide workouts and facilitate the SEAL PST (Physical Screening Test) that will ultimately qualify you for the SEAL Challenge Program and guarantee you a shot at BUD/S after Boot Camp. There is also an academic test (the ASVAB) to take, a great deal of paperwork to be filled out (to sign away your life), and a fun day of medical exams.

For those who would prefer to become a SEAL Officer immediately, this process is exponentially harder. Officers come from one of three commissioning sources: the US Naval Academy (USNA), ROTC (Reserve Officer Training Corps), or OCS (Officer

Candidate School). We'll delve more deeply into this ultra-competetive process a bit later.

Next is boot camp if you've enlisted, OCS if you're going to be an Officer. Boot camp is run at Great Lakes, IL, is 7(?) weeks long, miserable, and largely pointless. OCS takes place in Newport, RI, is 12 weeks long, miserable, and largely pointless. You will not enjoy a moment of either one.

After completing OCS, freshly-minted Ensigns travel to Coronado to check into PTRR (Physical Training, Rest, and Rehabilitation) at BUD/S. They're put in a holding class with pre-Hell-Week rollbacks ("white shirt rollbacks") to learn the basics of BUD/S. Soft sand runs, O-Course, underwater knot-tying practice, bay swims: this is their life until it's time to class up. Depending on when they show up and how many other Officers are waiting to class up, a new arrival might expect to spend between 2 and 14 months waiting his turn to join a class.

Enlisted men come straight to Pre-BUD/S from boot camp; Officers arrive at Pre-BUD/S a few weeks prior to classing up in order to meet the class, organize, and prepare the class for the culture shock coming from the friendly, supportive nature of Pre-BUD/S to the hostile, violent moshpit that is BUD/S.

Then comes BUD/S (Basic Underwater Demolition / SEAL training), the main event, and the focus of this book. The class flies from Great Lakes to Coronado, CA to begin BUD/S. BUD/S Orientation (BO) is a 3-week crash-course in BUD/S protocols: from the proper way to drop for pushups to the location of the chow hall to obstacle course techniques. Next comes First Phase, a 7-week "conditioning phase" whose signature evolution is the famous 5 ½ day ordeal known as Hell Week. After a small portion of the initial class finishes First Phase, they replace their green helmets for blue and begin Second Phase: Dive Phase. During Second Phase, you will become a proficient combat diver, starting in the pool with an open circuit familiarization dive and, on completion of Pool Comp (biggest hurdle in BUD/S after Hell Week), you will graduate to the Draeger LAR-V closed-circuit Oxygen rebreather - the Navy SEALs' combat diving rig of choice. You will learn to navigate underwater and hit a target undetected. After successfully completing Second Phase, you will put on the red helmet that denotes a Third Phase BUD/S class and begin learning the trade of land warfare. The first weeks of Third Phase are among the most pleasant in BUD/S: you will learn land navigation in a classroom environment and then travel to the Laguna Mountain Recreation Area just East of San Diego to hone your skills while finding blue posts in the middle of the hills, pastures, and woods. Next, you'll trade the peace of Laguna for the misery, cold, and isolation of San Clemente Island: "The Rock." Here it's just you and the Instructors. You'll learn pistol and rifle marksmanship, basic demolition, IADs (Immediate Action Drills), basic mission planning, patrolling, and to appreciate how much better life was back on the mainland. When (if) you return from the Island, you will stand on the grinder with your class, all in your cammies, and graduate BUD/S. There will be no fanfare or crowds - that comes when you finish SQT. There will be a moment for every student, immediately after graduating, of relief to know that you no longer need to run everywhere you go every day, that Instructors will speak to you like men, that you won't be dropped down again, and that you've completed the selection phase of the country's toughest military training course.

After BUD/S Officers are separated from their BUD/S class to attend JOTC (Junior Officer's Training Course); they are replaced by the Officers from the previous class who've just finished JOTC. At JOTC the Officers will delve more deeply into mission planning, leadership, and the current state of affairs overseas. The course culminates with a draining FTX (Final Training Exercise) week at Camp Moreno. The week is grueling (some students call it FTX Hell Week), but undeniably valuable - graduates of JOTC join their SQT class ready to lead.

Next is SQT (SEAL Qualification Training), where you'll learn the tools of your trade. In SQT you will learn CQC (Close-Quarters Combat), more advanced Land Warfare techniques, advanced combat diving skills, MAROPS (Maritime Operations) on Zodiac inflatable boats, cold weather combat and OTB (Over The Beach) techniques in Kodiak, AK), and a multitude of other skills required to become a SEAL. SQT will prepare you to join, and immediately contribute to, an operational SEAL platoon.

After SQT comes graduation day; you get your Trident - referred to as your "bird" within the Teams. Your family and friends watch and applaud as you join the ranks of the country's elite special operations unit. You did it: you're a Team Guy, a US Navy SEAL.

Then it's "Welcome to the Teams." It's your first platoon and you're a new guy and it's time to earn that bird every day.

A Common Vocabulary.

There is a language at BUD/S that you don't necessarily know yet. You probably know some of this information already. If you've been a good boy and you've already read other books, a lot of this should be a review. Regardless, these are the basic terms and concepts we'll be dealing with throughout this book, so we're going to establish some baselines here.

SEALs. We don't usually call ourselves SEALs unless the person we're talking to doesn't know the terms we prefer.

We call ourselves Team Guys because the Team is, without a doubt, the most important part of who we are. We go to bars as Teams. We occasionally hot-extract from that same bar as a Team. I don't condone bar-fighting, but it's a comfort to know that you're drinking with a dozen guys who will all go from jolly chipmunk to rabid wolverine in 0.3 seconds if someone outside the platoon talks to you wrong. The Teams are an unapologetic, hyper-aggressive brotherhood. We've got each others' backs. This is, far and away, the best part of being a Team Guy, which is why we most often refer to ourselves as such.

We call ourselves Frogmen in deference to the generations of Scouts and Raiders, Naval Combat Demolition Units (NCDUs), and Underwater Demolition Teams (UDTs) that paved the way for us. Some of these men went to war with nothing but a pair of canvas shorts, a haversack of C-4, a knife, and some huge balls. They were called the "Naked Warriors" with good cause. These men, our forefathers, did everything with nothing. We constantly strive to do their memories justice.

Today we have nearly every high-speed piece of kit we can think of. We're spoiled. But if you ask a Frogman, he'll tell you that all the 'Gucci' gear in the world doesn't make a Frogman. Fancy kit might make you a little more comfortable, but it won't make you elite. There's a reason you start shooting rifles with iron sights. There's a reason you swim with UDT shorts. There's a reason you learn to paddle a boat before you get a Zodiac with a motor. There's a reason you learn to swim long distance underwater before you touch a SCUBA rig. The Frogman is the real weapon. Strip him naked and drop him a mile offshore - he'll find a way to complete your mission. This is the attitude we carry the rest of our lives and a key to our successes throughout history.

A derivative phrase is that you're "feeling froggy," meaning you're feeling dumb and slightly masochistic and want to do something the old-school frogmen would approve of. For example (and you should never, ever, ever do this because it's stupid), when my class graduated BUD/S we had a party at a house with a pool. We filled a CamelBak reservoir with vodka and weighted it to the bottom of the pool. The idea was that the Camelbak had to be attended at all times by a drinker. You couldn't come up until you were relieved by another diver. This should not ever be done. Ever. It was incredibly stupid. It was also incredibly froggy. Still, you should never do this. Seriously.

We're Frogmen and we're Team Guys. We're SEALs only in reference to those who don't know what we're really like.

Enlisted. The majority of Team Guys are enlisted men. Junior enlisted are the "sled dogs." These men are your snipers, breachers (entry-men), medics, and radiomen. Senior enlisted are your chiefs. These men are the tactical decision makers. These are the guys with the most experience. They run the Teams in most ways. There is a saying, "Officers rent the Teams; Enlisted own them." This is, more or less, the way things run. Enlisted SEALs get all the cool-guy schools and badass jobs. They get more combat over their career. They have many, many more options to choose from. They also get so many large bonuses that they actually make the same (or better) money than their officer counterparts over the first 6+ years.

If you're looking to do a full 20-year career (or more), this is really the place to be. Not only can you stay operational longer (something every frogman should want), but you can always become an officer later. You can apply to the Academy, you can go to college under the Seaman to Admiral (STA) Program, or simply apply to OCS if you've already got your degree. You have all the options in the world.

Officers. Officers are the leadership of the Teams. Each Team has a Commanding Officer (CO) and an Executive Officer (XO). Each Troop (3-4 per Team) has a Troop Commander. Each platoon (2-3 per Troop) has a Platoon Commander, or Officer-in-Charge (OIC). Each squad (2 per platoon) has a Squad Commander, or Assistant Officer-in-Charge (AOIC). These men don't usually make tactical decisions. Their job is to look out for their men, both administratively and operationally. They spend the majority of their time dealing with "up and out" while the chiefs deal with "down and in." In a firefight the chief will be telling guys to shift left and take the high ground, the OIC will be coordinating a Quick Reaction Force (QRF), Close Air Support (CAS), Casualty Evacuation (CASEVAC), and any other assets in the air or on the ground. He will also be talking to the chief, making sure that they both have a clear picture of everything that's going on. The job is extremely difficult and it is not sexy, but a good OIC is the difference between a platoon of dead SEALs and 30 dead Taliban.

Officers are limited to 2-3 deployments of actual combat before they're relegated to more administrative jobs. There are exceptions, but this is the general rule and there is very little a man can do to alter this fate.

Officer Accession Sources. A civilian can get his commission and become an officer from one of three accession sources: The United States Naval Academy (USNA), Officer Candidate School (OCS), or the Reserve Officer Training Corps (ROTC).

The Academy is a four-year military college, the Navy's version of West Point. In your last year at USNA you apply for the billets (open jobs) you want. Jobs are largely awarded based on class rank, so if you're at the top of your class, you have a good chance to get your first choice. If you're a bottom-feeder, you're likely to end up with something you didn't want. In addition, BUD/S hopefuls come to a SEAL Team as part of their Midshipman Cruise between Junior and Senior years, where they are put through an evaluation process. The Teams make their recommendations based on performance and attitude during these few weeks, and this feedback is taken into account when awarding BUD/S billets from the Academy.

OCS is the shortest route to BUD/S and the only way to guarantee yourself a shot at BUD/S from the civilian world. Where, at the Academy, you're committed to years of service before you apply to go to BUD/S, a civilian can apply for a SPECWAR billet to OCS and, if not accepted, does not have to join the Navy. You can apply directly to the program you want and wait to see if you're awarded a billet before committing. That's not to say this route is easy. It's incredibly competitive. This is the only accession source we'll be covering in detail later on because if you're in the USNA or ROTC, you already know everything about the application process.

ROTC is the last accession source for officers. ROTC allows you to attend a regular college (as opposed to a military academy). You're required to attend military-themed classes and wear a uniform at school from time to time. It's no small commitment, but ROTC will also often pay for your school, making it a pretty good deal for those who take advantage of it. Again, we won't cover the BUD/S Application from ROTC because if you're in ROTC you already know the process (though the standards and methods from the OCS application will likely come in handy). And if you're not in ROTC already, you need to join, which is beyond the scope of this book.

DOR. When someone Drops On Request - or DORs - that means they're quitting. It's also called "ringing out" because in order to announce their intention to quit they have to ring the bell on the First Phase grinder three times, usually to the applause of every BUD/S student who can hear the bell ring. Those who stay gain strength from those who quit, and there are few things as exciting as hearing the bell ring without being the one who rang it.

Fleet. Fleet is the big Navy, the rest of the world outside Naval Special Warfare (NSW - the umbrella term for SEALs, SWCC, and even divers to an extent). DORs spend a little time at X-Div, or more properly, Students Awaiting Transfer, before they head to the fleet. Within NSW, the term "fleet" is derogatory. Call someone "fleet" in the Teams and prepare yourself for a fight. The men of NSW pride themselves on being nimble, logical, and elite - these are the opposite of "fleet."

Hooyah. "Hooyah" is the SEAL version of a Marine's "ooo-rah" or an Army soldier's "hooah." In BUD/S it's used as a universal acknowledgement when dealing with instructor staff. It's also used to display motivation, real or otherwise, as you're doing something you really don't want to.
"You understand you're failing, right?"
"Hooyah."
"Stop being a faggot and go hit the surf."
"Hooyaaaah!"
You get the idea. The liberal and universal use of "hooyah" is phased out in Third Phase. By the time you reach the Teams, a hooyah is most often ironic. It tends to mean "I can't believe how much this sucks." It can also be used to describe something froggy, like a killer "hooyah PT" that involves a 10 mile run and a 3 mile swim.
The single most powerful use of "Hooyah" is at a memorial service for a fallen brother. This is not ironic. It is a sign of respect and solidarity.

PI/BI. A Personnel Inspection/Barracks Inspection is called a "PI/BI." These are an excuse to beat you, plain and simple. They involve standing in formation outside your barracks in order to have your nice cammies inspected. Directly following the PI you'll stand by outside your barracks room and wait for an instructor to trash it, fail you, and send you to the surf. We'll discuss strategies for PI/BIs later on.

Getting Beat. The phrase "getting beat" doesn't usually mean you're getting beat up by the instructors. At BUD/S a "beating" is physical remediation. It's basically self-torture. The instructors tell you what to do and you have to do it. Getting wet and sandy or hitting the surf (these are different) are examples. There's also a First Phase favorite: backs, bellies, feet. When they say "feet' you jump to your feet; when they say "backs" you drop onto your back; when they say "bellies" you drop to your stomach. Mix this with "wet and sandy" on an asphalt surface, take into account a pissed off instructor, and speed it up - it gets painful quickly. This is a beating.

Instructors aren't allowed to physically assault you. But that doesn't mean it doesn't occasionally happen. I remember one time in First Phase during a Barracks Inspection when things got a little intense. One of my roommates was asked why we'd failed to polish the very corner of the floor behind the door. When he replied that he had no excuse, the Instructor exploded. He grabbed my roommate and threw him to the ground. Then he picked him up, screaming at him " 'No excuse' is NOT A FUCKING EXCUSE YOU LITTLE PISS-ANT. I'M GOING TO FUCKING KILL YOU RIGHT NOW." The rest of us remained at attention while he tossed my roommate around like an Orca tossing a seal. He had thrown my roommate half out the window and he couldn't get up right away, so the instructor turned. He ran to me, screaming "I'm going to fucking kill all of you!" Then he collided with me, hitting me square in the chest with a double hammer-fist, launching me off my feet and into my wall locker. He glared down at me and spit at the ground. "You all fucking fail. Hit the fucking surf." Then he left.

Grinder. The Grinder is the holy place of First Phase. It's a 50 ft by 50 ft asphalt square with white feet marked where you're to stand in formation before your "Grinder PT," which means you're going to get beat.

* * *

Evolution. An evolution is a training event. There are timed evolutions, like the weekly 4-mile run on the beach, and there are completion evolutions, like Log PT. Some evolutions are individual, like the timed run. Some evolutions are buddy evolutions, like the ocean swims, where you have to remain within 6 ft of your buddy the entirety of the swim. Some evolutions are boat crew evolutions, like Surf Passage. Some evolutions, like Grinder PT, are class evolutions.

Goon Squad. The goon squad is formed by the slowest people in a run, swim, or other competitive evolution. Even conditioning runs, where there is no time, has a good squad composed of the stragglers. The goon squad pays for its weakness with pain. For example at the end of a run the winners (who kept up with the instructor leading the run) might get to stretch. The majority of the class might have to do some buddy carries up a sand berm. The goon squad might get beat, get wet and sandy, and then do buddy carries up the sand berm.

Roll. A student might get held back a class, or "rolled" for medical or performance reasons. Failing two of the same evolutions will earn you a performance roll. You're only allowed one performance roll for the same evolution. If you fail runs in First Phase, get rolled, make it to Third Phase with the next class, and then get rolled for runs again, you're likely to be dropped.

Drop. A student can be dropped for repeated performance failures, for medical reasons, or for being considered unsuitable for the training. There was a guy in my boat crew during Hell Week that was constantly getting us beat. He was stupid (genuinely), he was lazy, he was weak, he complained, he didn't pull any weight, and he had nothing to offer. He was the very definition of worthless. But the instructors forced us to carry his weight during Hell Week (as a way to test our resolve, I suppose). I very nearly drowned him during the Around the World paddle. I probably should have. He was rightfully dropped a few weeks after Hell Week for being generally unsuitable for the program.

* * *

BUD/S Orientation. BO used to be called Indoc. The instructors aren't allowed to beat you anymore, so they tend to call it "Gaydoc" now. It is, more or less, a period to get yourself and your class in order. You'll learn basic BUD/S procedures so, when First Phase comes, you know what to do.

White Shirt. White Shirts are BUD/S Student who have not yet completed Hell Week. The moment you complete Hell Week you are awarded the coveted Brown Shirt, and the white shirt you used to wear begins to look repulsively dingy and loud. The term White Shirt implies that they've not earned any respect yet. They're unproven and it can be statistically assumed they're going to quit.

Brown Shirt. The brown t-shirt you're given at the end of Hell Week is the single warmest article of clothing you've ever worn. The moment you put that brown shirt on, the statistics are on your side: you're more likely to become a SEAL than you are to end up in the fleet. By no means is your work done. It's barely even started. But the numbers are on your side for the first time ever and that's cause for joy.

Helmets. Each phase has its own helmet color. Green helmets denote First Phase, blue helmets indicate Second Phase, and red means Third Phase. Your name is written on the front and back in white stickers. If you're an officer, you've painted a stripe down the middle of the helmet. If you're a petty officer, you've taped chevrons on the front and back. Helmets used to be metal and students used to have to paint them on a regular basis. Now they're plastic. This is a point of contention among the older guys who had to paint their metal helmets.

Proctor. Your class will have a proctor in each phase. The role of the proctor is to have a single point-of-contact between the class leaders and the Instructor Staff. The proctor is also charged with mentoring your class throughout training. Some proctors try to help. Some proctors are hands-off. Some proctors, like my Third Phase proctor, just use their extra interaction time to find more reasons to beat you.

Foreign Officers. Your class may have some officers from foreign military services. They will not take a leadership role, but they will go through the entirety of BUD/S with you. Some countries have a history of fielding spectacular performers. I've heard amazing stories about Poles, Russians, and Greeks. Koreans have a good reputation in the classes as well. If, on the other hand, you've got some foreign officers from the middle east, like Saudi Arabia or Egypt, you can bet that they will be the worst students in your class. I'm not being racist. You'll see when you get there. One of the foreign Os in my class almost shot an instructor on the Island. They're at BUD/S for political reasons - reasons so far beyond our pay-grades that it's not even worth talking about. Just be aware that you're likely to have one or two in your class. Hope they're good.

CSS. Combat Sidestroke is the required stroke for swimming at BUD/S. It's a low-profile, efficient stroke that doesn't take much physical effort to maintain a decent speed for an extended period of time. You have the option of taking your PST (Physical Screening Test) swim portion by swimming breast stroke or CSS. Take it by swimming the CSS. Not only can you go fast without smoking your pushup/pull-up muscles, but you'll be required to swim the CSS at Pre-BUD/S and in BUD/S. If you have a SEAL Mentor/Dive Motivator in your area, make a concerted effort to learn CSS from him. If you don't, there are videos on YouTube that show you each step of the stroke. Watch them a few hundred times and try it out. Get good at it. Concentrate on staying long in the water, keeping the point of your head underwater as you rotate to breathe, and keeping the number of strokes you have to take to a minimum. If you can get across the pool in 6-8 strokes, you're probably doing it right.

Call-Outs. A call-out is when someone in the class yells the name of an instructor and the class yells out a hooyah for them. When the class is "standing by" waiting for an evolution to begin and the instructors drive up, the class calls out every instructor, from senior to junior. Get the order wrong or skip an instructor and the class gets a little extra love.

"Drop Down" or "Push 'em Out". These are commands that you and your class will be expected to react to rapidly. "Drop Down" means to quickly assume the pushup position with a straight back facing the nearest body of water. If that means you have to turn around completely as you drop down, that's what you'll do. It's a reminder to students to always know where your escape routes are. For SEALs, the water is our refuge.

After assuming the position in the correct orientation, the class waits for the instructors to finish talking/yelling at them.

When the instructor is done, he'll say "Push 'em out."

And the class leader will yell "Push Ups! Ready!"

"READY!" The class responds.

"Down!" The class leader dictates the pace.

"ONE!" The class counts.

"Down!"

"TWO!"

First phase classes do 20 pushups prior to Hell Week. The numbers increase as your class progresses through BUD/S.

"Down!"

"TWENTY!" After the last pushup, the class remains in position as the class leader calls out the Instructor who originally dropped the class down.

"Instructor Smith!"

"HOOYAH INSTRUCTOR SMITH!"

If the Instructor says "push 'em out," the class will do another set. If he says "recover," the class will get to its feet and stand at attention. The proper way to recover is to pop up with both feet at once hopping from the pushup position to between your hands as you stand up.

TTP. Tactics, Techniques, and Procedures. A shorthand way of referring to "the best way we know how to do that thing."

Who Doesn't Make It? Case Studies In BUD/S Failure.

Here are some guys you don't want to be. Names have been changed in most cases.

The Over-Motivated Guy. Jason was pumped. Everything he'd ever read about SEALs pumped him up. He wanted to shoot, he wanted to fight, he wanted to travel and train. He wanted to bang some Frog Hogs (SEAL groupie women). He wanted to experience every minute of BUD/S. He was excited to feel the cold of the Pacific. He was excited to feel the adrenaline of the O-Course. He was inspired to excel. Every part of BUD/S and Team life looked awesome to him. When a Team Guy told him a large part of being a SEAL was trudging through a thorny swamp, boots full of mud, skin covered in ticks and leaches for days at a time with little sleep and less action, Jason said "that sounds AWESOME."

Everything was fun to Jason. He couldn't wait to get beat so he could see what he was made of. When, at BUD/S Prep in Great Lakes, guys in his class started to bitch about repetitive workouts, Jason told them that if they couldn't handle THIS, they'd NEVER be able to handle BUD/S. When guys in Basic Orientation/Indoc bitched about an inspection or a hard workout, he condescendingly told them "Dude, this shit is fun. If you don't think so, then you probably shouldn't be here."

Everything was fun until suddenly, on the morning of the first day of First Phase, Jason realized that maybe BUD/S wasn't actually all that fun. He realized that, just maybe, ringing the bell would be fun.

A few weeks later one of the guys found Jason's Facebook account, where he told stirring war stories about BUD/S and how unfair it was that he had been "medically dropped" right before he became a SEAL.

What can we learn from Jason's failure?

- *Have Realistic Expectations.* Jason quit because he'd created an alternate reality by ignoring those who'd been there and thinking he could use the momentum of false motivation to sail through BUD/S. Well, the thing about BUD/S is that, no matter what you tell yourself, it sucks. BUD/S is not fun. Not only will you be physically and mentally beat down for nearly the entire time, but you'll be miserable. Even when you're not getting beat, you will not enjoy it. The pipeline will take everything cool (SCUBA diving, shooting guns, land navigation, demolition) and make it miserable. You won't truly understand until you're there, but ask any Been There Done That (BTDT) Team Guy and they'll tell you - there is nothing cool about Demo Week on San Clemente Island. Nothing in BUD/S is fun. Know this. Acknowledge that you're committing yourself to a miserable 6 months (followed by a miserable 7 months of SQT). Embrace the suck and don't pretend the shit smells like daisies. Everyone will hate you and, if you believe your own talk, you'll probably end up ringing the bell.

- *Don't Talk Shit.* You're not a SEAL, you haven't finished BUD/S (or probably even been there), so you don't know what it takes. Don't pretend like you do. Don't be the know-it-all telling people why you're going to make it and why they probably won't. That guy doesn't often make it through the first week of First Phase even, so give yourself a fighting chance by shutting the fuck up.

- *Fail Like a Man.* I guarantee that you will fail at some point in your quest to become a SEAL. That doesn't mean you won't make it: if you go in with the right mindset (which we're working on right now) you actually have a very, very good chance. What I mean is that you'll fail at SOMETHING. A swim, an O-Course, an

Inspection, Pool Comp, Pistol Quals - you'll fail something. Fail like a man. Own your performance, make no excuses, figure out how you're going to improve/prevent a second failure, and execute. That doesn't mean tell every single person that you own your failure and filling them in on your 12-step self-improvement plan. Don't talk about it, just do it.

But, if that 'something' you fail is BUD/S itself, and you end up ringing out, ring out like a man. There are hundreds of DORs who, in order to save face, claim to have been Medical Drops or the victim of crooked instructors or political forces beyond their control. If you quit, own up to it. Be a man even if you can't be a SEAL.

The Bitcher. Brandon was such a negative force in my class that I've decided not to change his name out of disrespect for him. Brandon was small, but sturdy enough. In fact we were so worried he might not quit that some of us had brainstorming sessions on how to get him beat more often. Fortunately for us, Brandon ultimately quit during Second Phase.

What was so wrong with Brandon that everyone in the entire class hated him? If you asked him, nothing. Everyone *else* was jacked up, and he told them so.

He had obviously never heard the Irish Proverb that says "If you dig a grave for others, you might fall into it yourself."

Brandon was always in everyone's face, even the officers, telling them they sucked and that they should be as good as he was (when, in fact, he was often the problem.) His boat crew would come off the beach shaking their heads in disbelief as he was chewing them out and complaining that none of them were carrying their own weight, a refrain he would reiterate every other breath for the entirety of the evolution. Invariably the 6 other guys in his boat crew were 'jacked up,' despite the fact that they all thought Brandon was the problem. And if anyone contradicted his claims, or even told him to shut up, he put all 125 lbs of bitter little angry man an inch away from their face as he 'set them straight.' He failed to realize that if it was him against the world, he might want to look at himself.

Brandon's lucky he couldn't tread water, because if he'd made it to diving he was so strongly hated that he might've found himself the unwitting victim of a 'freak dive accident.'

What can we learn from Brandon's miserable existence and ultimate failure?

- *Don't be too negative.* I know we just talked about the dangers of being unrealistically positive, but Brandon was far worse than anyone with unrealistic expectations of how awesome surf torture was going to be. Doe-eyed kids with unrealistic expectations hurt themselves; Brandon made every single person around him miserable. BUD/S sucks, no doubt. You will be unhappy, no question. There's no reason to make it any worse. I'm not telling you to ignore the suck, just to deal with it. Acknowledge it and move on. I can't tell you how many times I turned to the guy next to me and said "fuck our lives" as we interlocked arms and marched out into the surf zone. Usually he'd give a fatalistic laugh and say something like "living the dream" or a wry "Hooyah" and then we'd start the class singing some gay song like "It's Raining Men" or "Poker Face" as we sat down in the icy waves. Laugh about your miserable fate instead of blaming other people for it.

- *Be aware of yourself.* When you're tired, chaffed, cold, wet, miserable, and despairing it's easy to lose your grip on reality. When you feel like the guys around you are all letting you down, put yourself in their position and see if you're doing the same thing. I guarantee that, if you look at it honestly, you'll see that 99% of the time you're failing the same way they are. Even if you're not, remember that there will come a time when they're carrying some of your weight, guaranteed. So don't think you're better than they are. You might be, but you probably aren't. Remember that and you'll have a much easier time.

- *Be a team player.* SEALs don't refer to ourselves as SEALs. We refer to ourselves as "Team Guys" for a reason. We succeed and fail as a Team. We are Team members as a way of life. Team Guys are our tribe, our brothers, and no Team Guy will violate that bond. BUD/S is the foundation of this team ethos. Don't be about "me" like Brandon was. Be about your boat crew. Be about your class. Not only will your class like you (and therefore help you up when you're down), but concentrating on your team members will take your mind off your own misery and actually make BUD/S more bearable.

The Relationship Guy. Jack was my best friend at OCS and a physical stud. He was the ideal 5'10", 200 lb, thick-necked, strong-legged, Academy guy. He was raised in Maine as a member of the Polar Bear Club, so icy water didn't even phase him, and he knew a great deal about BUD/S, SQT, and the Teams. We all, Jack included, thought he was a shoe-in. While under a boat in Indoc, Jack actually choke-slammed a pathetic member of his boat crew into the sand a few times until that guy (who we'll talk about in a minute) quit. Jack was legit until he quit 3 hours into Hell Week, during a short Surf Torture after the last Log PT ever, of all things. Because of his girlfriend of 3 months (who had recently promoted herself to fiancee). Rewind a few months.

Jack was a great guy until we got cell phone access at the end of OCS, when he ceased to exist. He was on the phone with this girl constantly, having the most emasculating phone calls one could ever imagine:

"What did you have for dinner?" "Oh, was it good?" "What did you have for desert?" "Well you should get ice cream then" "What flavor? I don't know. What flavor do you want?" "Then you should get chocolate." "One scoop or two? I think one." "Okay, then get two scoops honey." Barf.

I shared a room with Jack in BUD/S and spoke to him less in a month than I had in any given day of OCS. No joke. The kid was beyond reclamation and it showed. By the time we started First Phase, Jack was talking about marrying this girl during SQT. She came out to visit from the east coast on a regular basis, draining his bank account at an alarming rate. He proposed and they set a date for sometime in the middle of SQT when he thought he might be able to get a weekend off. He was so distracted that, at the beginning of Hell Week all he could think about was that she was too high-maintenance to deal with him being a SEAL. So he quit.

He was processed out of the Navy and got married while his class was in Kodiak, AK. (If he hadn't quit, he would've been in Alaska during his wedding, for which he'd already paid non-refundable deposits at his new wife's insistence. Which shows he - at least subconsciously - knew he wouldn't make it.) After months and months of feigning happiness, he finally came to terms with his regret and is trying to join the Army Special Forces. I hope he makes it, but I can tell you one thing for sure: if it wasn't for the woman, Jack would be a Team Guy already.

What do we learn from Jack's failure?

- *Get your household in order.* BUD/S is enough on its own. You don't need to add anything more to your plate. If your girlfriend can't deal with the hours, stress, or your absence, get rid of her. Despite how awesome you think your girlfriend is, this probably (statistically) applies to you. I'm not saying don't have a girlfriend when you're going through. I did, and she was wonderful. She made me food at all hours and helped me prep uniforms for inspections. Good women do exist, but yours probably can't handle BUD/S. And if she can't handle BUD/S, she most certainly cannot handle life in the Teams. Save yourself the stress and heartache and do some honest thinking about her expectations and needs. If she's not going to make it, cut her off now so you don't have to deal with THAT on top of the stresses of BUD/S.

- *Fully understand your commitments.* Jack was dumb in any number of ways, not the least of which was his expectations of life after BUD/S. He scheduled his wedding for a weekend when we'd probably be in SQT. He scheduled it during Basic Orientation/ Indoc. See any glaring problems with this? One: how did he know he wouldn't be rolled once or twice along the way, resulting in his being in BUD/S when he was supposed to get married? He didn't. Two: how did he know that weekend, even if he HAD made it to SQT, would be available? In reality if he hadn't quit or been rolled, he would have been on Kodiak Island in Alaska on the day he'd reserved that adorable little chapel in Cambridge. There is no excuse for this level of stupidity. Either he subconsciously knew he was going to quit, or he had no grasp of the commitment he was going to have to make in order to become a SEAL.

- *Don't make big decisions during BUD/S.* BUD/S is mental; it is the world's most effective mindfuck. You will not be in any condition, despite what you think, to make a big decision. You're not even going to be in a condition to decide whether you 'actually' want to be a SEAL, which is why I've told you to make your mind up BEFORE you get to BUD/S. If you can't even make a good decision regarding the very thing you do all day and night, how to you expect to be able to make a good decision about anything else? Do not get engaged. Do not ask for a divorce. Do not try to have a child. Here are the decisions you WILL get to make: *What should I eat for breakfast? What should I eat for lunch? What should I eat for dinner? How long should I stretch before I go to bed? How much more water should I drink? What should I do this weekend to recover and decompress before next week kicks me in the teeth?* If you try to make a decision beyond the scope of these questions, you are wrong. Being wrong very often results in ringing a bell three times and hanging your head for the rest of your life.

The Brick Shithouse. Abner was refrigerator-sized guy. Broad shoulders. Massive arms. Legs like stone pillars. A neck thicker than his head was wide. I was fairly certain that I would have a hard time hurting him with a baseball bat. But Abner was slow. Abner was mentally weak. Abner was a buddy-fucker (otherwise known as a "blue falcon" or a "bravo foxtrot" in polite company.)

Abner was, as I have said, a rather densely put-together fellow. A lot of guys think this is a real advantage because SEALs (and BUD/S students) need brute strength. That's not quite the mark. The ideal BUD/S student is a solid triathlete. The amount of running you do every day is staggering, and if you're carrying a great deal of weight around, even if it's muscle, your body is going to wear down much faster. Beyond the mileage, the fact that a large proportion of your running will be in the soft sand (and you've never felt sand this soft in your life), those extra pounds can kill you. The tree-trunk-sized guys are amazing to have in your boat crew during log PT, but you'll realistically only do 3-5 log PTs (usually 4) the entire time you're at BUD/S. The rest of the time, that guy is likely to be a weak link. If you're running under the boat, carrying the weight on your head (called Land Portage), you don't want to be the guy your boat crew is slowing down for. Heavy guys are at a disadvantage on the O-Course, during runs, on swims, during land portage, and when someone has to buddy carry them (not an uncommon occurrence at BUD/S, in SQT, or in the Teams).

Compounding Abner's size disadvantage was the root of his problems: Abner was mentally weak (in BUD/S, we refer to this as "being a pussy"). His size made life a little harder, but bigger guys than he were able to make it. Abner couldn't handle the physical or mental stress. He quit during Basic Orientation/Indoc during our "Intro to Land Portage" evolution. Land Portage involves carrying a large, floppy, waterlogged rubber IBS (Inflatable Boat, Small) on your head. A boat crew comprises 6-7 guys, all of whom run in unison under the boat while supporting the weight of the boat on their heads. If one guy doesn't carry his weight - called "boat ducking" - it dramatically increases the amount of weight the rest of his crew has to support. If there are two or more boat duckers in a crew, the rest of the guys risk serious injury due to spinal damage. Even knowing that, however, you simply cannot fathom quite how heinous a crime it is to duck boat until you're there. This was the first time we'd ever done "boat on heads" and Abner was ducking the entire time. Not only was he ducking, but he soon started hanging on the carry-straps, actually adding weight to the boat. After about 45 minutes of screaming at Abner to get his head under the boat, his boat crew leader, Jack, came out from under the boat mid-stride and choke-slammed Abner into the sand and screamed.

"Stay the fuck on the ground you piece of shit." Needless to say, this caught the attention of the Instructors, who swarmed like sharks in a pool of blood. They stopped all the boats, made Abner hit the surf, and put him back under the boat. He put out for a few minutes before he returned to strap-hanging and ducking boat. This time Jack choke-slammed him into the surf, put his foot on Abner's chest, and spit in his face.

"Just quit already you boat-ducking faggot." The instructors had been waiting for him. They gave Abner an armful of wood paddles and told him to run beside his boat since he was too weak to carry his own weight. The class forgot its own pain for a moment and cheered as Abner stumbled toward the boat, dropped all the paddles, and quit. Abner's weakness made us all feel stronger and we pushed on as Abner climbed into the bed of the trailing pickup truck with the other quitters.

What can we learn from Abner's failure?

- *Don't try to be enormous.* If you're a big fella, consider slimming down a bit. At the very least ensure you can run with the little guys. The instructors won't let you use your strength as an excuse for any shortcomings. If you're less heavily built, don't worry about bulking up. Pre-BUD/S will get you in the kind of shape you need for success. Before you ship, concern yourself with destroying the PST. Everything after that will take care of itself. There is no need to take creatine or steroids. There is little use in lifting weights beforehand. Pushups, sit-ups, pull-ups, running, swimming. Do some dips if you're feeling froggy. Everything else is pretty much cosmetic.

- *Carry your own weight.* No BUD/S class will tolerate weakness for long. Abner could've bench-pressed anyone in the class, but if he couldn't even carry his own weight under the boat, he was worse than worthless: he was a parasite we joyfully excised. Don't duck boat. Ever. Don't be a strap hanger. Ever. Choose death/ unconsciousness before you add one more ounce to your buddies' load. Be ashamed of any weakness that forces your classmates to pick up your slack. Fight to carry your weight AND your buddy's. Carry this attitude with you for the rest of your life, both in training, in the Teams, and beyond, and you'll find that success will meet you everywhere you go. Besides, if you don't carry your own weight you might find yourself taken over the berm by a handful of pissed-off BUD/S students while the instructors look the other way, not that it's ever happened before.

The Career BUD/S Student. When you finally reach Coronado, your class will be augmented by "white shirt rollbacks" - so-designated because they had been rolled before the completion of Hell Week, when you earn the right to wear a brown t-shirt. Generally, these guys are not going to make it. They will tell war stories of "Phase" if they got there and will be able to help you initially navigate the compound, but take their advice with a grain of salt. Some of them will have good reasons to have been rolled. Some of them may have even been rolled in a previous Hell Week. A lot of them, however, will have voluntarily rolled (though they certainly won't admit it - even to themselves) to avoid the pain. We'll talk about this phenomenon in a later chapter, but not every 'medical roll' is the same, and BUD/S medical is one of the easiest ways to get out of BUD/S without ringing out.

There will also possibly be a few fleet returnees: guys who quit, went to the regular navy, and came back. Previous failures are currently barred from returning, but the ban could be lifted at any moment. Some of these guys will be phenomenal - the Honorman of my SQT class was a fleet returnee; many will be pathetic - I call this group the "career BUD/S students." Some guys, it seems, take their previous failure and, like a rabid dog, snap right back with violence and focus on the big picture of completing BUD/S. These are the guys you want around you. Some guys come back and talk about "last time" all the time, like the experience of BUD/S was all they were after. You can tell who is who, generally, by what they concern themselves with and how they carry themselves. At first the career BUD/S students will be more helpful because they're caught up in the best way to change out, strategies for PI/BI, and the proper boot-tying technique. They'll often even tell you "my whole career has pretty much revolved around BUD/S... I know everything about it."

Ultimately, however, the career students are stuck there and fail to see the forest through the trees. The returnees you want around you don't really care much about the small details because they realize that the difference between a square-knot and a granny-knot in your boot laces might be the difference between 20 pushups and 100, but will not be the difference between finishing BUD/S or returning to the fleet. This difference in attitude becomes clear the morning of Day 1 of First Phase, when the career students are no longer in their comfort zone of Indoc: their faces will go grey, they'll look like they're about to soil themselves, and many won't stick around to see the afternoon. This phenomenon is so statistically represented that the community has increasingly limited the number of fleet returnees allowed at BUD/S, and is currently not allowing failures to return.

What can we learn from the Career BUD/S Students?

- *See the big picture.* BUD/S is a means to an end: becoming a Navy SEAL. Don't ever forget that. I know it probably seems like obvious advice, and it is, but it's also very valuable. It's easy to get mud-sucked into details that don't matter in the long run. By all means, pay attention to the details - sometimes they'll save you - but remember the ultimate goal and everything will make more sense.

- *Attack training before it attacks you.* Something you'll hear every day at BUD/S is 'violence of action.' Violence of action is how a small force of 16 SEALs can fight off an army. Extreme violence of action is the key to being a Team Guy.

A SEAL Senior Chief (E-8) once told me a story about a firefight in Ramadi, Iraq. He was a Troop Chief at the time and had two platoons maneuvering on some militants in the adjacent area. In that same area was an Army Airborne unit run by a Major (O-4). The Major and the Senior Chief were talking about their next moves while the platoons and the Army unit were hunting down the last few hostiles. They heard a few shots coming from the direction of their units. "Pop. Pop." Then, "bang, pop." The Major turned to the SEAL and asked "is that your guys in contact?"

"Nope. Not my guys," the Senior Chief replied immediately. The Major was taken aback by how quickly and confidently he answered.

"Are you sure?"

"I'm sure." The Senior Chief smiled to himself as he realized the Major had never operated with SEALs before. A few minutes later a firefight rang out like a violent chorus of chainsaws, bulldozers, machine guns, and cluster bombs - it didn't let up for almost two minutes. The SEAL smiled and looked over at the wide-eyed Major.

"*Those* are my guys." The Major nodded silently, awed by the extreme violence of a SEAL platoon in contact.

How does this violence of action manifest itself in BUD/S? Everything you do, from running to working out, to changing into and out of your cammies on the pool deck is done with a violent sense of urgency. If you fail to act with a sufficient sense of urgency, the instructors will be sure to motivate you with water, sand, and violent PT. Just like war, if you're not the violent actor, you will be the victim of a violent actor.

Don't wait to be a victim like so many career BUD/S students do. Attack training and you'll make it through.

* * *

Perceived Weakness. There was nothing really wrong with Brian. He wasn't an excellent performer, but, then, not everyone can be. His real failure was one of perception management. Perception is not reality, but when you're at BUD/S, you have to realize that there's no time to discover reality. Everyone, yourself included, will likely go based solely on your perception of others.

I kept a record of everything I did and saw throughout BUD/S, but you'll notice I still would never refer to it as a 'diary.' Because I'm not gay. Does that statement I just made *actually* make sense? Nope. Does it matter? No. That's how your class will look at it - and that's all that matters.

Brian not only talked about his "diary" openly and often, but asked Master Chief Will Guild, an ex-SEAL Team Six operator-turned SEAL Mentor if it was okay that he write in a diary every night. And he asked in a classroom setting for all to hear. Brian was soft spoken. He volunteered personal information, like how much he loved the way his girlfriend smelled, in large groups where such information was completely off-topic. Brian gave himself no chance. He may not have been weak, but to this day, I still think he probably was. Because he gave ONLY reasons to think he was a "pussy" or a "fag," that's what he was. That's what he is to me still, even though I know he might have been more. The entire class hated him because he seemed weak.

A friend of mine recently told me about an officer who graduated a few years after I did. This guy was well-read and used big words; he was also a vegetarian. Despite the fact that he never failed a physical evolution (and apparently was one of the fastest runner and swimmers in his class), this officer was largely disliked in his class because he seemed weak. Read that again: he was one of the top performers in his class, but because he didn't eat meat and he liked to read, he was "weak." It makes no sense, but you can absolutely see why his class thought what it did.

Looking at it logically, you could almost make the argument that completing BUD/S at the top of his class while on a vegetarian diet shows impressive discipline and strength. But the perception was that if he didn't eat meat, he couldn't be trusted to pull the trigger when the time came. According to my friend, the vegetarian is a Team Guy now and seems to be performing well despite his diet, but you can easily imagine events taking a different turn.

What can we learn about perception management from Brian and the vegetarian officer?

- *Inspire confidence.* The ideal SEAL in a BUD/S student's mind is strong, fast, competent, and a good team player. He is self-sufficient, he kills rattlesnakes with his bare hands and eats them raw. He shaves with rocks he sharpened with his teeth. His skin is made of leather and his blood is red and hot. He is supremely confident. He kills snakes with his bare hands and eats them. The closer you appear to this, the more confidence your classmates will place in you. A word of caution though: if you aren't these things but pretend to be, the guys will see through you immediately and your credibility will be shot.

- *Be different at your own risk.* The Teams are clannish and somewhat parochial. Differences are only tolerated in proven operators or when they're proven not to be weaknesses. In BUD/S there is little time to prove anything to anyone, and even making it through Hell Week or Pool Comp will leave you with an uphill battle. I'm not saying to hide who you are, but if you're looking to make it through BUD/S with the fewest distractions possible, I strongly suggest keeping the odd parts of your personality to yourself until your class knows you're a solid performer. Don't let your Barbie collection be part of the first impression you make. I had two former "male entertainers" in my BUD/S class, but neither one of them was found out until late in First Phase - long after the class recognized them each for their work ethic, physical strengths, and good attitude. At that point their previous employment was a funny aspect of a well-respected guy. Had they introduced themselves as male strippers, however, I have no doubt they would've had a *much* harder time winning the class over. They're both SEALs now, in case you were curious.

Who Makes It? Case Studies In Success.

   We've already talked about the biggest key to finishing BUD/S: the simple refusal to consider any alternative. This is the fundamental characteristic off all BUD/S graduates and the one thing none of the quitters had going for them. It's a simple answer for a complex phenomenon, but all truths are simple: they didn't quit because they wouldn't quit.
   But what does that look like? The SEAL teams are the single most eclectic organization you'll ever see. Ivy League graduates work alongside former longshoremen, contractors, high-school dropouts, computer programmers, federal marshals, mechanics, and Olympic athletes. This intense diversity is a very real source of strength in a platoon, so don't think you need to be a triathlete who hunts and shoots competitively to be of value. Your special skill set, whether it be networking computers, carrying heavy things, or shooting well will be of great use in the Teams. There are guys who don't drink, smoke, dip, swear, or fuck; there are guys who will do every one of these things every night. There are guys who, were they not SEALs, should probably be in jail; there are guys who, were they not SEALs, would probably be congressmen.
   Let's look at some examples of guys who did (and didn't) complete BUD/S with me and see what can be learned from each of them. Obviously, their names have been changed.

* * *

The dumb guy. Joseph was simply too dumb to quit. No joke, he "stupided" his way through BUD/S. When he failed a run and had to hit the surf, he wasn't worried because he barely understood he failed. He certainly wasn't thinking that if he failed the next run he might get rolled. He simply moved on and continued with his training day. Joseph never really felt sorry for himself because he never thought about what else could be. He just *did*. When he failed his Second Phase Dive Physics test twice and went to an Academic Review Board (ARB) to be considered for a roll, he told them he was trying hard and would try hard a third time if they gave him the test again. They gave him one more try, he passed, and ended up getting his Trident a few months later.

What can we learn from Joseph's success?

- *Don't stress.* Joseph didn't stress out over failures. He kept his head up and did his best. Worrying about past failures can be a serious distraction, and BUD/S is stressful enough on its own without you piling your own stresses on top. Stress not only distracts you, but has been proven to decrease the rate of physical recovery - an effect you cannot afford at BUD/S. We'll discuss practical ways to manage stress at BUD/S in the next chapter.

- *Perseverance wins.* Joseph was unremarkable. He was in no way gifted, had no advantage, but he never gave up and never stopped working. Failure did not discourage him and he never recognized he was disadvantaged. He kept on keeping on. Now he's a SEAL.

- *BUD/S doesn't take smarts.* I'm not being cavalier when I tell you Joseph was dumb. One time I asked him where he was from. He responded by telling me that his dad had a truck that could carry a whole deer in the back. But where did his parents live? The truck is red. A whole deer. That dumb. You don't have to be smart to finish BUD/S. Some would say being smart is actually a disadvantage - you might have more options elsewhere and you certainly can over-think things. Neither one of these things is particularly helpful when navigating BUD/S. So those of you who're downloading the Navy Dive Manual so you can pre-study for the Dive Physics test in Second Phase, hear me now. Cut it out. "Preparing for it now" will not only do you *no* good, but will also add stress. Seriously, stop it.

- *Focus on now.* Joseph was only really able to think about what was happening in the *now*. He never dwelled on the past or worried about the future. He only thought about what he was doing now, and so never became overwhelmed by the enormity of his undertaking. This one is incredibly important, so we'll discuss it further a little later.

The Clown. Erik Bishop was a happy-go-lucky clown. I never saw him unhappy and he always made me laugh. One time we were standing outside the First Phase barracks standing a uniform inspection and Erik turned to me and told me, half jokingly, "Gee Mr. O. I'm not too sure about my boots today."

I looked down and saw that his boots still had white salt deposits from hitting the surf the previous inspection. He hadn't done a thing to polish them. "Holy shit, Erik," I said, "what happened?"

"Well I really did mean to polish them, honestly. But I was watching a movie last night and then it got so late that I just sorta didn't get to them."

He smiled and shrugged and seemed to resign himself to fate. The Instructors showed up, we stood at attention, and the inspection began. Instructor L walked up to Erik and looked down at his boots. "Why is there shit all over your boots?"

Before he could tell him to shut up, Erik spit out, "Because I didn't spend enough time on them this weekend."

"And how much time did you have to prepare?"

Even more quickly this time, "Infinite time, Instructor L."

"That was a rhetorical question, Bishop. Don't you know what a rhetorical question is?"

Erik paused a moment, cracked a barely-there sheepish smile and asked hesitatingly, "Was *that* a rhetorical question, Instructor L?"

I couldn't hold back my laughter, Erik smiled, and the Instructor walked away. Somehow Erik passed the inspection. Erik is now a SEAL.

What can we learn from Erik's success?

- *BUD/S is a game.* Erik knew BUD/S was a game and didn't take any one thing too seriously. In the above interaction Erik risked only a failed inspection and a trip to the surf zone. Even a perfect uniform has a good chance of "failing," and Erik's boots should've guaranteed him a failure. But fortune favored his boldness. Either the Instructor passed him because he appreciated his bravery and honesty, or simply forgot to fail him because he was distracted by laughing. Either way, Erik's attitude won the day (and many other days, too). Be bold, don't fear failure, and you'll win more.

- *Keep it positive.* It's hard to keep a positive attitude at BUD/S. Everything sucks, your body hurts, nothing is fun. But you have to enjoy the small things, like peanut-butter packs stolen from the chow hall, dry socks, a 10-minute nap on dry concrete away from the Instructors. Erik basked in these small joys. He made them bigger than they were and, in doing so, made everyone around him feel better. Erik's buoyant, relaxed outlook helped us all decompress - a most valuable gift in such an unforgiving environment. Positivity is as contagious as negativity, but being negative does you no good. Stay positive by enjoying your small victories and you'll find everything else gets that much easier.

The Informed Guy. Steve had wanted to be a SEAL for years. When he checked in, an Instructor asked him to name the five SEALs who'd won the Congressional Medal of Honor. They ask questions they don't expect you to know so they have an excuse to make you get wet. When Steve promptly spit out "Bob Kerrey, Tom Norris, Mike Thornton, Mikey Monsoor, and Michael Murphy," the Instructors looked impressed for a hot minute before making Steve hit the surf for "being a smart-ass." Steve smiled all the way to the surf zone. Steve had read every book published on the Navy SEALs, fiction and nonfiction. He'd seen every documentary and could quote, in its entirety, the Discovery Channel's documentary of BUD/S Class 234. Steve had watched videos of people running the Obstacle Course, he knew every major evolution he'd have to complete, and he shared his knowledge with all his classmates. It should come as no surprise that Steve is now a SEAL.

What can we learn from Steve's success?

- *Do your research.* Steve knew what was coming. He knew what to expect and had heard dozens of guys talk about how *they* got through BUD/S. Information made him confident he could succeed. Steve was successful because he set himself up to win.

If you want to make it through BUD/S, you'll strive to be Steve. You're not a dumb guy like Joseph because you know enough to read this book and you're probably not a joker like Erik because he never really worried enough to learn much. They're the exceptions. A lot of guys who make it through BUD/S are guys who, like Steve, learned everything they could. If you're serious about becoming a Team Guy, you'll dedicate yourself to learning everything you can. Consider it gathering intel for your mission.

The Lessons of Statistics: How to Increase Your Chances of Success at BUD/S.

The statistics surrounding BUD/S can be incredibly intimidating. Depending on what you read, you'll find pass rates ranging from 5-30%. Numbers vary by class, but the last few classes have averaged 15-20% pass rate based on the number of SEAL-wannabes showing up for BO and the number of guys graduating in that class (including rollbacks who started BO with previous classes).

If you're being honest with yourself and taking BUD/S seriously, you should be asking yourself: "How do I know if I can make it? Presumably all of the guys who start BUD/S think they have what it takes to finish it, but so few really DO have what it takes. Why? Am I one of those guys who's going to quit and I just don't know it yet? What do the 15% have in common that the 85% do not, and do I have that?"

I have an answer for you, but before I get to it I need to put this out there: If you haven't asked yourself this question, why not? If you haven't, you need to think about the immensity of this undertaking. It's the same as trying to have a baby without asking yourself whether you can provide a decent home or whether you can afford the diapers. Do not get caught unprepared: there is no excuse.

Now, for those of you who are wondering whether you have that magical common ingredient the 15% share: I'm going to answer your statistical question with another statistic.

While Enlisted success rate at BUD/S is around 15%, Officer graduation rate is often over 50%. Despite the fact that the Instructors place considerably more stress on the Officers than the Enlisted and despite the higher academic standards, Officers graduate BUD/S at 3-4 times the rate Enlisted guys do. What can we take away from this? Are Officers better? Nope, not at all. Can we learn from this huge difference and increase your chances of success, regardless of whether you're Enlisted or an Officer? You're god-damned right we can.

A disclaimer: none of these attitudes are exclusive to officers. You can be a 17-year-old coming to BUD/S right out of high school, it doesn't matter. You can make it without considering any of these factors, but if you're that 17-year-old and you can understand some of the common factors that do contribute to the high officer success rate, you can incorporate these lessons in your physical and mental preparation. You can have all the advantages of being an officer without actually having to be one. With new policies regarding dropouts returning and higher admissions requirements for enlisted guys, this gap is sure to drop. But we can still learn from characteristics that previously created a large gap in success rates between Os and Es.

Pay attention: this is where you start to immediately increase your chances of completing BUD/S.

The Roots of Commitment. There is an immense difference in the amount of time and effort it takes to reach BUD/S as an Officer versus as an Enlisted man. My officer package took me over a year from beginning to put it together to shipping to OCS. I drove halfway across the continent to earn various letters of recommendation. I spent countless hours writing essays and personal statements. I got word that I was accepted to go to OCS with a SPECWAR billet no less than 14 months after I began. OCS is another 3 months. After OCS you'll sit in PTRR on Coronado from 3 to 14 months before classing up.

In contrast I could have gone to a Recruiter, taken a PST (which even my mom can, no joke, pass), and signed a SEAL Challenge

Contract within a week. Depending on available ship dates, you can be in Great Lakes at Navy Boot Camp within a month or two, and at Pre-BUD/S a few months after. You'll work out at Pre-BUD/S a few months before flying to Coronado to class up. The process has since gotten more competitive, but is still much more rapid than the Officer route.

By the time your average Officer has classed up, he's got years committed to BUD/S, where the average Enlisted man can have months. The psychological principle of cognitive dissonance comes in to play here. Cognitive dissonance means that the more pain, inconvenience, and effort a person endures for a goal, the more committed he is to that goal.

Why do you think Radical Islamists are forced to stop everything and pray 5 times a day? Why do they refrain from food during the day for the entire month of Ramadan? Why do they abstain from sexual relations and physical comforts? If you don't think cognitive dissonance comes into play there, you're not paying attention. They don't suffer solely because they're committed, they suffer, in part, to manufacture commitment. They are committed because they suffer, and in order to justify the suffering their brains make them believe the commitment is actually *worth* the suffering.

By the time an officer starts BUD/S, he has been influenced by this psychological force significantly more than his enlisted classmates. His quality of life has sucked for longer, but he's manufactured greater commitment.

Limited Opportunity. Another drastic and fundamental difference in mindset between officer and enlisted BUD/S students is that officers are never afforded a second chance at BUD/S. If they quit or get dropped, they can never return to BUD/S under any circumstances.

Enlisted men, on the other hand, were permitted three chances at BUD/S. This is currently on hold because returnees aren't allow to return, but the thought process is still important to take note of. This was a psychological out. They were given the luxury, crutch of thinking "You know, I'm not sure if this is for me. Maybe I should try something else and come back if I don't like it." Or, even worse, "This sucks. Maybe I'm not ready for it and I should come back in a few years." Even if you didn't look at this as a truly viable option, the fact that it's available can be a hindrance.

Sometimes the world gets so dark during BUD/S that the little crack in your plans allowed by the simple option to return is enough to let yourself quit.

On the upside (depending how you look at it), fleet returnees have such a poor success rate at BUD/S that their applications are being turned away. The door to return is closed and now even Enlisted men have only one opportunity to make it through BUD/S.

Maturity Helps. The funny thing about having to attend at least 4 additional years of schooling to be eligible to become an officer is that the youngest officers are about 4 years older than the youngest enlisted men. BUD/S tends not to be their first experience away from home. Many have held jobs and lived on their own for years. The maturity gained by life experience cannot be over-valued.

Officers are not the only ones with degrees and independent lives, but every officer has had to fend for himself in some way for years. Not every enlisted man has. Those enlisted men with college degrees and life experience reap all the benefits from that history that the officers do, and thereby increase their chances of success from what they would've been going to BUD/S right out of high school.

The substantial level of maturity gained by years on one's own, regardless of who you are or what you've been doing since you left your parents' house, is a wellspring of strength and perspective that lets you deal with adversity in a more collected, even-keel manner.

Preparation is Key.
To be eligible for a SEAL Challenge Contract, you need to be able to meet the following standards:
500yd Swim - 12:30
Pushups - 42
Sit-ups - 50
Pull-ups - 6
1.5mi Run - 11:00

If you can meet these scores, you are eligible to ship to Boot Camp. Compare these scores to the bare minimum scores an officer hopeful must surpass in order to be considered competitive:

500yd Swim - 9:00
Pushups - 100
Sit-ups - 100
Pull-ups - 20
1.5mi Run - 9:00

An officer applicant who submits these scores would be at the bottom of the stack and would need to distinguish himself further to be seriously considered. A more likely selectee would furnish scores like these:

500yd Swim - 7:00
Pushups - 120
Sit-ups - 120
Pull-ups - 30
1.5mi Run - 8:00

Let me be clear: **If you can pass the SEAL Challenge, you are fit enough to complete BUD/S.** There were a dozen guys who graduated BUD/S with me who could barely pass the SEAL Challenge when they shipped to Boot Camp. They made it and are strong, contributing members of their platoons now.

But you don't want to be those guys because I know that every time I was hurting on a run, under a boat, on a swim, or during any other physical evolution, those guys were hurting twice as badly. They were digging deep when fitter guys were breathing easy. They were sweating timed evolutions when everyone else was relaxed.

The better shape you're in when you get to BUD/S, the better off you are, but no matter how fit you are, you will hurt during BUD/S. Every man meets his physical challenges and pushes through misery. If you can raise your threshold by being in amazing shape, however, you're going to meet your match less often. If you're a terrible runner and every single timed run (there's one every week) is a challenge to pass, your stress levels are going to be markedly higher than a good runner who can cruise to a pass every time.

Fitness is a cushion. If you're sick or injured (and you will be sometimes, no doubt) and you're only running at 70% cardiac capacity, you want that cushion. If you can pass a swim with pneumonia because you normally crush the swim, you're fine. If you normally struggle to pass and you have pneumonia, you don't stand a chance. If you normally finish a run at the front of the class, shin splints might put you in the middle or near the back of the pack. If you normally finish a run at the back of the class, shin splints will put you in the surf zone, the goon squad, and ultimately get you rolled.

Nearly every officer will have that cushion of physical fitness because of the scores he had to achieve to even get to BUD/S. Because the physical requirements to get a SEAL Challenge Contract are significantly lower, enlisted men are not required to build that physical cushion and many never do. With the advent of the "draft system" enlisted applicants are being required to field more and more impressive PST scores, and these scores will only help increase their success rates.

Enlisted success rate is improving in recent years, however, since the advent of the Pre-BUD/S training program in Great Lakes. There are exit standards every SEAL-hopeful has to pass at Pre-BUD/S in order to get to BUD/S that are greatly elevated from the SEAL Challenge scores:

1000m swim w/fins: 20:00
Pushups: 70
Sit-ups: 60
Pull-ups: 10
4mi Run: 31:00

If you can pass the minimum SEAL Challenge scores before you ship to Boot Camp, Pre-BUD/S will get you in shape to pass the Exit Standards. The Exit Standards set you up for success at BUD/S.

External Focus. There is a fundamental difference in expectations of officers and enlisted men at BUD/S. Enlisted guys need to be good "sled dogs." They need to be able to put out, to take direction, and to act with aggression and speed. They need to carry their own weight and pass the standards. They can put their heads down, pull for 6 months, and graduate. This is an awesome luxury, but also a major disadvantage at times.

Officers, on the other hand, are expected to lead. They have to ensure each and every man in his boat crew is working together, to know what's going on in all of their lives (and heads). They have to coordinate collateral duties like painting statues, sweeping sand from the grinder, and do all the administrative work for the class. All these things are in addition to completing the evolutions and being the sled dog when called upon. Officers will sleep less and get in trouble more. They will be held under a microscope and will be culled if they don't measure up to the instructors' expectations. Officers are spread thin during BUD/S.

As much as it sucks, being required to manage dozens of things at a time has an unintended benefit. If you're concerned about making sure that the swim pair list is 100% accurate up-to-the-second, you're not going to stress out about the timed swim. If you're busy taking down scores during an inspection, your own failure affects you less. If you're watching all your guys under the boat to see who needs to be rotated out next, you don't notice your own pain as much. If you're motivating your boat crew during log PT, you don't have time to reflect on how miserable you really are.

"But" Nothing. It couldn't matter less whether you're trying to attend BUD/s as an enlisted man or an officer: you can use these tools to set yourself up for success. Even the 17-year-old fresh from his high school graduation can emulate these characteristics that make officers statistically more likely to graduate BUD/S. You can play the statistics game and set the board in your favor. Even if you can't match the characteristic on your own, just being aware that these small things make such a big difference can help you reach your goals.

For instance, you probably can't (and shouldn't) increase the amount you suffer before you get to BUD/S in order to increase your cognitive dissonance and, thereby, your commitment. Simply resolve to have the same level of commitment that the longest-suffering man in your class has. What does that mean, really? There's nothing special about that officer who's put two years into getting to BUD/S: he has simply sacrificed so much that he won't quit. You don't need to suffer to match the result of his suffering. Just emulate the result of his suffering: don't quit either. It might seem overly simple, but it's not. It's the right amount of simple.

If you refuse to quit, then you won't quit. You don't need to suffer any more than is necessary; you can have the same commitment to success of your own volition. Just don't quit and you're the same.

The same can be said for that officer's single opportunity to complete BUD/S. He's fully committed to completing the program this time because he has no other option. If, in your mind, you eliminate the possibility of ever coming back to BUD/S, you'll again have the very same advantage that officer does. If it helps, remember that opportunities for prior DORs to return to BUD/S are currently gone. Imagine those opportunities will never come back. You may not have to fool yourself because, regardless of who you are, you may likely get only once chance to play.

Maturity is a harder advantage to emulate, but anyone can improve. Remember that the strengths of maturity are perspective and the ability to control one's emotions. You can accelerate your personal growth in these areas by doing any number of things. You can read to expose yourself to hardships others have endured. There is a reading list at the end of this book that I highly recommend you complete - it will start you in the right direction. If you don't have a job, consider getting one. The discipline it takes to work a regular job you might not always enjoy will help bridge that gap between boy and man and help you keep your mind focused when you're in the surf zone or under a log.

Here's a life raft in case you're in a desperate moment during Hell Week and you lose sight of your goals: The ultimate result of having perspective and a calm mind during BUD/s is being able to realize that, as terrible as this moment is, it will pass. All the misery and bullshit will pass and will ultimately be worth having endured. That's a shortcut. If you can truly believe this, if it comes from inside you, if you say it to yourself because you've come to that conclusion by yourself (instead of just repeating it because I told you to), you're well on your way to finishing BUD/S. As a bonus, you'll find that this level of discipline will help you wherever you go regardless of whether you become a SEAL.

One of the easiest characteristics to emulate is the physical fitness cushion. Work out more and harder. This is the one exception I would make to what I said above about not increasing your suffering in order to increase your commitment. If you absolutely must make yourself uncomfortable, work out more and harder. Put a pull-up bar on your bedroom door. The price of admission through the door starts at 10 pull-ups. Up the numbers as you get stronger. Want to use the bathroom? That'll cost you 30 pushups. Need to eat? Give me 50 pushups before you touch that refrigerator. A little discipline with these rules and you'll be jacked diesel before you know it. Add more running and some swim technique with a local Dive Motivator/SEAL Mentor and you'll be golden. If you ship with bare minimum PST scores, that's fine. You have plenty of time to get yourself there. Work out in boot camp. Get the most out of Pre-BUD/S. Pour yourself into your workouts, invest in fitness, and you'll have plenty of cushion when you finally class up in Coronado.

The last of the characteristics we want to match is the easiest: when you get to BUD/S, volunteer to help with everything. Don't just put your head down. Help your buddies. Help push the jet skis over the berm. Help paint the dots on the Grinder. Not only will you be respected by your class for being a team player, but focusing on things other than yourself will help you ignore the pain/discomfort/misery/torture/conditioning you're enduring on a daily basis. Be that guy and you'll be a Team Guy one day.

Now Go Do It.

We may have originally found these keys to success at BUD/S by looking at why officers complete BUD/S notably more often than enlisted men, but that doesn't mean you can't bend these tools to your own use. Nothing here is exclusive territory. Snake-eating survivalist bear-men DOR; Bambi-eyed boys make it to the Teams.

If you want to set yourself up as well as you can, you'll take these ideas to heart. You won't quit, you'll work hard, and you'll have done everything humanly possible to complete BUD/S. Not only will these 5 characteristics help you succeed, but the fact that you know you've done everything you possibly can do will help you set your mind at ease when the shit hits the fan. You'll know you can weather the cold night because you're not going to quit. Your confidence will get you the rest of the way there.

To Enlist, Or Not to Enlist. That is the Question.

This section is not going to be a comfortable read for some of you because I'm going to tell you the truth about officers and enlisted men. If you know you're going to enlist and you don't care about the issues some of your compatriots are going to have to grapple with, please feel free to skip this chapter. If, alternatively, you know you're going to have to be an officer because you're in your third year at the Naval Academy or you've signed some sort of irreversible ROTC contract, you might consider skipping this chapter because you're not going to like what I'm going to tell you.

If you're considering applying to go to OCS with a SpecWar billet, I want to strongly urge you to reconsider enlisting. If you are anywhere in the officer pipeline and you have the option of enlisting instead, do it. By all means, feel free to get your degree before you enlist. More than half of enlisted SEALs have a degree. It's a great thing to have and gives you options down the line. But a degree does not mean you have to become an officer.

I am an officer. I went to OCS with a SpecWar billet and then reported to BUD/S. If I could do it all over again, I would enlist. Let me count the reasons and, I hope, save you from making a similar mistake.

I know that you've likely heard that if you want to be a SEAL more than an officer, enlist. If you want to be an officer more than a SEAL, get your commission. That's bull. I wanted to be a SEAL

58

more than an officer, but I knew I could do both, so that advice was entirely worthless to me. You can obviously be both a SEAL and an officer. The question isn't which you want to be more, it's how you want to spend your time. An enlisted SEAL spends his life doing SEAL stuff. A SEAL officer is going to end up spending a great deal of his time doing officer stuff (including creating epic PowerPoint presentations) that will crowd out SEAL activities from his schedule. The last time my platoon had a range week, where we shot all day every day, do you know how many rounds my OIC shot? Zero. He was too busy with administrative work to shoot. That's the job sometimes. Are you sure you want it right away?

Officers make more money than enlisted men on their paychecks. This cannot be argued. But if you factor in the amount of money available in the bonuses for enlisted SEALs (vs. the nearly nonexistent bonuses for officers), the pay isn't better. In fact if you were to factor in the $40,000.00 SEAL Challenge Bonus that enlisted men receive upon completion of SQT (officers don't get any bonus), it takes 4 years for an officer to even catch up with the enlisted SEAL. He will be an O-3, a full Lieutenant, before his higher paycheck adds up to more money than the enlisted SEAL he went to BUD/S with. And guess what? Right about that time the enlisted SEAL is going to find himself in the market for a Selective Reenlistment Bonus (SRB). This SRB has, at times, been as high as $150,000.00 and is currently hovering around $80,000.00. If you're considering becoming an officer because of better pay, you're wrong.

On a ship in the regular Navy, the life of an officer is exponentially more pleasant than the life of an enlisted man. This is not the case in the SEAL Teams. If you're looking to maximize your quality of life in the Teams, you need to enlist. Unless, of course, PowerPoint makes you pitch a tent. If you love PowerPoint and email, you may just love being an officer. We're constantly reading and submitting reports. There is a lengthy report due after every training block the platoon undertakes. There is an even more painful report every time someone gets hurt in training. From time to time a senior officer will demand reports on reports, this actually happens, and reports on the status of the report on the reports. Then you have to factor in the incredible amount of time taken by writing FITREPS and Evals, the Big-Navy mandated grade sheets of everybody's job performance. Let's just say that these are the worst thing you've ever been done because saying someone is "Incredible" actually means "mediocre." In order to indicate that someone is incredible, you have to say something like "Superb Operator with Superlative Leadership Qualities." And don't you dare write "Superlative Leadership Potential" because, in the fucked-up world of Evals, that means they haven't shown any real leadership. If this sounds fun, get your commission.

Take mine.

If, on the other hand, you'd rather come in to work, work out, take care of your gear, go shoot, surf at lunch, work out again, and leave in the early afternoon, you should seriously consider enlisting.

Beyond the actual daily grind, you'll find that job expectations are a great deal clearer for enlisted guys than they are for officers. Enlisted men take care of their personal gear and their department gear, they stay organized, they stay on time, they stay in good shape, and they stay proactive. This is a stellar enlisted man. Every single person will give you a different expectation of a good officer. Most will include phrases like "looks out for his guys," which are definitely important, but you can see how two different people would interpret this guidance differently. There is a grey area here that does not exist for an enlisted SEAL, and figuring out the balance takes time and effort that enlisted men don't have to expend.

Both enlisted SEALs and officers can get 'screwed' by the SEAL Team itself from time to time. But let me give you the most recent example I have of an enlisted guy and an officer getting 'screwed' and you can see the difference. Two enlisted guys in my platoon got volun-told for a course on a Wednesday. They were going to leave on that Friday and have to be at the school all weekend. They got screwed because they were sent on a trip on short notice and they missed out on the weekend. The school, however, was a tracking school. Their weekend was not a loss. They spent the entire time tracking men through the woods and camping out around a campfire by a river at night. Alternatively, an officer I know was also recently volun-told for a job working for the Team's operations department (they run the day-to-day of the Team based on the Commanding Officer's guidance). He has been the admin bitch of a civilian working in the Ops shop for over 4 weeks straight now. He has done nothing the entire time other than create PowerPoint presentations for a woman's readiness group associated with the Team and plan a party for the outgoing XO. Oh, he also had to decorate the newly-painted wardroom. He went to OCS, BUD/S, and SQT; he finished his platoon's pre-deployment workup. And now he's been a secretary (not even a glorified secretary) for a civilian for 4 weeks and counting. Pick your poison, gents.

Enlisted SEALs go to Sniper School. They go to Breacher School and learn to blow up doors. They learn to be Corpsman (medics), Joint Terminal Attack Controllers (JTACs - they guide munitions from air assets, they put 'warheads on foreheads'), and radio operators. Officers go overseas and work in a headquarters and prep, you guessed it, PowerPoint presentations for big-wigs. This is how SEAL officers get their "professional development." Even if there's no reason not to go to a school, like JTAC, an officer is not likely to get the green light to go simply because officers don't usually go. As an enlisted man you will go to cool-guy schools. As an officer, you will likely fight for every school you get and you will rarely, if ever, get a fun school. Cool-guy schools are the almost exclusive domain of the enlisted man.

The jobs that most officers do are incredibly important, but they aren't fun. They're not in the same league as shooting a suicide bomber in the head from 800 yards.

On the other hand, a headstrong new officer is going to make more headway in getting things done than a headstrong "new guy" enlisted man. A junior officer, depending on his level of knowledge and the personality of his platoon commander, can actually find himself able to contribute and help shape his platoon. (A headstrong new enlisted guy, however, is likely to find himself taped up and thrown in an iced-over pool.) This ability to rise above the fray of low-level politics and pack dynamics from time to time also affords a young officer the ability to learn a bit of everything. On training trips he is not committed to being a breacher or sniper 100% of the time, and so finds himself able to join the snipers one day and the breachers the next, becoming familiar with every skill set in his platoon but not being a master of any.

New guy officers fill the roll of the Assistant Officer in Charge (AOIC) during their first workup and deployment. This role is largely defined as "shut up and learn from the Chief." They often end up doing the majority of the administrative work for the platoon while the Officer in Charge (OIC) teaches them how to do his job.

In his next rotation, an officer will most likely be the OIC of a platoon. On the battlefield it's his job to think "up and out." He's managing all the assets (helicopters, drones, close air support, etc) while the Chief is controlling the tactical situation on the ground. Additionally, the OIC is the face and voice of the platoon (and the SEAL community in general). Since NSW doesn't own any battlespace overseas, SEAL platoons typically work for a more senior officer from the Army or the Marine Corps. In order to conduct operations in that man's battlespace, the OIC of a platoon has to get approval. As dumb as it sounds (and is), if the SEAL OIC makes a poor impression on that Army or Marine Corps officer, his platoon might sit around and play XBOX the entire deployment because they're not allowed to get out the door. This is yet another reason why having (or being) a good OIC is mission-critical, though nowhere as cool as being a sniper or breacher or point man.

The whole issue of whether you should enlist or join as an officer is a personal one. If you want a long, rewarding career as an operator, enlisting is the way to begin. Often the best officers are the mustangs, guys who were enlisted Team Guys before they got their commission. This is always an option for an enlisted man who wants to be a leader and pull a more respectable retirement check. Most enlisted men prefer their lives in the enlisted world and wouldn't become officers even if you paid them handsomely.

On the other side, if you don't intend to stay in the Teams, joining as an officer makes an amount of sense. You get a good amount of experience, get to see every side of the business, and get to lead some bad ass men. Day to day, however, your life is often not nearly as rewarding. And after just a few deployments, you've worked your way out of the field into a desk. Most guys don't join the Teams to ride a desk - which is why the majority of Lieutenants process themselves out of the Navy after their OIC tour.

The choice is yours, and there's no one 'right' answer, but be sure to give consideration to all your options.

Chapter 2

SEAL Mental Toughness Techniques.

Possunt quia posse videntur.
"They could because they thought they could."
- Virgil, Aeneid 5:231

People experience BUD/S two different ways. Most people will tell you that BUD/S is heinous, violent, and impossible. Guys who make it will tell you that it sucked but wasn't the worst thing in the world. Both groups endured the same program, the same tortures, the same water, the same instructors, the same sand. In fact the guys who made it endured a great deal more and worse - you'll find nearly universal agreement that the worst part of BUD/S isn't Hell Week or First Phase. Confounding the question even further is the fact that often the best runners, the best swimmers, and the strongest guys are among the first to quit. Why, then, do some men complete BUD/S with ease where other men are incapable of enduring?

The answer is so simple it has to be true: mental toughness.

There is no secret ability or unmentionable spiritual gift I possess that you do not. I'm a SEAL because I chose to be. Plain and simple. I proved my mental toughness under the boat and in the surf. Your turn to prove yourself is coming sooner than you realize, so I'm going to share with you some mental techniques you should be using in BUD/S.

This won't be the last time you see these techniques either: the major concepts actually come from the Naval Special Warfare Center's (NSWC) psychiatrist, the very same guy who created that C-SORT psychological fitness test you're going to have to take as part of your application to go to BUD/S. If I were telling you this in person, I would be elbowing you and winking when I mention this because not only will these techniques help you succeed at BUD/S, they'll also help you score higher on the C-SORT. You'll get these techniques again, at great length, when you get to BUD/S and have your first Mentorship session. You'll be so far ahead of the curve, having practiced these techniques for months prior, that you'll smile and say to yourself "I've got this."

These techniques will save you from yourself. Face it, as far as your mind and body are concerned, BUD/S is a stupid idea. It's cold, it's long, it hurts. Your mind - if allowed to run free - will sabotage you. Your body - if allowed to speak - will convince your mind to quit. At the time these urges will seem logical, will be backed up by every fiber in your body, and will convince you that you don't really need to stick it out. Your mental weakness is the serpent, seducing you to eat the fruit and ring that bell. These techniques will help you short-circuit these reactions, redirect your energy, kill that serpent, and keep your head in the game. You've got this.

Mental Toughness: Segmenting.

Ben Saunders is a British explorer and endurance athlete, famous for skiing to the North Pole solo and unsupported. He is one of three men to reach the North Pole alone and on foot, and the youngest by over a decade. When an interviewer asked him how he was able to wrap his mind around such an epic undertaking, Saunders replied that he never did. He told the interviewer that his mind rarely strayed from "getting to that bit of ice a few yards in front of me." He maintained this for 1032.3 km while pulling all his supplies behind him on a sled.

The first mental toughness technique I want you to learn is segmenting, or goal-setting. Segmenting is what Ben Saunders did when he concentrated on the ice in front of him and ignored the 800km he still had to ski. He broke an epic undertaking down into palatable lengths of ice. He always had the energy to take a few more steps. Then a few more steps. Then a few more. Soon, a few more steps added up to a further distance than he ever imagined. He never had to make a huge decision to continue or give up. After all, he only had a few more steps to take. Ben Saunders never allowed himself an "out." So he succeeded.

Have you ever been running and, in order to push yourself, decided to sprint to the second telephone pole? Do you think you'd have run as hard for as long if you'd just picked up the pace for a little while? This is the same effect.

How do you eat an elephant? One bite at a time. This is a joke, but it's also segmenting. And it works.

Eat BUD/S one bite at a time. You can break it down any way you want to, but the most common is chow to chow, day to day. Wake up in the morning and want to quit? Just make it to breakfast. When you're eating breakfast you'll say to yourself, "This isn't too bad" and you'll continue. When you're done, get to lunch. Then get to dinner. Then you've got one less day to do. Get to tomorrow's breakfast now. That's all. Don't concentrate on graduating or even finishing the phase you're in. Get to lunch. When you find yourself in the surf zone, remember that it can't last forever because you're getting to lunch. When you're at lunch, get to dinner. When you're at dinner, get to bedtime. That's one more day of BUD/S you'll never have to do again.

I hated Log PT more than anything in BUD/S. I would run 10 miles wet and sandy before I willingly did another Log PT. Every time we finished a Log PT I'd check it off and it would be a good day. It didn't matter if we went straight from Log PT to a surf torture: I was one more Log PT closer to completion.

Becoming a SEAL is an epic undertaking. When you get there you'll look back and marvel at all the shit you put up with to get there. But not while you're in training. While you're in training you will eat one bite at a time.

Homework:
Practice segmenting today by living your life one evolution at a time. If you're in school, segment class to class. If you're working, segment break to break (if you don't already). If you have chores, segment chore to chore.

Practice breaking your existence into palatable segments. If Ben Saunders can eat his elephant one bite at a time, and hundreds of students eat BUD/S one bite at a time, you should give this mental toughness technique a serious effort. It just might mean the difference between a brown shirt and a ticket to the fleet.

Mental Toughness: Visualization.

The ancestor of every action is thought - Ralph Waldo Emerson

Alan Richardson divided volunteers into three random groups. Group 1 was required to come in and practice shooting free throws 20 minutes every day for 20 days. Group 2 was told not to shoot a basketball, think about basketball, or have anything to do with the sport for 20 days. Group 3 was required to come in and participate in vivid visualization sessions about shooting free throws. At the end of the 20 days Dr. Richardson tested each group for improvement over their beginning averages. Group 1 (practice) improved their free throw accuracy by 24%. Group 2 (did nothing) made no gains. Group 3 had not touched a basketball in 20 days; their practice had been strictly limited to the visualization sessions. How did they fare? Group 3 improved their free throw accuracy by 23%, only 1% less than the group who'd actually been shooting free throws.

Jack Nicklaus has famously said that he attributes 90% of his golf success to mental preparation and only 10% to skill. Nicklaus would religiously visualize putts, chips, and drives. "I would never hit a shot, even in practice, without having a very sharp picture of it in my head. First I see the ball where I want it to finish...then see the ball going there. I watch its path, shape, and even its behavior on landing, then a sort of fade out, and the next scene is of the swing that will turn the previous image into reality." Jack Nicklaus used visualization to win 18 major championships over his career and is considered one of golf's all-time greats. It worked for him, make it work for you.

Effective visualizations are vivid and detailed. If you're picturing the balance logs on the obstacle course, make sure you know which side has a log of larger diameter. Make sure you know which log tends to roll which way. Make sure you visualize your pants being unbloused, feel the sand in your waistband from the low-crawl, and the slight rope-burn on your palms from the cargo net. The more detailed and visceral your visualization is, the more effective it will be. Use all your senses. Smell the sea-breeze. Hear the crunch of sand under your boots and the screaming of instructors into the bullhorn. Hear the guys in front of you yell "Hooyah" when they hit the Hooyah Logs. Taste the sand and sweat in your mouth. Feel the grinding of the raw rope fibers of the cargo net and the burning of sweat in your chafing. Don't leave anything out. The more you put in, the more you get back.

Effective visualizations are repeated. If you do it one time, you're not gaining much. You need to gain the muscle memory (which visualization is proven to help with). You need to put in the work so when the real deal comes, you've been there before and it's old news to you. Practice in bed as you're falling asleep every night. Practice at chow if you have an extra minute. Visualize success at every turn and you'll find it when you get there.

Effective visualizations are largely positive. If you're having trouble with the balance logs or the Slide For Life obstacle, use visualization to help yourself. Picture yourself succeeding. Do not picture yourself failing. There are times to visualize negatively, but when it's an issue of performance, you want to practice doing it right (and visualization is practice). Vince Lombardi said "Practice does not make perfect. Only perfect practice makes perfect." If you're practicing mentally, there's no reason to practice anything other than perfection. So keep your visualizations positive, except in the following instance.

If you really want to discourage yourself from quitting, visualize the consequences.

Do not visualize the actual quitting.

I repeat. Do not visualize yourself quitting. Keep that image entirely out of your mind. It's fucking poison.

If you want to do this, visualize that you quit a day ago and you haven't told anyone. Now visualize that call to your parents. They're disappointed but always supportive. Visualize the conversations you have with the other quitters you now live with. Everyone has an excuse and their weakness makes you hate yourself for yours. Hear them all say they were medically disqualified (even though you know they weren't) and hear yourself agree "Yeah, I'm hurt too, but the doctors just would't believe me so I had to quit." Visualize the conversations your friends have about how they all knew you'd never be able to make it. Imagine having to explain quitting to every single person who knew you were going to BUD/S. You have to face them. You have to live with many of them. Imagine trying to find a way to overcome the shame of failing. How long is it going to take for them to stop thinking of you as a failure, a quitter, a pussy? How long until anyone takes anything you say seriously again? Visualize being sent to a crappy ship, an undesignated Seaman. Imagine, if you will, a life below deck where you spend 18 hours chipping paint and repainting the spot you chipped. Imagine not seeing the sun for days or weeks at a time. This picture is worse than anything in BUD/S. Experience the shame and humiliation of quitting once in your head. Feel how much you hate yourself for giving up on your dream. Then never, ever, ever experience it in real life.

Homework:
Practice visualizing your next step in your quest to become a SEAL. If your next step is getting in shape, visualize yourself running and doing pushups. Picture perfect form and a good performance. If your next step is taking the PST for real, visualize the entire PST. Every lap of the swim, the order in which you change out during the transition/rest time, each pushup, each sit-up, each pull-up. Feel yourself walking to the track, staying as relaxed as possible, before the run. Feel yourself sounding off as you cruise through each lap of the run, slowly pressing the pace until you're at 100% on the last lap. Picture yourself finishing and

getting your SEAL Challenge contract right there. Feel that pride and accomplishment.

Now visualize your next step. Remember to include all your senses. Get after it.

Mental Toughness: Arousal Control.

Nearly every person who quits BUD/S will tell you they feel a flash of relief followed by a tsunami of regret. The regret is earth-shattering and nearly instantaneous. It's worse than anything that happens to you while you're in BUD/S.

Why, if they were going to regret their decisions so quickly, did they quit in the first place? What pressed their DOR button? If you talk to them you'll find that they weren't thinking about much when they quit, they just did it. They weren't looking at the big picture; they lacked perspective and they let their stress get the best of them.

We all know what the fight-or-flight response is. In times of stress or perceived danger we revert to our most basic human urges: avoid pain, pursue pleasure.

BUD/S is a lot of pain. Your brain will naturally want to avoid it.

If you get broken down to fight-or-flight, you're on the verge of quitting: it's very easy to make the pain stop.

All you have to do is quit.

This stress-induced adrenaline rush is caused by a release of cortisol (a stress hormone) in your brain. Not only does cortisol control the release of adrenaline, but it also suppresses your immune system and decreases bone formation. The adrenaline itself will make your movements jerky, making marksmanship difficult or impossible, and will wear you out, making you more vulnerable to injury or disease. Both hormones can - for obvious reasons, decrease your chances of completing training.

There is a technique to control your physiological responses to stress. In your mentorship sessions at BUD/S, you'll hear this referred to as your "4 and 4 for 4." The technique: inhale for 4 seconds, exhale for 4 seconds, repeat for 4 minutes. Focus completely on breathing deeply and smoothly. At the end of four minutes you'll find yourself in a much more controlled mental state.

People have been using controlled breathing techniques for centuries as an integral part of yoga, meditation, and martial arts. You'll find that there are times you'll rely heavily on your 4-and-4-for-4 in BUD/S. While you're locked down in the classroom the Sunday before Hell Week kicks off, you'll often find yourself beginning to breath quickly and your mind racing. Stop. Do your 4-and-4-for-4. You'll be back on even keel. On the pool deck before your name is called to enter the water for Pool Comp, you'll see every single man doing his 4-and-4-for-4. Before the 50m underwater swim, before the Day One Grinder PT, before a marksmanship test - you'll find students concentrating on their breathing in order to control themselves.

Trust the technique. Practice it. You'll find it comes in handy more than you'd you think it would. I did it before combat ops in Afghanistan. It works.

Homework:
The next time you find yourself nervous, use your 4-and-4-for-4. Before your PST, before your ASVAB, before a test in school, before a track meet or wrestling match, controlled breathing techniques will help you calm down, remain collected, and perform better. Incorporate it into your everyday life and you'll find it's much easier to maintain your composure.

Mental Toughness: Self Talk.

Life is what your thoughts make it. - Mark Aurelius

Self-help infomercials make me laugh. My favorites are those sleazy guys who try to sell CDs of compliments and positive thoughts to middle-aged housewives who live on a steady diet of Mary Kay makeup and Jenny Craig meals, who work out with a shake-weight, and watch the Home Shopping Network all day (wearing their Snuggies) until Oprah comes on and they have a spiritual connection to women across the world. These guys sell dreams of success to those too weak to go get it themselves.

That's what I think of when I hear the phrase "self talk" or when I hear someone mention "affirmations."

I think of those guys who spend money on The Secret, a mystical key to success that tells you to put your wishes and positive energy out into the universe and your dreams will come true. No joke. Simply ask for something and you will get it. No effort on your part is required. There are some excellent YouTube video excerpts I strongly recommend you watch. In fact, put the book down and go watch them for a few minutes. They're worth the time. Just search for "The Secret."

Can you believe that book made it to the top of the New York Times Bestseller list? Neither can I.

Snake-oil wishy-washy 'techniques' like this make me self conscious when it comes to using actual mental techniques that center on positive thinking. I don't want to be anything like those limpwristed losers who buy The Secret. But there actually is value in positive thinking, and we can't let those people arrogate this valuable technique from us.

The first thing we should recognize is that nobody can affect our minds, only we can. Epictetus, a Stoic (Greek) philosopher, tells us that "men are disturbed not by things, but the view they take of them." He means that there's another layer between someone else's words and actions and our reaction. I'll give you a perfect example of the sort of mind-fuck you'll experience in BUD/S.

Log PT, baby, the last Log PT before Hell Week.
I hate Log PT. I'm skinny. The logs are heavy. I like having skin. The sand-coated logs like to remove skin. The logs and I disagree on a number of things.

There's a foreign officer in my boat crew, we'll call him Shareef. Shareef is a pussy. My entire boat crew is smoked. We're all dying. We've been doing lunges and 12-counts (you'll learn about these awesome little exercises later) and running in soft sand with the log at a chest carry for over an hour. Now we're lined up doing lunges. The calls for the lunges are coming out fast and cruel from the instructors and we can't keep up. I look over and, as my boat crew is straining to get the log up, I see Shareef leaning on the log.

That motherfucker is not only NOT helping, but he's actively damaging his boat crew.

This is a mortal sin thou shalt never commit. I move myself on the log to be next to Shareef. I'm hoping to get him to put out; I intend, at least to try to carry as much of his weight as I can and save my guys. After two more lunges, I'm smoked to the bone, but the calls keep coming. "One. Two. Three. Four. One. Two. One. Two."

An instructor, a Chief, comes over and squats directly in front of me. "Mr. Xavier," he says, "You are failing."

His voice is cold and mechanical and I'm afraid maybe I am failing. I know Shareef is weak. Am I? It certainly feels like I might

77

be.

Fuck me. If I'm weak they'll boot me out. I'm gonna hold on and make them do it. I won't do it.

"Hooyah." I gasp as I try to keep up with the lunges. Shareef looks like he's putting out for a moment. Of course.

Really, am I a shitbag? Am I weak and blaming it on Shareef instead of myself?

"Mr. Xavier, if you're too weak for this, maybe you should just quit. You're hurting your boat crew. You're a fucking disgrace."

"Hooyah, Chief," I gasped between lunges, "I'm not fucking quitting." Inside I know they might actually think I'm weak and unsuitable for the program. But I don't let it affect me because I know they'll pull me out if I'm really too weak. I'm not scared. I simply keep putting out because that's all there is to do. Inside I'm thinking "if they really want me gone, they'll drop me. Otherwise, I'm going to assume they're just messing with my mind." I try not to let them get to me.

"Hey Tony!" Chief calls over the instructor with the megaphone. "Mr. Xavier here is too weak to keep up. I think we should start over, don't you?"

"Starting over for Mr. Xavier because he is too weak to keep up." The class groans silently, hating me with grumbles and curses, and grits its teeth as it begins lunges again. Legs and backs are on fire. I shrug it off because I'm just going to go until I pass out or die. If they don't like it, that's their problem. They'll have to drop me to get rid of me.

We start lunging. I look over between breaths and see Shareef, right next to me, leaning on the log again. That's it. I turn toward him and Spartan kick him in the ribs. He flops to the ground whining and holds his side.

I don't care.

He's a buddy fucker and, as far as I'm concerned at the moment, that should be punishable by death. I slide down to the end of the log and the rest of my crew silently adjusts its spacing. All of a sudden we can keep up. After two full, glorious, luxuriously easy lunges, Shareef gets up and watches us. Chief comes back over with a little smile on his face.

He knew what was going on the whole time. He was just testing my reaction to failure and humiliation. Good thing I didn't get down on myself.

Now he's on Shareef. After being humiliated, Shareef regains his position on the log. One lunge later and he's leaning on it again. I push him off the log and he collapses. One of my guys spits on him and I can't help laughing. He tries to get on the log again and we don't let him. The instructors are laughing now, and tell Shareef that his team has finally realized it's better off without him. Our boat crew never got one-on-one attention from the instructors again.

Parenthetically, Shareef was the single foreign officer I saw get sent home early. He failed Drown Proofing with 4 classes before the BUD/S command decided he simply could not be trained. His other countryman in my class ended up graduating, but not before getting lost beyond all reason during Land Nav and almost shooting an instructor on San Clemente Island.

Here's what we can learn from this story of Log PT: The instructors will, at every turn, try to get you to quit. It's not because they want you to quit - they don't even know you. It's because they want quitters to quit. So they tell everyone to quit. They're good at it too: they'll make it seem like they're talking to you specifically. They'll make a spectacle of you from time to time. You have to remember that the things they say and do cannot touch your resolve. Only you can. Quitters might quit, but fighters stick it out and say "fuck you."

The chain reaction goes like this:

Event - Belief - Consequence.

The event, in my case, was public humiliation and denunciation. They were kicking me while I was way, way down.

My belief could have been that they truly didn't want me there; the consequence of that belief would have been me quitting. Instead, my belief was that I didn't care what they said. I believed I was capable of succeeding, despite what they said. I believed I was strong enough. I believed they were just messing with me and that they would drop me if I was truly not fit to become a SEAL.

The consequence of that series of beliefs was that I solved my boat crew's problem, we completed the evolution, Shareef got sent packing to his home country in shame (I wonder if they executed him in dishonor), and I ultimately became a SEAL.

Now nobody touches my resolve but me. Nobody dampens my spirits but me. Like Epictetus said, we're not affected by the things that happen to us, but by our reactions to those things. React correctly and nothing can truly affect us. The best way to control your reaction is through self-talk.

Some guys might memorize phrases to repeat, a mantra of sorts. I, personally, found myself repeating "this is what I'm doing" throughout Hell Week. It's not profound or insightful, but it's simple and I found that it redirected my attention. Any time I thought about picking my head up and seeing myself in the intimidating context of Hell Week instead of the individual evolution, I would start to ask myself why I was doing it. "Because this is what I'm doing right now."

Why am I putting up with this?

"Because this is what I'm doing right now."

If you want something with a little more bravado, try this:

"This is the shit that separates me from weaker men."

Homework:

Your self-talk homework comes in two parts today:

One. Come up with a phrase or two that you feel will motivate you in hard times. Make it short. Make it easy to remember. I don't care where you choose it/them from, but make sure it's something that doesn't require much thinking to understand. You want to be able to use it when you're scraping bottom. You want something you can use just as easily during a PST or bootcamp as you can on Wednesday of Hell Week. Give yourself some mantra to take strength from when you need it.

Two. The next time someone makes you mad or upset, remember that they don't have the ability to change your mood. Only you do. If they're having an effect, that's you allowing them to affect you. Separate their actions, the event, from the consequence. In this case, the consequence would be your change in mood. Choose to react differently. Believe they're having a bad day and you shouldn't take it personally. Believe they don't know what they're talking about. Believe what you need to in order to change the consequence. Do not allow them access to you.

Practice this every time you sense yourself becoming angry or upset. Not only will you find it helps you when you get to BUD/S, but I'll wager it'll help you in your everyday relationships as well.

Mental Toughness: Small Victories.

If BUD/S is a game you're playing against the instructors, then you're going to lose every day. There is no question. You can do everything perfectly, you will still be "fucked up beyond repair." You will still be punished. They will find something. If they can't, they'll make it up. Believe it or not, the majority of the beatings you get for messing up are scheduled. They are planned, premeditated.

You cannot escape them.

You will lose every battle and it will get very old very quickly. In fact you'll start to get mad in Second Phase because you'll see through their bullshit. Our first day of Second Phase, we had a solid beating on the beach. They tried to run us to death, but we were pretty fast. So they stopped us down the beach, away from the prying eyes of the command who would save us if things got bad. The beating lasted over two hours. We bear-crawled. We filled our cammie pants entirely with sand and ran with mouthfuls of seawater. During this beating they screamed at us that this was because we kept messing up the same things. "Same names!" they yelled. "Your proctor has done everything in his power to set you up for success and STILL you fuck up."

The only thing was that when they yelled "same names" they didn't even know our names, so there's no way they could've been actually mad at those guys. Our proctor had apparently done "everything in his power" to help us, and so we were being punished. We hadn't met our proctor yet. We hadn't done an evolution yet, aside from this beating, so there was nothing we could've messed up. We were pissed. We were losing a battle we didn't know was being fought.

This is BUD/S. You can't take it personally. It's like Hoot says in Black Hawk Down, "See you're thinking. Don't. 'Cause Sergeant, you can't control who gets hit or who doesn't or who falls out of a chopper or why. It ain't up to you. It's just war."

See, you're thinking. Don't. 'Cause, buddy, you can't control who gets beat or who doesn't, or who gets wet and sandy or why. It ain't up to you. It's just BUD/S.

You will lose the war every day and the only way to really keep your head up is to enjoy the small victories. Just finished a Log PT? That's one less Log PT you'll ever have to do in your life. Winning.

Dig out the low-crawl on the obstacle course a little bit. Don't do it too much because they'll notice. Do it some, though. When you go through the low-crawl, enjoy the extra room, because you pulled a little one over on the instructors. Sure, you still had to run the o-course. They won the war. They're going to beat you afterwards. Yup, they win again. But the low crawl? On the low crawl you were the victor. Winning.

Stash some peanut butter packets in your pockets from the chow hall. They're small packages of calories (read: energy) and positive mental attitude (PMA). They can survive the surf and the sand and live to be eaten another day. Eat them and share them. You're not supposed to do this, but I only ever saw one guy get caught with them and all he had to do was hit the surf. Well worth the risk. You're going to hit the surf anyway. Peanut butter packets: winning.

My roommates and I failed a barracks inspection in First Phase. We thought we could beat the system. Because we'd passed the uniform inspection we were allowed to change into working cammies (vs. Immaculate "inspection" cammies) before going down to get beat for the sins of our barracks room. We closed the door to change, changed out, and decided to turn the light off and wait in the room. We figured they didn't actually count how many guys were getting beat, so they'd never miss four guys. Apparently we weren't the first or only students to try this strategy, because as we waited in the dark room, we heard instructors burst through the exterior door of the barracks and yell.

"Anyone still in the barracks, DROP THE FUCK DOWN AND FUCKING BEAR CRAWL TO MY VOICE."

We looked at each other. I looked at the window.

"Window?" They all looked at the window. We looked at each other.

"Window."

We helped each other out the 2nd-story window, dropped onto the ground, and ran around the barracks to the drying cages where those lucky few who'd actually passed were getting ready for a conditioning run. We ran into the cages and got ready for the run. We never got beat and we never got caught. That day, we were winning.

Here's another fun fact: I didn't hit the surf the entirety of Breakout (which is the chaotic evolution that kicks off Hell Week). Breakout is insane. There are mortar simulation rounds going off, explosions, instructors shooting .50 caliber blanks into the air. There are smoke grenades obscuring everything. There are instructors running everywhere screaming at everyone. It's complete and utter chaos. You're supposed to run from the Grinder, where you're getting beat, to the surf zone to get wet, and back to the Grinder to get beat again.

You know what my boat crew and I did? We ran like madmen, arms over our heads like Kermit the Frog when he gets excited, screaming "Hooyah" at the tops of our lungs. We realized that if we entered the Grinder, we'd get beat, so we ran to the entrance of the Grinder and turned around toward the ocean. We ran down to the surf and turned around right at the water's edge. On the rare occasion an instructor asked us what the hell we were doing, I would tell him that another instructor (usually I chose a name that outranked him) had told us to do that very specific thing. There was so much chaos there was no way to tell what was going on. They couldn't even see who we were, so if the same instructor asked us the same question twice, he'd never know it. We used their own chaos to our advantage and started Hell Week off by pulling one over their eyes. We won the battle. But we still had to do Hell Week, so they definitely won that war.

Gain momentum and rekindle your spirit in the small victories. They're all you're going to get, but they're enough to see you through.

Now some guys, some Team Guys even, will tell you this is bad advice because you're cheating yourself out of the full training.

Bullshit.

BUD/S is the modern Spartan "agoge," where young boys were trained and tempered for war and put into difficult situations. In Sparta they were punished severely, not for stealing, but for being caught stealing. Cheating wasn't wrong if you got away with it. In fact it was part of the training, teaching budding warriors to think out of the box and take advantage of every opportunity. Any man who furrows his brow at the thought of braving the possibility of soul-crushing punishment for an advantage has his mind in the wrong place.

BUD/S is selection for a warrior culture. BUD/S is mental and physical conditioning for the pain and shock of war. There is no other purpose. A man who moralizes on the right and wrong of cutting corners in BUD/S forgets this: there are no rules in war. The storied British Special Air Service (SAS) believe this so ardently they've immortalized the spirit in their unit's motto: "Who Dares, Wins." Their maritime counterparts, the Special Boat Service (SBS), echo the spirit of unconventional thinking in their ethos: "Not By Strength, By Guile."

Be smart, be brave. My first covert op wasn't in Afghanistan. It was in OCS where we created a ratline for smuggling food in. I polished my skills and whetted the edge in BUD/S doing things like crawling out of the window. Some of us swam food out to classes before and after us while they were in Thursday night of Hell Week as they did the Around the World Paddle. Against the rules, yes. Who cares? We were winning.

Weigh the possible consequences against the possible gain and the likelihood of getting caught. Grow some balls and act. Make those small victories count.

Homework:
Begin to recognize the small victories in your life. Get a smile

from a hot girl? Victory. Hit two green lights in a row? Victory. Take joy in the small things and see how it boosts your spirit. If you take the time and get in the habit now, you'll find it's much easier to find small victories while you're at BUD/S.

Next, make victories for yourself. Read about the unconventional tactics SEALs used with unprecedented success in Vietnam. Read about the Spartan agoge and begin to prepare yourself for the closest thing the modern world has to offer.

Mental Toughness: The Man Next to You.

"How did I get through Hell Week?
Well, I kept looking around and there were still guys there.
I figured if that guy can do it, so can I.
He's no better than I am."
LCDR Joe Burns

Ask any Team Guy how he got through Hell Week and BUD/S, and you're likely to hear this. The man next to us helps us all. We can derive strength from his presence and he from ours. If he can do it, so can we.

This is an easy way to keep your head in the game, but beware its backswing.

Make sure that you're not only keying on friends when you tell yourself this, because those friends might not be there on Friday of Hell Week. I've seen good guys quit because their friend did. They apparently only related their ability to succeed with their friends', and when those friends don't cut it, it's like someone came along and cut their legs off at the knee.

So take strength from your classmates. Tell yourself that if the man next to you can do it, so can you. Just don't be too specific. As long as there's one other man in your class, that should be good enough for you.

* * *

Homework:

None. If you don't care about the guys next to you, don't even go to BUD/S. Become a banker or something.

Chapter 3

Pre-Ship Steps for Enlisted Tadpoles.

"Who Dares, Wins."
- SAS Motto

So now you've found yourself dreaming of becoming a SEAL. You want to enlist, crush BUD/S, learn everything you can in SQT and become a consummate professional warrior. You want to be one of the world's elite special operators. Fuck yeah. Get some.

There's only one problem: how do you even get there? Where do you start? What sort of bullshit do you have to endure, what tickets do you need to punch, and who do you need to talk to in order to even get to BUD/S? The process isn't terribly complicated, but a mis-step can cause your quest to come to an untimely, screeching halt.

The good news is that, after reading this chapter, you'll know what to do and what to avoid. If you end up not getting a contract because you're dumb and didn't take my words to heart, then I suppose the Teams are better off without you. Here's where you start with discipline; here's where you start to show dedication. Start now and don't look back.

Enlisted Pre-Ship: Key Tasks.

In order to become a Navy SEAL, you first have to be in the Navy. It would be a terrible risk, however, to join the Navy hoping to go to BUD/S without a written guarantee you'd get a chance. Big Navy isn't easily moved, and there's always grey paint that needs to be chipped on some ship in the middle of nowhere.

Thank goodness, then, for the SEAL Challenge, which contractually obligates the Navy to give you a chance to attend BUD/S (provided you pass the standards leading up to it.) The two most basic requirements for a SEAL Challenge Contract are as follows:

Passing Armed Services Vocational Aptitude Battery (ASVAB) Scores.

Passing Physical Screening Test (PST) Scores.

The best way to get both of these scores on record with the Navy without making any true commitment is the Delayed Entry Program (DEP). DEP is a way to join the navy, get access to NSW-NSO Mentors, SEAL Motivators, and take the PST without signing your life away. DEP allows you to slowly ease yourself into the Navy over a year. You can decide not to enlist at any point. The only limitation is a requirement to restart the enlistment process if you've been in a DEP pool over a year. For our purposes the program is fantastic; there really aren't any drawbacks.

Joining DEP is as easy as finding a local Navy recruiter (they're everywhere) and telling them you want to DEP in with the intention to get a SEAL Challenge Contract. At this point they're going to look at you like you've got a dick growing out of your forehead and ask you what your second choice is. You shouldn't settle for anything less, so tell them as much.

The problem with most recruiters is that they really don't know anything about the SEAL Teams or BUD/S. A recruiter I spoke to when I was considering enlistment told me that being a fireman on a ship was almost the same thing. My guess is that he had a quota to fill and he was low on firemen. Let me be clear about this: a fireman on a ship is not a Navy SEAL. Neither is SWCC. Neither is a Diver or a Search and Rescue (SAR) Swimmer.

Remember this about your recruiter: that fat fuck works for you. You don't owe him a god-damned thing, so don't feel compelled to entertain a second choice. Be civil, but don't take "no" for an answer, ever. If a recruiter won't help you get your SEAL Challenge, you go find one who will.

Once you find a recruiter who's willing to work with you, you'll have to take the ASVAB. The test is usually administered on an old-school computer and will take a few hours. The test itself isn't difficult, the standards you have to meet aren't incredibly high (they're detailed in the SEAL Challenge Requirements chapter at the end of this book), and most guys will surpass the minimum score fairly easily. If you're a poor test-taker (or just dumb) don't fear: you can retake the test every month until you pass. If your recruiter tells you otherwise, he's probably misinformed. Remember, he works for you. If he's not helping, you fire him and get someone new. If you do need to score higher on your ASVAB, there are study guides available in bookstores that are well worth the money. Just look at this as the first of many evolutions on your road to becoming a Team Guy.

So you've passed your ASVAB. One more test: the C-SORT. Taken directly from the Navy's SEAL/SWCC website:

"The Computerized-Special Operations Resilience Test, or C-SORT, is designed to assess a prospective SEAL candidate's mental toughness or resilience. The test includes multiple sections designed to assess a prospective candidate's abilities in three areas: performance strategies, psychological resilience, and personality traits. Performance strategies test for capabilities such as a person's goal-setting, self-talk, and emotional control. Psychological resilience focusses on assessing several other areas like an individual's acceptance of life situations and the ability to deal with cognitive challenges and threats."

If you don't recognize that we've already talked about these very specific attributes in the chapter of "Mental Toughness Techniques," you should go back and read that chapter again.

Here's a fun fact: those techniques were codified in the BUD/S Mentorship curriculum by the same Psychologist, Dr. Potterat, who developed the C-SORT. Even if you think they're hoodoo mumbo-jumbo bullshit (which they are not) you should still study them for when you take the C-SORT because you only get one opportunity to take it.

Here's the thing about the C-SORT: you can still get to BUD/S even the test says you're mentally weak. You just have to be physically stronger. If you bomb the C-SORT (which you shouldn't, since I've given you the tools used to design it), you just have to achieve elevated PST scores. And all that takes is more working out on your part, which shouldn't be a big deal because physical fitness is a labor of love for you by now, isn't it? So the C-SORT might be an inconvenience, but it will never be a roadblock.

Now you can "DEP in." Depending on your DEP pool, you may be required or "encouraged" to attend DEP meetings. These are the tax you pay for being able to work out with a SEAL Motivator or NSW-NSO Mentor (these terms are largely interchangeable). Some Mentors will hold workouts 3 times a week. Others will only have one workout a month. Some only administer PSTs. I hope, for your sake, your Mentor is active and holds workouts on a regular basis.

My Mentor was an absolutely phenomenal Team Guy. He held workouts 2-3 times a week, helped me navigate the paperwork, and kept track of my scores and workouts. Regardless of how active he is, your Mentor is your new best friend because he's the gatekeeper. Attend every single event he sets up. Take every PST you possibly can. Remember that if you take a PST and don't pass, you lose nothing. Worst case, you got a killer workout. Best case: you get your contract.

You have everything to gain and nothing to lose.

Somewhere between the ASVAB and DEPing in, you also have to go to MEPS (Military Entrance Processing Station), where you'll have a fun day of semi-demeaning physicals. They'll test for color-blindness, visual acuity, hearing sensitivity, and, to finish off your day, you'll spend a few joyful minutes duck-walking back and forth across a cold tile floor in your underwear with a dozen of your (now) closest friends. The guy next to you will probably be fat and pungent. Maybe he falls sideways onto you because he can't duckwalk. Maybe you can't get his disgusting smell off you until you get home. MEPS is a delight.

If you've done all of the above, you will be entered into the pool of applicants. From this pool the Navy will periodically select the top applicants and award them SEAL Challenge Contracts. It is entirely possible to compete BUD/S having only achieved minimum passing scores, but these days it's more competitive and minimum passing scores probably won't get you selected. You see, all applicants enter the same pool.

If you're number 201 in the pool, with 200 applicants having better scores than you, then when they choose the top 200 for a class, you'll be number 1 on the list. But if 200 more competitive applicants enter the pool before the next 'draft,' then you're back to 201 and you'll be passed over again. While you're in the applicant pool you can - and should - continually improve your scores. Continue to work out and take PSTs. Your Mentor can submit updated scores, which would bump you up higher in the draft order and increase your chances of getting picked up.

Once you're selected you will be able to sign your SEAL Challenge Contract (which probably also includes a juicy little bonus payable upon SQT graduation.) At this point you're ready to ship, though you may have to wait a while before there's an opportunity to leave. While you're waiting, get your life in order and prepare to give your all.

Ship as soon as you can - there's not a single good reason to wait. We'll cover boot camp in the next chapter.

Enlisted Pre-Ship: TTPs.

Crush that PST fo sho. The single most important thing in your life now is working out. You should strive to become an unstoppable pushup juggernaut. You should find ways to run more. You should swim like a fish. Pull-ups should be your religion. Get some.

The swim. You have to complete a 500 yd swim, using Combat Side Stroke (CSS) or breast stroke. Learn CSS and do your PST with it. Not only is it the only stroke you'll be swimming at Pre-BUD/S and BUD/S, but it won't wear you out for the rest of the PST. Try powering through a PST using breast stroke and compare your pushup/pull-up performance to when you swim the CSS. There will be a huge difference. Breast stroke uses a large number of the same muscle groups as pushups and pull-ups, where CSS doesn't. You also have to put out the whole time while swimming breast stroke. In the CSS good technique can make passing the swim effortless. And you'll be fresh and rested for the rest of the PST.

It's impossible to teach you the CSS in a book. Use YouTube. Use a SEAL Mentor. Once you get the basic idea, I can offer you these three solid pieces of advice for turning a mediocre time into a spectacular time:

1) Keep the crown of your head, the top point of your skull, in

the water at all times. Imagine a pole is running through your spine, lengthening it and straightening it. That pole continues out through the crown of your skull and connects to a point on the wall ahead of you about 6 inches under the surface of the water. When you rotate to stroke, your whole body rotates around this axis. When you breathe, don't lift your head. Simply roll, keeping the point of your skull submerged, until your face breaks the surface. You don't need to keep your head out of the water for an entire exhalation and a slow inhalation. You can exhale throughout the stroke so you're ready to suck a good breath in when you rotate to your breathing position. It will seem like you're almost rolling onto your back to do this. That's fine. You'll start there and slowly, as you get more comfortable, scale back until you're getting a full breath in a fraction of a second with the least movement possible.

2) Practice efficient technique. There are a number of things you can do to make your stroke more efficient. The single best thing you can concentrate on is keeping your stroke count low. Try to get across the length of the pool in the fewest strokes possible. This drill isn't for speed. It's to teach your body how to eke out every bit of power from every stroke. If you can consistently swim a length with 6-7 strokes, you're doing pretty well. If you take more than 8 to get across the pool, slow down and experiment. The CSS is highly sensitive to technique changes. Once you get your stroke count in a decent range, you can even add a little dolphin-style undulation to the beginning of your glide. The moment you pull your top arm down and initiate your glide, do a slight dolphin kick (using your whole body). If you do it wrong, you'll feel awkward and you'll slow your glide obviously. If you time it right, you'll find it feels natural and your glide will be notably extended. Remember that in order for the dolphin kick to work, you need to be swimming at a decent speed already. If you try it on your stroke-count drill, you'll suck. Work it into your speed work and it'll pay off.

3) Be an ambidextrous swimmer. When most guys learn the CSS, they learn it on only one side. You're either swimming on your left side or your right side, but not usually switching off. If you're really committed to crushing your PST, you'll learn to swim on both sides. And you'll alternate sides every time you touch a

wall. Doing this serves a number of purposes. First, it's more efficient to touch the wall, bring your feet under you, and push off. You don't need to spend time or energy rotating your whole body while you're on the clock. Second, if you're swimming outside, you can keep the sun out of your eyes. Third, and by far the most important reason, every time you switch sides, you give one set of muscles a rest and work its complementary set. Over the PST the majority of your muscles will only be working 250 yards. If you don't alternate, those same muscles will have been working 500 yards. Not only will your muscles have worked half the time, but they'll have had 10 sets of rest roughly equal to the amount of work they just did. This alone can drastically reduce your swim time. Add the benefit of being more rested for the remainder of your PST and you'll see that anyone who takes the PST seriously is going to be alternating stroke sides every time he touches the wall. You're significantly stronger on one side than the other? Fucking work on it. If you're not willing to do even that, how can you reasonably expect to make it through BUD/S? Trust me when I tell you that your ambidextrous swimming will pay dividends in your weekly 2 mile swims, the 3.5 miler, and the ultimate 5.5 mile swim at the end of Second Phase.

The Pushup. I'm going to unveil for you the best-kept secret to getting better at pushups: do some fucking pushups. That's it. That's all there is to a pushup. Do pushups to max with good form. Do them often. Do sets of pushups. Do slow-motion pushups. Just do some pushups.

Some SEAL Mentors (the guys who administer the official PSTs) have different rules for pushups. Some say you need to touch your chest to the ground. Some say you need to touch your chest to a fist held under your sternum. The official guidelines for the PST say that your elbow must break 90 degrees. If you don't know the rules used by the Mentor who's going to administer your PST, train to the hardest standard possible. That way, you can never go wrong. But don't worry so much about these things. Mostly, just do some god-damned pushups already.

The Sit-Up. Sit-Ups are all about momentum. Get going fast and it's not that hard to keep going. Some Mentors are harsher than others about rules, but all will require that your hands stay in contact with your chest or your shoulders. When you go down and your back touches, some will require that your shoulder blades lay flat on the ground. Most are content if your shoulder blades just touch.

The guy holding your feet can just kneel on your feet, but that hurts and isn't very stable. The boys in the big leagues hold their buddies' feet like this: sit on their feet with the pad of your ass and cross your legs under their knees to secure the heels of their feet. Wrap your arms around and hug your buddy's knees, holding tight. This form provides a significantly improved base for your buddy, permitting significantly less energy to be lost by trying to help you control his feet. It feels gay but it works. And BUD/S involves a lot of gay moments, so get used to it.

The best advice there is for sit-ups, aside from "go fast," is that your elbows do not have to touch your knees. Your elbows only have to touch your thighs. If they touch your thighs 2mm above your hip, that counts just as much as if your elbows went over your knees and touched your kneecaps. The less energy you can expend per sit-up allows you to do more and faster.

The Pull-Up. Pull-ups are a weakness for a lot of guys, but before you complain about them, let me tell you this. There was a girl in the DEP pool I worked out with. She wanted to be a Diver. When she showed up to the workouts for the first time, she couldn't do a single pull-up, just like you'd expect. By the time she shipped to Boot Camp, she could do 11 pull-ups. More than most of the guys in the workout group. I guarantee she crushed Dive School. Still feel like making excuses for your poor pull-ups?

Get a pull-up bar to put up in a doorway in your house. Use it. Every time you pass through that doorway, force yourself to do a certain number of pull-ups. Discipline yourself and knock them out. You'll see that intimate familiarity with that pull-up bar is going to get you further than any other pull-up workout progression on its own - and it takes almost no effort to do.

When I was training I required myself to do 10 pull-ups before I went to the bathroom. Every time. And 10 before I showered.

Every time. No exceptions. When 10 got easy, I went to 15. Discipline and consistency are key here.

The Run. No portion of the PST claims more failures than the run. People are fat, lazy, and hate pain. Running is easier when it's done on the XBOX playing Madden 2012 than it is in real life. More than this, however, the run is at the end of the PST. You've been crushing the swim, pounding out pushups, screaming through sit-ups, powering through pull-ups, and now you're smoked.

Some advice for the run. Keep your pace even. Don't try sprinting away from the crowd at first. You'll die, fall back, and suck. Try to find someone who's a few steps faster than you are. Run with him. Stay smooth. Keep your jaw loose by shifting it side-to-side a few times - that'll prevent your shoulders from locking up. Stay relaxed. Breathe evenly and controlled.

The best way to do well on the run, though, is to have run a shit-ton before you even get there. Run every other day, working up to 5-7 miles a day. Then, after a month or so, fill a few of the rest days in with sprint workouts to get your speed up. Ultimately a good run schedule looks something like this:

Monday: 4-5 miles

Tuesday: 8x200m sprints with 5 minute rest in between each sprint

Wednesday: 4-5 miles (you'll be sore at the start, but you'll feel amazing by the end)

Thursday: 8x100m sprints with 5 minute rest in between

Friday: 4-5 miles (again, you'll feel awesome at the end)

Saturday: 5-7 miles (easy pace, be able to have a conversation with running partner the whole time)

Sunday: Rest

Your schedule needn't look exactly like this. This is only a guide. Work up to something like this. Not only will it pay off majorly when you take your PST, but the work you put in now will pay off in Pre-BUD/S, BUD/S, SQT, and the Teams. Running is an integral ability from this moment until the day you get out of the Teams. Get it in your system now and you'll save yourself in the long run.

* * *

Pre-Contract vs Post-Contract Workouts. Always work out, regardless of where you are in the pipeline. From this moment until you die (or at least get out of the Teams) working out will be your way of life. But you won't always work out the same way. Before you get your SEAL Challenge Contract (or SPECWAR OCS Billet) you will be working out to one end and one end alone: in order to crush the PST. Every single thing you do will be to increase pushups, pull-ups, sit-ups, swim, or run capabilities. You may do some kettle-bell swings to help your core. You may do dips to help balance your upper body. You may run varying distances to work on speed or endurance. You may do kick-ass swim workouts and you may do a day in the pool concentrating solely on technique. But every single one of these variations needs to have in mind a specific reason revolving around the ultimate goal. Superior PST scores are all that matter.

Once you've got your sweet little contract (or OCS Billet), you can de-emphasize the PST. Notice that I didn't say completely forget it and join an MMA gym. You should always be prepared to crush a PST, but you don't need to focus solely on the core exercises anymore. In fact, you shouldn't. If you were to work out 4-5 days every week for a year and do nothing but the PST exercises, you would hate your life. You would hate working out. When you hate something, it's much easier to stop doing it. It's not mental weakness, it's human nature. So now that you've got your contract, vary your workouts. Stay in good shape, but don't be afraid to do a triathlon, play basketball, lift a little more (if that's your thing), or even do CrossFit if you're gay like that. Note: CrossFit is for fags, but Don't Ask Don't Tell is no longer in place so feel free to wear those Vibram toe-shoes and do the CrossFit WOD. It doesn't really matter what you do, so long as you stay in shape and stay motivated.

Do NOT burn yourself out before you even ship. There's going to be plenty of time to be "over it" in the next shitty year (or more) of your life, so make this enjoyable. Hang out with your friends, go out at night, drink some (if you're over 21, of course), chase women. You don't need to be that "warrior monk" who is 100% focused on training. I don't know a single Team Guy who's like that. Focus on your training when you must. Focus on something else when you can.

Get comfortable in the water. You'll be spending a good amount of your time in BUD/S, SQT, and the Teams in the water. And you won't just be swimming. You'll be put in the water under some pretty demanding (sometimes heinous) conditions and expected to perform. I strongly suggest you put some effort into becoming more comfortable in the water. Tread water. Tread water keeping your hands dry. Tread water holding a dive brick.

Get some of those dive sticks that kids use at the pool during the summer. Toss them into the deepest pool you can find and pick them up in order. Do pushups and pull-ups on the pool deck and swim a lap. Get used to being in the water under massive fatigue, where you're gasping for breath and accidentally get a lungful of water.

The more comfortable you are in the water, the easier your life in Coronado is going to be. Put in the work and it will pay off.

Know Your Enemy. Your enemy, for the moment, is not the Taliban. He is not al Qaeda or Iran or the politician your parents happen to dislike. There will be plenty of time to study these enemies when you're in SQT and in the Teams. Besides, it'll probably be at least 3 years from now before you get overseas and nobody can really say who we'll be fighting then.

When I say "know your enemy" I mean BUD/S.

BUD/S is your immediate enemy. Read everything you can get your hands on. There's a reading list at the end of this book. It would be beneficial for you to become intimately familiar with the books listed. Learn everything you can from these books. Knowledge is power, baby. There are serious books on the list like The Warrior Elite, from which you can get good information, and there are crappy fiction like Suffer in Silence, from which you can get atmospherics from a guy who quit during First Phase. Don't turn your nose up at anything. Just digest it and take what you can.

You should also watch every video/movie you can. Again, some good things to watch are listed in the back of this book. From a Discovery Channel documentary on BUD/S (which I probably watched 250 times before I shipped out) to the Navy SEALs movie with Charlie Sheen (which you should watch because it's pretty funny to use some of the cheesy lines when you're doing the things for real: when you're doing a hostage rescue training mission, "Navy SEALs, here to get you out!" will give everyone a good laugh.) There are some interesting videos on YouTube even, but you have to wade through the heavy-metal-themed photo montages and Airsoft 'action' videos made by chubby, Cheetoe-eating pubescent know-nothing wannabes.

The other side of knowing your enemy is never assuming you know everything. Always, always, always know there's more to learn, and good information may come from unexpected places.

Write. I know, you want to kick down doors and shoot Osama bin Laden in the face (sorry guys, somebody already did that). The single best weapon you can bring to the table in your quest to become a door-kicking badass is self-awareness. The single best way to achieve a high level of self awareness is to write. It sounds gay, I know, but so does sitting nut-to-butt on a pool deck, arms and legs wrapped around the guy in front of you for warmth. Just because it sounds (and might be) gay doesn't mean it won't help.

You need, at very least, to write down a solid statement of your motivators. Why do you want to be a SEAL? It needs to be clear and, most importantly, honest. You don't need to show it to anyone - it's easier to be honest with yourself if nobody's going to read it - you just need to write it. Writing something down forces it to materialize. Aristophanes wrote that "by words the mind is winged" and he was right. Work hard at putting words to your thoughts and motivations and they will become much more real to you.

You can't write vague feelings down. You can only write concrete words. This process sucks, but solidifying your passions into real motivators provides you a strong foundation. You don't want a weak foundation on Monday night of Hell Week. And this is groundwork you can do now to improve your chances of success later. Writing these motivations down forces you to simplify them which, in turn, makes them stronger.

This personal statement should be a personal requirement to yourself. If your SEAL Mentor doesn't require you to write one, I do. If you're serious about becoming a SEAL, you'll start on your personal statement the moment you finish this chapter.

If you want to help yourself out even more, you will continue to write. Don't call it a "diary" or "journal," because that sounds pathetic. Call it a training log or training record, but don't limit it to things directly related to training. Sure, include workouts, things you learn, and advice you're given by SEALs and other people you admire, but don't limit yourself. If you want to give yourself the most self-awareness you can, you will include everything that's on your mind, no matter how peripheral it may seem. Einstein, Edison, Roosevelt, Patton, Darwin, Rommel, Churchill, Bonaparte, Lincoln - these men were all prolific writers. It's no coincidence they had such an effect on the world. Having to distill your thoughts into words will help you better understand where your head is and where it's been. Writing is a fantastic way to constantly evaluate yourself, to figure out what works for you, and what doesn't.

But I know that most of you won't even really entertain the idea of a training log. It's an extra commitment that you don't think you need. And you don't. Plenty of guys who get their Bird haven't written anything like this. But it will help, I promise you that. The most serious among you will keep a log. The rest of you need to at least write the personal statement - there is no measure to how much it will help.

And let me end this discussion about your personal statement on a note about honesty. Don't write that you want to be a SEAL because Pat Tillman, Michael Murphy, and Michael Monsoor all inspired you. That's bullshit and everyone knows it. You're not joining out of pure patriotism either. There are so many things you could do to 'serve your country,' so why would you choose BUD/S of all things? If you think these are your real motivators, prepare to ring that bell, because these things will not fuel your fire in the cold and dismal night. These reasons all smack of that false motivation we talked about. If your motivators are flimsy, you're fooling yourself and you'll pay.

If you're joining to prove to yourself that you can do the hardest thing there is, that makes more sense. If you're joining because you want excitement, that sounds honest. If you're joining because you want to be the best and you want to kill terrorists, I'll buy that. If you're joining because you've lived a soft life and want to temper yourself in the fire, bring it on. Whatever your motivators, make sure they're real. Make sure they're honest. Remember, you're not showing this statement to anyone. This is for you and you alone. This way you have no reason to lie or put up a front. Those of you who don't take this seriously will stand a much higher chance of quitting than those who take this suggestion from me and take the message to heart. Always be honest with yourself.

STFU. Perhaps the most profound advice I can give you as you try to get to BUD/S is to Shut The Fuck Up. Seriously. We SEALs consider ourselves "quiet professionals" for a reason. If you and I were to meet in the street, you'd never know I was a Team Guy. I won't tell you because you don't need to know. Hell, this book is written under a pseudonym because it's not about me - I wrote it for you.

You can start practicing the important skill of Shutting the Fuck Up today. Train and don't be ashamed of your goals, but you don't need to tell everyone. In fact you'll soon find life is less annoying if you don't tell people what you're training for. Everybody thinks they know something about SEALs and will give you asinine advice. Examples:

- "Oh damn! I know a guy who finished SEAL Training but his fingerprints kept growing back when they burned the tips of his fingers off, so he was medically disqualified!"
- "You know that only 0.5% of all people can be SEALs, right?"
- "Did you know they drown you and bring you back to life 3 times to become a SEAL? That's how those guys are so hard!"
- "I heard they give you a puppy when you get to BUD/S and you have to raise it yourself until the end of training. Then they make you kill it with your bare hands to show that you can kill without remorse!"
- "You know you'll have to be able to hold your breath for 15 minutes at a time, right?"
- "They shoot SEALs a few times during training so they know

what it feels like!"

- "My friend's brother's friend's cousin is a SEAL. He said they train with the CIA to assassinate world leaders with a knife and a garrote."

- "When you get your Trident they line you up and beat it into your chest, if you make a noise or show any emotion, you're done."

- "SEALs can do 1000 pushups in a row with no rest."

- "G.I. Jane is a great movie!"

- "You should be a CCT instead! You know they have to go through SEAL training AND Ranger School, right?" - (not true at all, in case you were wondering)

- "I was going to be a SEAL, but I got medically dropped because of chaffing."

These comments are funny, but they get old quickly. People don't know anything about the Teams, but that won't stop them from trying to be part of the coolness. The worst part about talking about your goals is that people tend to treat you with a patronizing, mocking deference - and they won't take you seriously.

There was a guy in my class that never even told his *parents* that he was going to BUD/S. In fact, they thought he was in corpsman training until a few weeks before he graduated SQT. Needless to say, they were *shocked*. But you know what? There had been no mention of his SEAL aspirations made on his Facebook, there were no family newsletters or Christmas cards that mentioned his training. There were no distractions.

I'm not saying you have to be like that guy - that was pretty extreme. What I'm suggesting is that when someone approaches you in the gym and asks why you're working out, you don't tell him "Because I'm joining the SEALs!"

Get rid of (or at least anonymize) your Facebook. The same goes for MySpace, Twitter, LinkedIn, etc. You should have *zero* online presence. At *very* least, ensure there are no references to or mentions of your SEAL-related goals. Make sure your parents or proud grandparents don't call your local newspaper and tell them about you. People will look for you. Instructors will search every name online, looking for anything connecting you with the program.

When we were in Second Phase, the instructors found military-related pictures of two guys on their Facebook pages, and they got beat, wet and sandy, for almost an hour. You don't need the extra BUD/S.

When you make it to the Teams, it's even more important to keep your internet footprint to a minimum. The problem with the internet is that everything's cached. If you have something on a website connecting you to BUD/S and take it down, that information can still be found. If you think that al Qaeda and its affiliates aren't scouring the internet for targets related to bin Laden's killing, you're stupid. Why potentially put you and your family at risk? Just don't do it. And make sure, once you decide to head to BUD/S, that your parents/relatives are on the same page. It's good for you now and it's good for everyone when you make it to the Teams.

Get your life in order. Tie up loose ends. If your girlfriend isn't going to be able to handle the stresses of BUD/S, SQT, and the Teams, you're better off ending things now. You don't need a distraction or a reason to second-guess yourself. BUD/S is generally easier if you're single because you can't really afford to think about someone else (a requirement in a healthy relationship).

In the same vein, automate all bills. Eliminate as many as you can. Get rid of most of your stuff. The things you own own you, right? Simplify and downsize everything you can. Cut all ties, memberships, and property but the essential. Anything that might be a potential distraction should be eliminated. Keep only what is essential.

Enlisted Pre-Ship: Don't Be That Guy.

Don't take "No." for an answer. You've probably heard that "where there's a will, there's a waiver." Do not give up on getting to BUD/S. I've heard countless stories of guys who wanted to go to BUD/S, but their recruiters weren't interested in them because they had a DUI, because they were colorblind, or because they'd had some knee surgery in the past. They ended up signing with some other contract into a program that was not their first choice. I had guys with multiple DUIs in my class. There were a handful of guys who were colorblind. A large portion of guys had had some major joint surgery in the past. These guys didn't take "no" for an answer from a recruiter. Like I've told you before, that guy works for you. Make him work. If he won't, fire him and get someone who WILL go to the mat for you. In all likelihood you *can* get to BUD/S - you just have to want it badly enough.

Another note in the same theme: don't take any contract with the intention of switching from the fleet or during training. **This does not happen.** If you sign a contract for something other than your program of choice, chances are you'll end up doing THAT job instead. Because you're stupid. Don't be stupid. There's not really an excuse. Sign only the contract you want. Nothing else.

Don't Exaggerate. Only SEALs can lie about what we do.This goes hand in hand with my urging you to Shut the Fuck Up, but it goes further. Don't let your school newspaper write a story about you that says you're going off to join the squad that killed Osama bin Laden, that you're going to be a Sniper, that you're going to be fluent in 5 languages, or that you're going to learn 23 ways to kill a man with a straw.

Don't Wear SEAL Gear. I don't care if your SEAL mentor gives you a T-shirt with a Trident on it when you get your SEAL Challenge Contract. I don't care if your mom buys you a hat at a truck stop that has a Trident on it. I don't care and neither will any frogman who sees you. Until you've earned it, you don't wear a Trident in any way.

Avoid "Hooyah Me" Posts in Online Forums. Avoid "Hooyah Me" in general, actually. What do I mean by that? Avoid conversations and online interchanges whose primary purpose is attention or extrinsic motivation of any sort. Nobody really wants to know about how much time you're sacrificing to prepare for BUD/S. Nobody is going to call the First Phase Instructors and tell them that you're so dedicated they don't really need to put you through Hell Week. Don't fabricate dreams or situations in the gym where you had to talk tough to some poser before putting your headphones in and working out at a heightened state of being because your cause is true and pure. You're not inspirational and you don't really think anyone's going to be able to answer your "Do you think I'm working out enough?" question.

People who do this are not looking for help, they're looking for reassurance and they're looking for a good-game. Your motivation should come from within you. You should not care if people know how hard you're working out. A coach of mine once told us that "champions aren't made during practice, when everyone's watching. Champions are made in the dark hours of the morning, working, while everyone else is sleeping." Take the same attitude with your training.

Don't become an MMA Fag. This really isn't so much training advice as life advice. If you want to learn to fight, great, do it. But don't become what I like a call an MMA Fag. The MMA Fag wears

TapOut clothes with Prada sunglasses. He listens to Bas Ruten tapes in his car and to grandiosely-named self-made techno-remixes of tween-pop, techno, and MMA fight announcers. Fight, by all means. Don't be a fag. Words to live by.

Don't Get Tattoos. Don't get any tattoos until after you're done with BUD/S. If you get one after you sign your contract but before you ship out, you can find yourself in a world of administrative hurt. You might find yourself with a fully-voided contract or worse: they can void your SEAL Challenge Contract but not your Navy contract, meaning you owe time in a different rate. Who gets to choose what rate you end up in if this happens to you?

Surprise, cockbag! The Navy does! So don't do it.

There is a great time to get tattoos, however. As of right now, you don't get in trouble for any tattoos gotten between BUD/S and SQT. If you *must* get ink, do it then and you'll be safe. Unless this advice alerts some bean-counting 'shoe' (derogatory term for non-operators) somewhere that there's a loophole, in which case this last little gem I'm sharing with you might be a relic of the past. Moral of the story: check before you get that hardcore dragon or celtic knot.

Do not get a DUI. Along the same lines as drugs here. Guys get kicked out of the Teams for Alcohol-Related Incidents. Guys periodically get dropped from SQT (even if they're only a day from graduation) for getting DUIs. If valuable members of our community - combat veteran operators - get kicked out for DUIs, how tolerant do you they they'll be if you get one? We're not even going to mention the danger you expose yourself and others to when you drink and drive, so let's just all agree to have a plan before we go out. Everyone wins.

Do not tell them everything. I'm not saying you should lie to your recruiter, but I'll put it like this: nobody really cares if you tried marijuana a few times. They really only care whether you can pass a drug test *now* and whether you've been to rehab. Nobody, even the people conducting your Top Secret background clearance are likely to care if you've had some experience with an herbal remedy. Nobody is going to scour your childhood bedsheets looking for hair to sample. They care whether you're an addict, a terrorist, or a criminal. Other than that, you're not that important to them.

That being said, **Do not pop positive.** Personally, I don't have problem with drugs. A great many of my friends partake in recreational drugs on a regular basis. But I'm in the Navy, and one of the sacrifices we make in joining the Navy is that we simply cannot partake ourselves. Do not do drugs. Do not smoke weed, do not take the Vicodin from your mom's hysterectomy, do not take your little brother's ADHD drugs. They will test you. You will be immediately processed out of the Navy and on your ass. They don't test for hallucinogens or steroids, but I'd recommend avoiding those bad boys for entirely different reasons.

Do not give up. It needs to be mentioned. Ask your local Mentor how many guys come to him interested in becoming SEALs and how many of those even *ship*. Don't even get started on how many *make it*, just ask him how many get a contract and ship out. I bet he'll tell you 1 for every 5-10 interested young men even gets to the PST. Now factor that into the actual percentage of people who make an attempt to become a SEAL and those who make it and you're looking at a 2-5% success rate. The good news? By simply *taking the PST*, you're already beating the odds and increasing your chances, all else equal, 5-10 times. So don't give up before you even have a chance to quit. You'll always wonder what would have happened if you'd gone to BUD/S. Don't wonder, just get there.

Enlisted Pre-Ship: Mark's Parting Wisdom.

This chapter was full of very specific advice for you to follow before you ship out with your SEAL Challenge Contract. If you follow my advice you'll be on the right track to demolish BUD/S. You'll enter the program at the right point, so downstream from here you'll enter BUD/S right where you need to be. If you've ever done any whitewater rafting, you know that even though there might be 4 different ways to go through a specific rapid, the veteran rafter is always going to navigate one set of rapids in order to set himself up to enter the next set in the right place. Sure, if he doesn't know what's coming next he'll probably be able to get through the first set of rapids, quickly judge the next set, and hurriedly get into position. The more times in a row, however, he has to guess his route, rush to position, navigate the obstacle, and then quickly formulate a new plan, the greater his margin for error. He's playing a game of chance. It might work out for him, particularly if he's good, but it's not ideal. Ideally he knows everything that's coming so he can ride the cleanest, smoothest, safest line.

I'm a veteran of this river. So are all the Team Guys I've consulted regarding the content you found in this chapter and the chapters that will follow. I'm giving you the cleanest, smoothest, safest line. I advise you take it.

But if you only remember one thing from this entire chapter, I want to emphasize this:

Ship as soon as you can.

Seriously, you can always be in 'better' shape, but if you wait until you feel 100% prepared, you will never ship. If you can pass the SEAL Challenge PST, you're ready. Get started now. You've got years before you get downrange, our commitments overseas are quickly winding down, and it would be a shame to show up in the Teams and not have any real Team Guy work to do. Get yourself in the program so you can get yourself in the fight as soon as possible.

Chapter 4

Advice for Navy Boot Camp.

"STTG: Submit to the Gayness."
- Unofficial West Point Cadet Motto -

Boot Camp: Key Tasks.

Stay in Shape. It's easy to get fat and weak in boot camp. Sometimes you're lucky and get put into a special "SO" group of recruits and you'll get more sanctioned workout time. But not everybody gets that opportunity. Even those that are in the "SO" groups find themselves losing fitness. You'll be required to perform a SEAL Challenge-passing PST at boot camp, so maintain as high a level of fitness as possible.

Finish. Boot camp is easy and boring and will suck. You will not enjoy it. You will not benefit from it. But you have to do it. We're not going to waste much time discussing it because it's not important or interesting - you just have to get through it and get on with your life. It's the price you pay for an opportunity at BUD/S.

Crush Your PST. You will take a PST in boot camp. Crush it. If you don't produce good enough numbers, there's a possibility you'll be dropped from the program long before you get to BUD/S. If you can get scores that pass the SEAL Challenge basic requirements in your boot camp PST, you will be just fine.

Boot Camp: TTPs.

Work out at every opportunity. It might seem like I'm belaboring the point, but I'm not. Physical fitness is paramount and boot camp does not prize it. There is enough activity and little enough decent food that the fatties in your class will likely lose weight, but if you go in in shape you're going to be hurting as you atrophy.

So find as many opportunities to work out as you can. Do pull-ups in the bathroom at night. Do pushups in your spare time. Do goblet squats while holding a heavy bag of laundry. Get creative in order to stay fit.

Stay positive. Boot camp is dull and disheartening. Even depressing. Don't let the stupidity or pointlessness of it get you down. Find fun when you can. Make fun. Play pranks on one another. Play some practical jokes on the Recruit Division Commanders (RDCs) - you'll find they take themselves far too seriously anyways. You might get in a little trouble, but there's a big difference between a prank and something overly destructive that will get you in *real* trouble.

Consider it an opportunity to grow some balls and make something fun out of a shitty situation. I've found that the guys who got in 'trouble' a lot at boot camp make the best SEALs and often had less trouble with BUD/S.

* * *

Know that boot camp is the worst part of BUD/S. It sounds ridiculous, but most guys would rather do First Phase over again than go back to boot camp. First Phase might hurt, but you're getting exercise on the beach, doing challenging things, and actually achieving something. Boot camp is dull and uninspiring. You will respect your BUD/S Instructors. The same cannot be said for your RDCs at Boot Camp. It's all uphill from there, man. It only gets better.

Boot Camp: Don't Be That Guy.

Don't drink the Kool-Aid. The RDCs at boot camp are trained to condition you to obey. Don't give in to them. They will try to convince you to enforce stupid rules within your own class and try to convince you that's what discipline is. Don't ever forget that your RDCs don't matter and that some of the guys in your boot camp class will be with you in BUD/S.

One of the guys in my platoon told me a story about how he got caught jerking off on the toilet in bootcamp. Jerking off on the toilet is unauthorized at boot camp apparently. The guy who was on watch came into the bathroom and banged on the door of the stall and then told the RDC. When they got to BUD/S, everybody in the class knew this story and made sure that guy didn't make it past Indoc.

Your boys are the only important thing. You'll be with them in BUD/S and in the Teams. They will not forget your actions in boot camp, so establish your reputation early.

Don't talk. Don't talk smack about BUD/S. You haven't earned shit yet. I know I sound like a broken record, but some guys get to boot camp and brag that they're going to destroy BUD/S. We've talked about them again and again. They don't often make it and people don't usually like them anyways. Be humble.

Boot Camp: Mark's Parting Wisdom.

Like I said, boot camp is boring and easy, but it's so boring and easy that it's worse than BUD/S. Suck it up, knock it out, stay in shape, and have fun when you can. 7 weeks goes by fast and you'll be done with the worst part of the whole pipeline.

Chapter 5

Applying to OCS.

"Not by Strength, by Guile."
                    - British SBS Motto

If you've taken all my advice into account and realized that my urging, for whatever reason, doesn't apply to your particular situation/personality/skill-set and you want to go to OCS, you're going to need to start putting together an OCS package. You also have the options of going to the Academy or going through the ROTC program to gain your commission and subsequently going to BUD/S, but if being a SEAL is your primary goal (vs. becoming and officer) that's not the way to go.

Both USNA and ROTC send young Ensigns (O-1s) to BUD/S every year. Many of them go on to become fantastic SEAL Officers. The problem for a man with the singular dream to become a SEAL is that both USNA and ROTC require you to commit to years of service before you know what job you'll be doing during your commitment. This is the price you pay for having your college paid for: uncertainty. Alternatively, you can apply for a SpecWar (BUD/S-to-OCS) billet at OCS without making a commitment. You don't sign anything or join the military until after you've submitted a SpecWar application, received a SpecWar offer, and accepted the offer. There is not a single chance you'll end up on a ship without having had a chance at BUD/S. If you go the ROTC or Academy route, you might apply for a SpecWar billet, be rejected, and end up on a ship for half a decade fulfilling your commitment.

Another advantage to going through OCS is that, in the event you get dropped (or, heaven forbid, quit), you'll be the first demographic of officers to be released from service. Outside NSW, big Navy is downsizing. If you don't make it through BUD/S, they probably don't want you at all. Officers that quit or were dropped from BUD/S in my class (and most classes over the last 3-5 years) weren't sent to another program; they were processed out of the Navy entirely. There is no guarantee this will happen, and it doesn't happen for everyone, but it happens more often for OCS officers than ROTC or USNA officers because the Navy paid for the ROTC and USNA guys to go to college. They've invested a great deal of money in them. The Navy has invested almost nothing in OCS officers, so they're the easiest to get rid of. Not that you're going to quit or be dropped, but if you were you wouldn't be doomed to a slow, lingering death in the engine room of the USS Haze Gray.

As you contemplate the OCS application, it's important to know that it's a long process. Many guys take upwards of a full year to put together a successful package including a spectacular PST, strong letters of recommendation, a memorable personal statement, a solid college transcript, and good Aviation Selection and Testing Battery (ASTB) scores. There used to be two selection boards every year and no required personal interview, but that has recently changed. There is now only one board selecting applications for the entire year and there is a personal interview that helps inform the board's final decision. Getting everything together in time for the board is of utmost importance and, based on when you start compiling your application, you might well end up waiting over a year from the time you submit your application to the time you ship to OCS.

If you're applying while still in school, you're still going to need to find some sort of employment after you graduate. Or you can mooch from parents and friends until you have no more friends and your parents hate you. That works for some guys. The point is that you should have a plan.

If you're out of school and working, don't quit your job. I wouldn't recommend even mentioning the whole application until you're offered the billet. If you don't get it and try again it'll be another full year before you get another shot; it would be terrible to continue another year at a job where you've already burned bridges.

Besides, you have a statistically-low chance of actually getting a billet, so it would be horrible to have to face co-workers who can only think of you as a failure.

The other alternative course of action, upon receiving a rejection, is to enlist. There would be nothing preventing you from using the PST you submitted for your OCS package to get a SEAL Challenge Contract. Since you have your college degree you'd be eligible for a college-graduate bonus right off the bat, too (Usually $3-8k). With all your paperwork (MEPS, etc) done already, you could potentially ship within the month.

The OCS route is incredibly competitive, but that doesn't mean you can't do it. You can. Lesser men than you have succeeded. But you'll need to commit fully to building the strongest application possible. Otherwise you're just wasting time.

OCS Application: Key Tasks.

Find a SEAL Mentor. SEAL/SWCC Mentors (also called Dive Motivators and NSW/NSO Mentors) work with DEP pools around the country to run workouts and administer PSTs. Some Mentors run a few workouts a week; others run a few workouts each year. The more active your Mentor is, the better off you are. If you don't have an active mentor in your area, consider relocating to an area with an active and supportive Mentor. Areas that always have active workout groups are San Diego and Virginia Beach (for obvious reasons). There are also unusually solid programs in the Northeast (Maryland, Massachusetts, etc) and in the Phoenix area. If you have the option to relocate, it might be worth your time.

You can find your local Mentor by calling a recruiting office and asking for his name and contact information. If they don't know what you're talking about, you can either call a different recruiting office or ask them to put you in contact with the person who runs the local DEP pool. That person will certainly be able to connect you to the local mentor.

The SEAL Mentor's only job is to run workouts for the DEP pool, so you are outside his job description. Be sure to respect this fact. Call him, tell him you're putting together an OCS package, and would love the opportunity to work out with him. When you go there, you had better put out and be the best there. You want him to take you seriously. The only way to do that is performance. It doesn't matter what you say. Your performance, attitude, and effort will tell him the real story.

Find a good officer recruiter. A good officer recruiter is hard to find. I actually had to call three different offices to find someone who would be willing to help put together a SpecWar package. One recruiter even hung up on me when I told him I wanted to be a SEAL officer. No joke, the majority of the people in these offices have never met a SEAL and don't know a thing about the program. They took one look at me and dismissed my chances at even getting a billet. They thought it would be a waste of time. ("That silly faggot won't make it a day in BUD/S.")

Even the recruiter I ultimately had submit my package didn't think I was going to be worth his time until after my SEAL Mentor submitted my PST Scores. Find someone who is at least willing to submit your package for you. And stay on top of them. You'll have to know more than your recruiter, or you'll end up getting screwed.

Crush the PST. The PST is the very first, most important indicator that you might succeed at BUD/S and in the Teams. If you destroy the PST you stand a good chance when you get to the board; if your scores are below average, you had better blow them away in person. And when I say "average," I mean average for your fellow applicants. The generally accepted minimum competitive PST scores for a SpecWar candidate are:

> Swim: 9:00
> Pushups: 100
> Sit-ups: 100
> Pull-ups: 20
> Run: 9:00

Score better than this and you're in the running. Knock a minute more off the run, cut two minutes off the swim, add 20 pushups, 20 sit-ups, and 10 pull-ups, and you've got yourself a PST that will set you apart from the crowd. That kind of PST will make the atmosphere of your board interview a bit friendlier and push you to the top of the pile. I cannot overemphasize the importance of impressive scores.

* * *

Obtain Letters of Recommendation. This is perhaps the hardest to accomplish. You're not looking for letters of recommendation from college professors (although you can include those, too). You're looking for letters of recommendation from retired and active senior officers (preferably Captains and Admirals). You're looking for references from SEALs (or, at very least, from other SOF units). And you want these letters to be powerful, telling, and specific to you. It's obvious when a letter of recommendation is a form letter and that detracts greatly from the weight of the letter. Obviously you can't tell a SEAL Admiral what to write; what you *can* do is make such a strong, positive impression on him that he *wants* to write something better for you. Network. See if your mentor knows someone of note (he probably does) who might be willing to grab lunch with you, etc.

Personal Statement. A few chapters ago I recommended that guys preparing to ship under a SEAL Challenge Contract should write a personal statement telling why they want to be SEALs. What they wrote was for them and them alone. Your personal statement carries a bit more weight. It will be read by the men deciding whether to give you a shot at BUD/S as an officer. This statement is your chance to differentiate yourself from your peers. Make the most of it because it will be among the last things they look at before they meet you in your interview. If it's good, you'll start off on solid ground; if it's crap, you'll find yourself starting off in the hole. It's hard to dig out of a hole when a Team Guy is on guard. And you might think that SEALs wouldn't care about your writing skills, but you'd be wrong. SEAL officers are not only expected to be athletic studs, but also academic beasts. You'll do a great deal of professional writing and public speaking and they'll be evaluating your accordingly.

Take the ASTB. You will also be required to submit an OAR (Officer Aptitude Rating) score, which is a subset of the Aviation Selection and Testing Battery (ASTB). The Math Skills Test (MST), Reading Skills Test (RST), and Mechanical Comprehension Test (MCT) comprise the OAR. You are not required to take the other three portions of the ASTB because unless you're applying for aviation billets as well. The OAR score is more of a formality than anything, and if you've got a basic grasp of math, english, and understand how cogs/gears work, you'll be fine. Your officer recruiter should be able to provide you with study material. Study for a few days or a week, but don't stress over it. The test is a check in the box and not even close to as important as the PST, LORs, or Personal Statement.

Complete SF-86. The SF-86 is a terrible online process that provides a huge amount of information to the government in order to facilitate a background check. It requires references for every place you've lived in the last 7 years. It requires dates of travel, even if on vacation, for the last 7 years. This process takes a long, long time. Start it as soon as you get in touch with a recruiter, finish it as soon as possible, and print a few copies. This will save you from having to redo it in the future when (not if) your recruiter or the navy loses your information a week before the board deadline. Again, when you finish it, PRINT yourself a copy. Somebody will lose it along the way and you don't want to have to go through that again.

MEPS. This is the same process enlisted guys go through and will medically clear you for military service. Set aside a full day for this and get there early - the earlier in the day you start, the faster the whole process will be.

Submit your Package. You spent all that time preparing it. Make sure it's perfect. Make sure it's on time. Scratch that, make it early. The navy sucks at paperwork and if you submit it anywhere near the deadline you're taking an unnecessary risk.

Personal Interview. This is the most important part of your entire application. In fact you should think of the rest of the application as laying the groundwork for a stellar interview. Until the recent past, there was no personal interview. Now OCS candidates will be interviewed just like their USNA and ROTC counterparts to ensure the right guys get into the program. I cannot stress the interview enough. There are guys who look like shoe-ins on paper who end up not getting a billet because of the interview. Conversely, there are guys who don't distinguish themselves on paper but show so much promise in the interview that they're given a billet.

The interviewers are looking for confidence and force of character. Remember that your job, should you succeed, will be to first usher a class through BUD/S with maximum completion rate. And second, you will be expected to lead men in combat. This is the lens through which you will be evaluated. Are you capable of thinking ahead? Are you in the habit of working out contingencies? Can you think of others in a stressful situation? Do you want it enough, for the right reasons? Can you endure staggering hardship with a smile on your face? Are you able to speak to power without pandering or waffling? Do you have a backbone and a functional brain? Do you use them? How? How do you show attention to detail? They'll be looking for these things from you, so starting thinking about your answers and relevant experiences now.

Your best chance lies in crushing every single aspect of the application. Submit an application they simply cannot reject. That's your goal.

OCS Application: TTPs.

Assume your recruiter doesn't know anything. Most officer recruiters don't know a thing about the SEAL program. If your recruiter suggests otherwise, great, but act on the assumption he's wrong. Verify any information you get. Get a feel for whether he knows what he's doing. Compounding this problem is the fact that your recruiter probably doesn't take you seriously. He doesn't think you can make it. He probably won't put much effort into you or your application and will likely make dangerous assumptions. Never forget that you only have one board a year and a small administrative mistake on your recruiter's part can severely damage your chances.

The SpecWar application process is different in a number of ways from the usual packages your recruiter puts through, and the process is constantly changing, so your recruiter is likely to operate on a number of assumptions that are simply wrong. He will get dates and requirements wrong, so remain vigilant. If he tells you something that doesn't match what you know or have heard, ask him for the reference. Be a pain in his ass. A polite pain, but a pain. Verify information yourself. If he tells you he sent something to the security clearance people, ask for a confirmation from them. Make it impossible for him to drop the ball, but don't be a dick.

Befriend your recruiter. Your application is a lot of work for your recruiter. It's outside his routine. It's unlikely to be accepted - and he only gets credit for those who are actually accepted. Your recruiter has very few reasons to be motivated about your package. Give him a strong one: personal friendship. Befriend your recruiter and you'll see he doesn't drop the ball on your application. He's not working on a low-probability application, he's helping a friend out. Not only will a friendship cause him to take greater care with your package, but you might find he's willing to stretch himself to help you, whether it be rushing paperwork or taking a chance to get you a connection and a letter of recommendation.

Your officer recruiter also puts together a cover letter for the front of your package. This is the very first thing anyone sees. If your recruiter thinks highly of you, you'll come out the gate looking head and shoulders better than your peers who didn't take the time to develop a relationship with their recruiters.

Save your SF-86. You will spend hours upon hours completing your SF-86 online (or, worse, on paper) in order to begin your security clearance. You will submit it online or fax it through your recruiter. It will touch at least 3 other pairs of navy-employed hands before it reaches the place that needs it. The place that needs it also employs navy hands. The thing about navy hands is that they lose paperwork. They love losing paperwork and blaming it on someone else. And that someone else mysteriously lacks a phone, email address, or pulse. Save a copy of your completed SF-86 and hold onto it yourself. When somebody loses it down the road, you won't have to do the entire thing over again.

Work out with your SEAL Mentor. You should be doing every one of the DEP workouts your SEAL Mentor puts on. You should win every race and push everyone else to perform better. Make the most of every workout. Not only are the workouts often beneficial, but putting out every workout will help your SEAL Mentor see that you're the real deal. Your SEAL Mentor is either a former Team Guy or he works with former Team Guys. If he realizes you're serious about going to OCS and BUD/S, respects the workouts you do, and sees leadership potential in how you interact with the guys in the DEP pool, you'll find he's a good way to get letters of recommendation. I was working a menial retail job after college instead of a something in my field because a retail job offered me the flexibility to schedule around the DEP workouts. I didn't miss a single workout in almost a year. You should do the same.

CRUSH the PST. There is no way to overstate the importance of the PST. A stellar PST will put you at the top of the pile. A mediocre PST will put your application in the shredder faster than anything else. Your entire life should be scheduled around working out. You should dream in pushups and combat side-stroke (CSS). You should have nightmares about pullups. Take multiple PSTs along the way to gauge your progress and assess your weaknesses.

When you know your weakness, formulate a plan to make it a strength. Pull-ups were a weakness of mine. My first PST I got 12 pull-ups, so I bought a pull-up bar I could mount in my doorway. Every time I passed under the door, I would owe a "pull-up tax" of 10 pull-ups. When that got too easy I, upped the tax to 15, then to 20. On my final PST I got 32 pull-ups because of my pull-up tax. Do the same thing for the aspects of your PST you need to improve and I guarantee you'll see a great deal of improvement. It's about consistency and discipline. Not only will the fitness help you, but the resulting discipline will serve you well in BUD/S as well.

Make connections. Use your officer recruiter and your SEAL Mentor to generate as many connections to the SEAL community as you can. Keep your ears open. Scour the internet for any connections you might be able to make. Once you make a few inroads, use them to get even more connections. If you can, find a way to visit a SEAL Team. Following an AOIC around for a few days is not only a great way to get a letter of recommendation (likely from the CO), but it's also an opportunity to answer any questions you might have. A visit will also show you the SEAL life and allow you to decide for good whether it's worth the sacrifice to you.

Get letters of recommendation from SEALs. While a solid letter from an Admiral or Captain from the fleet will carry some weight as a character reference, it will not tell the board a thing about how suitable you are for the Teams. A well-written letter from a SEAL Chief would be infinitely more helpful to a board than a fleet officer because SEALs really only listen to other SEALs when it comes to a person's suitability for the Teams. Only SEALs truly know what it takes to be one of us. Get as many strong letters of recommendation as possible, but emphasize letters from within the community.

Make BUD/S your only option. On your OCS application, you are afforded room to Mark a first, second, and third choice. When my recruiter asked me what my second choice was, I looked at him and said "Nothing." He was shocked.

"Are you sure you wouldn't want to be a pilot?"

"I'm sure."

"What if you don't get the SpecWar billet?"

"Well, I think I will. But if I don't get it this time, I'll get it the next time around."

This should be your mindset already. If you don't get a SpecWar billet, you should not be okay with being a Pilot or Submariner. If you are, then forget putting SpecWar down at all. Even if you were to get a billet, you probably won't make it through BUD/S. You should have a singular focus on BUD/S. Nothing else should suffice.

Make your personal statement memorable and easy to read. The selection board is going to have to read hundreds of personal statements. If yours doesn't make you stand out, you've missed an opportunity. If yours is difficult to read, it will not be read. Include an "X-factor" that will differentiate you from the crowd, but be sure it's relevant. The fact that you learned East Coast Swing dancing on the west coast and West Coast Swing dancing on the east coast will certainly get you remembered, but in what light? You want to be remembered for how suitable you seem for the job, not because you wasted the board's time with something stupid and irrelevant.

Remember one of the Teams' simplest maxims: "Don't be a fag."

Your personal statement should also flow naturally, with no breaks in momentum due to grammatical problems, unnatural word use, or clarity issues. Keep in mind that your board reviewers are going to have to read dozens upon dozens of crappy essays. If you're the light in the darkness, you'll be remembered fondly. If you're the blackest hole, they're either going to hate you or, worse, put your statement down before they finish. And you can't blame them for this - an unintelligible essay is the result of poor communication skills and attention to detail, two characteristics at the heart of what makes a good SEAL officer.

If you're not a great writer, get assistance. Find an old teacher, a friend, or a parent to help you.

Fifteen minutes early. Any time you're interacting with Team Guys (or anyone upon whom you want to make a good impression), be fifteen minutes early. Show up to your interview early. Show up to your PST early. Show up to the recruiter's office early. When you're meeting someone who's going to write you a letter of recommendation, mix things up and show up fifteen minutes early.

Begin preparing for your board now. If you're in the process of putting your package together, you really need to start preparing clear answers for likely questions. If you're further away from your interview, it would benefit you greatly to prepare for your board by learning everything you can about the SEAL community. Read heavily. You should be able to answer any number of questions about SEAL history, notable SEALs, ethical situations, and your own potential involvement in the Teams.

Here are some possible questions:

- Can you name the five SEALs who have been awarded the Medal of Honor? Tell me how each got his award.
- Which president commissioned the SEAL Teams? What year?
- Who is Draper Kaufman? Who is Roy Boehm? Who is Rudy Bosch? Eric Olson?
- Who were the Scouts and Raiders?

- Who were the UDTs?
- Tell me about Operation Redwings. What do you think you would've done differently, if anything?
- Why do you want to join the SEALs, as opposed to the Rangers, SF, or Force Recon?
- Why do you want to be an officer in the SEAL Teams instead of an enlisted man?
- If we give you chance to go to BUD/S, what will be your biggest leadership challenge?

Practice your answers to these and other questions aloud. Practicing in your head is entirely different than saying your answers and hearing your words. All great speakers practice out loud. Speaking clearly and without hesitation, you will come across as strong and confident - a very good attribute for the board to sense in you. You will need to be confident but respectful; the scent of arrogance or disrespect will sink your application faster than you can blink.

You only have one chance at a first impression, so take care in how you present yourself. This applies down to your clothing. Dress up. Be clean and clean-shaven. Introduce yourself with a firm handshake, a smile, and solid eye contact. Address the board with respect, but don't let respect progress to fear. Sit straight up. Be polite. Show them that you are strong, courageous, educated, passionate, and personable. Remember that your job, should you make it to the Teams, will not only be to lead men in battle, but also to be the face of the platoon and the Teams. The men evaluating you are determining your suitability for that job in addition to your ability to complete training.

There is a lot involved in the SpecWar OCS billet application, but if you follow my advice you'll find yourself in the running. Remember that the easiest way to have your application thrown out before it's given any serious consideration is to submit unacceptable PST scores. Everything else in the application is viewed in light of your physical fitness. Work out as though your future depends on it, because it does. Spend your spare time learning as much as you can about the SEAL community by reading as much as you can. Prepare yourself to submit the strongest application you possibly can and stay on top of your recruiter to make sure your completed package gets to the right people at the right time.

OCS Application: Don't Be That Guy.

Don't give up. This process plain sucks. It is, as we say in the Teams, "a dick-dragger." It takes an absurdly long time and takes a lot out of you. You will sacrifice a great deal for upwards of a year without any concrete reward. In fact it's statistically likely that, at the end of that year, you won't even get the billet.

That being said, if it's truly your dream to go to BUD/S through OCS, don't give up. Be tenacious; stick to your guns. I was hung up on by a handful of officer recruiters before I was even able to have a real conversation with one, whereas the enlisted recruiter was practically begging to have me sign and ship (and give me $8,000.00 up front for my degree). But I stuck to my guns.

You'll probably get a call at work (or school) at some point during this application process that your recruiter has hit a snag. "It's not going to happen," he'll tell you.

"Yes, it actually *is* going to happen," you'll reply. If this is what you want, don't let anybody get in your way. And don't, above all else, get in your own way. Just make it happen. Everything else is details.

Keep it to yourself. Similar to the STFU advice I give the enlisted guys before *they* ship, don't talk about this process to everyone around you. The fewer people know about your ambitions, the better.

The moment it gets out is the moment people stop taking you

seriously. The moment people associate you with the word "SEAL" is the moment people will make the leap and begin mocking you and introducing you as a SEAL. Uncomfortable, distracting, and unnecessary conversations will inevitably follow. Often these conversations will conclude with stupid advice to "practice being cold before you go" and a condescending look that says "you'll never make it but I don't have the heart to tell you."

Beyond this, if you don't get picked up by the board, you'll find that most people around you have already discounted you. And the moment they find out you didn't make it you'll be a failure in their eyes (even if they themselves couldn't do a single pushup). Do yourself a favor and keep your aspirations private. Act like the quiet professionals you want to join.

Don't miss the deadline. Particularly now that there is only one board per year, it is incredibly important that you get the entirety of your package turned in on time. If you don't, you'll be waiting a whole year before the next board comes around. That's a long time to stay motivated and in BUD/S shape.

You can help prevent being late to the board by intending to be two months early. You should also be on top of your recruiter and get confirmations for every single thing you've submitted. Keep a running checklist of everything you have to do; have a plan to complete everything early. Verify your plan with your recruiter and anyone else who might know if you're missing anything. Stick to your plan, or, as we say in the Teams, "Plan your dive; dive your plan."

Don't submit a typo-ridden personal statement. Your personal statement is the board's first chance to get to know you, so make a good impression. A personal statement with typos and grammatical errors gives the first impression that you are lazy, lack attention to detail, and don't really care about becoming a SEAL. None of these are a good idea.

Have multiple people - the people who correct you when you say something wrong - read your statement. A high-school english teacher who remembers you would be a good option, as would a college professor of literature. Make sure your statement does nothing to distract your detail-oriented readers from what you're telling them.

Don't overstudy for the OAR. It's tempting to spend a lot of time studying for and putting off the OAR/ASTB test. You can kill a lot of time on it without reason. Not only is the test easy, particularly if you're pretty fresh out of college/high school/6th grade, but it doesn't really matter.

You need to spend your time where it's going to pay off the most. The OAR score is not even remotely as important as anything else in your package. Even if you're dyslexic and illiterate you should have no trouble scoring over the minimum of 35. If you can score over a 50, you're good. Nobody cares about anything beyond that. Pass the test and move onto the things that matter, like your PST, personal statement, LORs, and interview.

OCS Application: Mark's Parting Wisdom.

Statistically, you won't get this billet. It's too competitive. The same thing, however, could be said for completing BUD/S - that you won't make it. That's the crazy thing about statistics - no matter how true or predictable they might be, they don't determine your fate. The trend has no bearing on the individual.

No matter what the statistics say about success rates at BUD/S, you can beat them.

You can join the winners.

All it takes is the right preparation and mindset.

The SpecWar OCS billet is slightly different because there are a very limited number of billets, and your resume makes a difference. That being said, you know what they're looking for, so you know how to shape the next years or months (whichever it may be) of your life to maximize your chances of being selected.

If you aren't selected the first time, you have the option to reapply and try again the following year. This would be absurdly difficult, mentally, but could be done. In that year you'd have to improve upon your PST scores, gain more and better letters of recommendation, and perfect your personal statement. You'll have advantages over the guys who are a applying for the second time: not only will you already know the entire process, but you'll be medically cleared, your security clearance will be completed already, and, most importantly, the fact that you were willing to wait a whole year to try again will speak highly of your tenacity and mental strength. Your determination would not go unnoticed by the board.

But a year is a long time to wait, and you don't want to miss the fight. Maybe, if you aren't selected, you might consider enlisting. More than anything else, you don't want to miss the fight - you'd be hitting yourself if you put off joining another year and ended up missing the last few gunfights.

Chapter 6

Enduring OCS.

"Mix a little foolishness with your prudence: it's good to be silly at the right moment."
- Horace, *Odes*, Book 4

So you got into OCS. Congrats, bro, that's no small feat. Now, let me be clear here: OCS was the worst part of BUD/S. I would do Hell Week again before I went back to OCS, no joke. The other OCS graduates in my BUD/S class would tell you the same thing. OCS isn't hard, but it's miserable. In the politically-incorrect parlance of today's youth, OCS is "gay." In fact a buddy of mine who was prior-enlisted before he went to OCS told me, without hesitation, that he'd rather do boot camp twice over than deal with OCS again.

You will get out of shape in OCS. I know it seems ridiculous, but you will undoubtably lose a substantial amount of fitness. OCS is designed to get "fat bodies" in shape. And the fat, lazy guys and girls (called, exclusively, "females") will lose a bit of fat off their soft bodies while in training, only to gain it back five-fold when they get out of OCS. They do this through a minimal (and heavily controlled) amount of exercise and a highly-restricted calorie intake. The level of exercise is probably more than most people in your class stick to, but pathetic in comparison to the physical regimen you've been on to this point.

The amount of food is good for starving fat off soft bodies, but entirely insufficient to even maintain the body composition you will be reporting in. Persistent, gnawing hunger will rule your daily existence until you figure out a way to cheat.

You will hate life at OCS. I don't know a single person who didn't, but it did some good for the undisciplined and childlike members of my class. You will see the same - they're gaining something from the training not because the training is good, but because your classmates are pathetic. And you will have to interact with them as they complain about having to run a half mile or do twenty pushups. You'll hate your life from the moment you get there until, at very earliest, you become a Candidate Officer (Candi-O).

The progression at OCS goes something like this: When you arrive you are an Indoctrination Candidate. Your life will suck more this first week than any other. It's supposed to 'break you down' so they can 'build you up' over the following weeks. If you have the constitution necessary to become a Team Guy, you won't get broken down so much as you'll get pissed off.

After you complete Indoc Week, you'll become an Officer Candidate (OC) and remain an OC for the majority of your awesome time in Newport. As an OC you will endure the keystone OCS evolutions and complete your academic coursework (all of which is geared specifically for the SWOs - Surface Warfare Officers). Read: this phase is almost entirely irrelevant to life as a SEAL officer. On the upside, OCS will inspire you even more not to quit because it's a glimpse of life on a ship, which is where quitters go.

When you become the senior class, you will officially be Candidate Officers. Finally, you will be allowed to eat what you want, use the salad bar, and even go back for seconds. You will be responsible for helping run the rest of the classes, inspecting after "sweepers" (cleaning), and shepherding the Indoc class around in the absence of their DI. Being a Candi-O is like having a weight lifted off your shoulders: you can even work out on your own. The only thing better is getting your commission and setting the building on fire as you run off base with your Ensign bars. I'm kidding about the fire. Arson is a serious crime. Don't do it. But you'll want to.

Your biggest savior in OCS will be a few of your classmates who also see that OCS is stupid. If there are other SpecWar guys in your class, you've got it made. They'll probably be the only ones bold enough to have much fun because they're not afraid of being 'remediated' by the drill instructors. You may get lucky and get some cool Pilots, NFOs (Naval Flight Officers), or even an Intel guy/girl. The rest of your class is likely to live in a psychological prison of fear the entire time - and they will hate you for anything you do that might get them in trouble. Do it anyway.

Officer Candidate School: Key Tasks.

Indoc Sunday. You will check in, probably in a gym, on a Sunday morning. You'll sit down in a calm environment and fill out all the paperwork to officially enroll yourself in OCS. Fun fact: if you don't show up, or show up and tell them you don't want to do it, you can walk away with no commitment. After you sign your life away and have your bag inspected, you will be shuttled to the barracks with a van full of other doe-eyed Indoctrination Candidates. The Candi-O driving you will probably tell you it's going to be a quiet Sunday, that pretty much nobody is there, and that you'll have a nice intro to the staff tomorrow morning after breakfast. That guy is a liar.

You can't see it yet, but the entire building is poised to pounce on you. You'll probably be walked to a stairwell where there are lines or "V"s taped to the floor. You'll stand on them, the Candi-O will teach you the OCS way to tie your shoes. Then the world will explode for a moment as the doors burst open and 6-10 other Candi-Os descend on you, screaming in your face. They'll make you tear your shoelaces out and put them back in. There's a huge snare-drum being pummeled at the top of the stairs to add to the confusion and chaos. You won't see it, but there are Lieutenants, Chiefs, and Marine Corps Drill Instructors just beyond the next door. They're not there to watch you. They're there to make sure the Candi-Os don't cross the line. For example: they can't touch you.

Then you get to run upstairs and go through a series of loud "learning stations" where you'll learn proper Navy greetings, you'll get a "Poopie Suit" uniform (green dungarees), and you'll be issued other gear like a canteen and a "gouge book" full of Navy knowledge (like the General Orders and Rank Insignia). You'll be expected to memorize the information in the book while you're at OCS. For the next few days, the Candi-Os will be your only contact with the world. You will be confined to your hallway and permitted to use the bathroom only when your entire class goes.

Meet DI. That Wednesday you'll meet your Drill Instructor - a Marine Corps Gunnery Sergeant or Staff Sergeant. The morning you meet him or her will be a long one - with a good, solid beating to show you who the boss is. The nice thing about having a real DI (instead of Candi-Os) is that they're hilarious. If you just watch them and listen to the ridiculous things they say, you'll be laughing a lot. Maybe it'll get you beat a little more, but the laugh is worth it. And you could use the extra PT - you'll be atrophying rapidly.

RLP. RLP (Room, Locker, Personnel Inspection) is the single dumbest thing I've ever done in my life. You will spend the entire 3rd or 4th week doing things like starching and folding your underwear into a perfect 6"x6" square (measured from any point). If any spot is more than 1/16" off, or the starch browned under the iron, or the shape and measurements didn't hold up to being tossed across your room, that's a hit. 10 hits and you fail. A buddy of mine failed because he had IPs ("Irish Pendants," or stray threads) on the underside of his mattress. He got a hit for a stain on his mattress that was recorded on his check-in sheet.

When a DI comes into you room to grade you, you'll be on your bed getting beat while he throws everything out of your locker and drawers onto the ground as he screams the things you did wrong and the grader (a Candi-O) records them. It's called "hurricaning" your room, and you'll understand why when you see it. The air will be thick with your carefully-prepared clothing items; it will seem like 2/3 of your belongings are simultaneously airborne.

RLP has ridiculous standards, is graded based on the violent whim of whichever DI grades you, and is relevant to nothing you'll ever do again. If you fail the first RLP, you have a second chance to pass it a few days later. If you fail again, you get rolled to the next class.

ORLP. In your 8th week you will be graded on your Summer White uniform, the specific layout of a few Navy items on a desk, and your knowledge of the gouge book. There is no hurricaning here, but the Lieutenants conducting the inspection do have a strong predilection for douchbaggery. Remember that OCS is most often the last stop for a LT as he processes out of the Navy (either willingly or unwillingly), and the LTs there are often (but not always) bottom-of-the-barrel from the fleet. This is their opportunity to assert superiority and they probably don't know the gouge book as well as you do, so you may find yourself getting hit for correct answers (this did happen to me). The good thing is that nobody fails ORLP.

There was a brain-dead Supply Corps candidate in my class who couldn't name a *single* General Order of a Sentry - something we'd been practicing for almost two months. The LT grading him kept asking him different questions until he got a few almost right (by repeating the LT's prompts). That fat slob is now a LT in the Supply Corps on some ship somewhere.

Candi-O. Once you're a Candi-O you're almost done. Enjoy eating a meal in peace like a regular person. Enjoy being able to walk somewhere by yourself. Enjoy a little responsibility. You'll be in charge now and, based on the fact that you were capable of getting a SpecWar billet, you'll probably rank pretty high in your class's Chain of Command. Remember how pointlessly mean the Candi-Os were to you when you were in Indoc and when you were a regular Officer Candidate. Don't be like that. Just do what you have to and get out of there.

Officer Candidate School: TTPs.

Memorize the "Big Three" gouge beforehand. When you get to OCS you will be expected to quickly memorize your Chain of Command, the General Orders of a Sentry, and the Code of Conduct. An updated Chain of Command can be found online in Navy OCS Forums. The General Orders of a Sentry and the Code of Conduct can be found in the back of this book in the Appendix.

Memorizing these things will make your life a bit easier. You're expected to spend a great deal of time studying your gouge your first few days at OCS. The problem is that you're supposed to study the 3"x4" notebook held inside a plastic bag by a fully extended arm. Your arm gets tired quickly and the small print is hard to read through the distortion of the plastic bag. If you know the Big Three already, that's all you'll need to know for the first 6 weeks. That's a lot of time you should be studying that you can spend napping.

Instead of holding the book out in front of you, you can put it in your lap and close your eyes. Doze a little. When someone yells at you, just tell them you're reciting your General Orders in your head to make sure you've got them. Then start reciting them until that person shuts up and leaves you along to sleep in peace. It won't work every time, but it will work sometimes. And a Candi-O can do *nothing* to you. In fact, your Candi-Os are so scared of your DI that they won't say a thing to him about how often you sleep, etc.

The minor inconvenience of practicing before you ship is well worth the morale-raising restorative power of a nice little nap while everyone else is submitting to the suck.

Have a good last night of freedom. You will likely arrive in Newport the Saturday night you report. For the love of all things sacred, do not eat a bowl of Ramen in your hotel room and go to sleep. Go out for a nice meal. It's the last nice meal you'll have for a while. I walked off base from the Navy Lodge where I was staying (you're allowed to get a room there if you're reporting to OCS in the morning) and found a pizza place. I sat down at the bar, and, over the course of two hours, ate a whole pizza and drank 4 pints of Sam Adams Boston Lager while I watched a basketball game on the TV overhead.

I strongly recommend a similar night. If you're more social than I was, then go out with a few people from your class. Often classes will meet up that Saturday to have a meal together. This is a great idea. Go, do it, enjoy yourself. Just don't hit it too hard because you're already going to have a migraine from all the yelling and drum-banging you're going to live the next few days. Doing Indoc Day hung over would be *pure* hell.

The point is that you should relax. Do something to charge your batteries and enjoy your freedom. You won't have an opportunity to do either one of these things for quite some time.

Check in late. I know I told you always to be early, but this is an exception. You will be given a time window within which you're supposed to show up to OCS and check in. Show up at the very last minute.

They have a schedule they have to stick to. There are tasks that the Candi-Os need to accomplish, like issuing you your uniform and getting you to lunch. If you show up at the top of the time window, then you're going to have to deal with hours more hazing and mind-games and yelling than you would if you showed up at the end. If you show up at the end, you will probably be rushed through all the gear issue and, the moment you join your class, you'll go to lunch. It may seem like a small thing, but why expose yourself to more mindless bullshit than you have to?

Get a large "poopie suit." They size you for the "poopie suit" rapidly. Make sure the one they give you is big. Bigger and baggier the better. If you get one that's too small, you won't even be able to stand up straight for a full week. And that would be terrible.

Laugh. Laugh whenever possible. It'll make the Candi-Os mad during Indoc, but who cares? Test those guys. And remember, the people who are around you the most during Indoc are actually the lowest ranking Candi-Os in their class. They really don't have much say in anything. They're just following the orders of the DI and their superior Candi-Os. And they're far too scared of the DI to say anything other than "Aye Sir," etc. Don't take them seriously.

In fact you might find it amusing to mess with them a bit. I spent a while in Indoc pretending to be clueless. They would tell me to go in my room and bring out a pair of socks (this is the sort of game you avoid by not showing up early like I did). I would come out of the room with a pair of gloves. Someone would come down the line and yell at me for being stupid and not knowing what socks were. "Go get your socks Candidate!" I'd shuffle into my room and grab a pair of shorts.

You can see where I'm going with this. The game was amusing for me, frustrating for them, and had zero consequences. Had anyone seriously pulled me aside and asked what I was doing, I was planning on telling them one of two things, depending on the tone of the conversation: (1) I would just tell them that the yelling and screaming was so shrill that I couldn't understand what they were saying, or (2) I would tell them that if someone told me to do something stupid, it would only be reasonable that I would do something stupid in return. It's good to goof off when it doesn't matter. It never matters at OCS.

I actually laughed a lot at OCS, despite the misery. When you eat by the numbers (a barbaric process you need to watch online to fully appreciate), goof around. Eating by the numbers is an inventive form of torture you'll endure at OCS:

* * *

A Marine Corps Drill Instructor, Class Chief Petty Officer, or Candidate Officer (a member of the senior class on deck) says "one," and every student snaps their heads to within 4 inches of the plate of food. At "two" they pick up their "War Spoon" (the official name of an OCS soup spoon); "three" and we scoop up as much food as we can. "Four," the spoon and food go in our mouths. "Five," we remove the spoon, replace it on the tray, and check that everything is properly "grounded" (touching): the tray is flush with the edge of the table, and the two glasses are grounded in the upper left hand corner of the tray, touching the edge of the tray; the plate is grounded to the bottom center, with the War Spoon grounded to the bottom edge of the tray and grounded tangent to the plate. On "six," we snap back up to attention, with our feet at a 45-degree angle, heels touching, feet on the port side of the table support (even if that table support is well to the side — which often leads to significant contortion), and with the "thousand-yard stare." On "seven," we are allowed to chew, and on "eight," we are allowed to swallow. The process then repeats.

(Levitt, Steven D. http:// www.freakonomics.com/2007/12/27/eat-by-the-numbers/)

On step three, when everyone is greedily scooping up food to fill their spoons fully, extend your arm fully and steal a huge mound of food from the guys across from you and quickly bring it back under your mouth as if nothing happened. Your buddy across the way won't be able to react because doing anything will draw attention to both of you and you'd *both* in trouble. If he's smart, however, he'll get back at you by doing the same thing to you next time. But instead of eating the food he takes from your plate, he'll just drop it in your drink(s) on the way back to his plate. He may be out a bite, but you'll be out an entire drink - and you'll both have a good laugh unless your victim already drank the KoolAid and is scared of getting 'beat'. In that case, stand by to be scolded about being a mature leader. You'll remember that scolding with joy when you're leading Team Guys into combat and that guy is triple-checking his inventory on some ship in Japan.

Another good way to have a laugh is to have your wife/girlfriend/ friend/brother/sister send you some ridiculous packages. The Drill Instructor makes you open all your packages in public. When guys, particularly the fat ones, got boxes with candy in them, he'd make them stomp the candy into powder while the rest of the class got beat. It was hilarious. If you know that the DI is going to look through all your packages, have people send you packages with impossible-to-explain contraband or in them, like anal beads or some revolting pornography. Or, if you're feeling a little less froggy, try explaining a large box full of nothing but packing popcorn, or a small box with a single adult diaper in it (preferably unused). The ultimate goal is to get your DI to break character and laugh - there's really nothing more gratifying than beating him at his own game. These sort of shenanigans can really make your day, week, or even month. Strongly recommended.

Your class may begin to hate you and your friends because your practical jokes run them the risk of having to do a few pushups or wall-sits here and there, but they're all fat and lazy and could do with the extra workout anyways. Embrace their hate because it shows that you're not scared and they are. Plus you'll want the extra workout anyways.

Have fun with the OCS Forums. There is a popular forum at www.usnavyocs.com. This forum is a terrible source of information regarding BUD/S and the SEAL Teams (in fact, it's worse than no information at all) but you can use it to make plans to meet for dinner out in town before your check-in day. If you're looking for some good laughs, though, you can use it for your own purposes.

The Candi-Os who will be conducting your Indoc week will all be reading the posts for your class. Go ahead and post some ridiculous things. Maybe make multiple accounts and post things about how much you love ballet dancing and how you're going to teach the Candi-Os and drill instructors to have natural grace. Then post, as someone else, that you heard from a friend there that there are 4 or 5 really hot guys in the Candi-O class who will be doing your Indoc. Get some ridiculous stuff out there, and you'll reap the hilarious benefits as you see them trying to figure out who's who from the forum.

Shave your head before you show up. I know this is exactly the opposite of what they tell you to do. They also tell you to show up early. Fuck that. Shave your head. Not only will it save you the money and pain - they charge you something like $15 to shave your head, the barbers tend to crack you over the head repeatedly during the haircut, and the result is so poorly done that you'll probably have to get it redone by a classmate with hair clippers. (On that note, consider bringing a set of clippers so you can shave your head on a regular basis instead of paying ungodly sums to have it done at the barber shop.) Besides, having your head already shaved is a small, but poignant, middle finger to the whole process.

Shower during Indoc. Here's a little secret about Indoc: they control every moment of your life until they put you to bed. After you're put to bed, you can do pretty much anything you want. Everyone in charge of you is too tired to care. Nobody is watching.

After they put you to bed that day, you can feel free and confident to shower and brush your teeth at your own leisure. It may seem like a small thing, but it's not. The morale you'll recover by doing this is priceless. You'll sleep better and you won't hate your life quite so much. I didn't figure this out until the end of Indoc Week, and I was kicking myself for being so slow to figure it out.

Find the black market. There is a constant flow of Snickers and PowerBars into OCS. If there's another BUD/S-bound OC or Candi-O ahead of you, you'll probably find yourself the grateful recipient of a Chocolate PowerBar behind closed doors. If there are SpecWar guys junior you, be sure to hook them up, too. If they're at OCS while you are, chances are they'll be in your BUD/S class, so take care of them.

When you're in Indoc, and especially when you're a new OC (just out of Indoc), you'll find yourself needing a lot more food. Find a Candi-O or more senior OC who has more access to the Naval Exchange (NEX) and pay them to bring you goods. There are ALWAYS a few different sources running food into the junior classes and it's not hard to figure out who to ask. You'll quickly see the guys and girls who take themselves and the program too seriously. These are the douche-nozzles who will rat you out to the DI. Avoid them. There are guys who will talk to you like a regular person. If they won't make a NEX run for you, they can probably find someone who will.

When you're particularly hard up, you can pop your "covert op" cherry and sneak down into "DI Country" to use their vending machines. Get a couple of guys who have the balls to make it happen and go down there after dark. Alternatively, if you can't do that, you can volunteer to be the crew that vacuums DI Country every night. Not only will vacuuming down there give you authorized placement in an otherwise off-limits area, but it will also allow you to recon the whole floor to make sure you're alone while simultaneously drowning out the noise of the vending machine under the roar of 3 vacuum cleaners running. You can even use vacuums to set a security perimeter/early warning system by fanning them out around each corner of the corridors downstairs so you'll know someone's coming long before they see you raiding the vending machine.

Until we got a fully-functional black market and distribution chain set up in our class (around week 4), we survived almost solely on PowerBars, Pop Tarts, and Snickers secreted from the vending machines both at night and during cleaners. It helped us maintain a reasonable weight and, more importantly, was incredibly fun.

One warning, though: don't let the majority of your class know what's going on with your black market. There was another group of guys, separate from my SpecWar guys, who were also bringing in food (though not from the vending machines...nobody else had the balls to do that). They got a little too bold and altruistic and shared their stash with a few too many people. Some Supply Corps female turned them in. They got burned hard by the OCS staff and we had to live off our stockpile (and our covert vacuum ops) for a week because they were inspecting every bag in and out of the building. Don't trust the self-righteous douchebags in your class to be any better, so keep your supplies to yourself and those you know you can trust.

Loose lips sink ships.

There's one other item you want to get ahold of in the first few weeks: caffeine pills. You will be so incredibly tired from lack of sleep, stress, and malnutrition that you'll find it difficult to stay awake. This first starts to become a problem when you're preparing for RLP, folding, ironing, starching, and contemplating suicide. Caffeine pills would be a godsend this week and will only get more valuable. By the time you're into Ocean Navigation, Mo-Boards (an old-school way to predict the movement of your ship in relation to other ships), and other academic courses, you'll be a walking zombie. I kept falling asleep in class, so I stood up in back. I'd fall asleep standing up, so I'd stand on one leg. When I continually nodded off on one leg, I resorted to doing pushups on the floor of the classroom in the back. When I fell asleep *while doing pushups* for the third time, I gave in and got myself some caffeine pills. I only wish I'd been smart enough to get ahold of them sooner.

Store food in cars. If you're in the area, bring your car. It's a great place to store snacks for when you get your weekly trip out to the seawall (where your vehicle is parked). Even if you don't bring your car, you'll arrange to store some of your bags and extra stuff in a classmate's car. Make sure that you bring a box of PowerBars and some of your favorite candy (as well as a bag of assorted candy to share with those less prepared than you).

You'll get some time (depending on your DI) to walk out to the cars as a class to get underwear or an iron or money and the like. You'll end up using it to call home and gorge yourself on junk food. Some guys take the opportunity to bring goods and cell phones back to the barracks, which is a risk. It paid off for people in my class - we were never inspected and guys had their cell phones hidden in their rooms very early on. It's not unheard of, however, to have your bags searched on the way back from the vehicles, so be prepared for that should it happen.

Go to church on Sundays. I'm not saying you should go to the service, I'm saying you should go to 'church.' I take no part in the ancient superstitions of church, but I went and stayed in the room with the food and newspapers. Most people don't go to the service, they sit in the back room, eat donuts (and other goodies), read the paper, watch the news, and talk. The church, regardless of whether you're religious or observant or atheist, is the single place you can fully let your guard down. No OCS staff will bother you there.

The alternative to 'church' was to read or write letters in a room with an OCS staff member. That's not so bad, but you're still at OCS and live by OCS rules. You can't really relax there because it isn't an opportunity to decompress, so go to church and read there.

Work out on your own. This should go without saying, but work out. At first this will be difficult. It will mean doing pushups and sit-ups in your room and pull-ups from the shower-stalls. As you gain more freedom, you will be able to use a few of the paltry fitness facilities. Use them. Medicine balls and kettle-bells will help you maximize your fitness levels. Kettle-bell swings can go a long way to keeping you in decent shape.

As a Candi-O you'll be allowed the freedom to go outside. Get a handful (3+you=4) and do a base-tour run with a large kettle-bell. Run a certain amount of time with the kettle-bell before passing it to the next guy. This is a fantastic workout, it's pretty fun, and will help you prep for BUD/S.

Assembly line for RLP. This strategy is *only* good if you have a friend or two (or three) you can trust absolutely, if you can trust them to take as much care with your RLP items as they would with their own. If you don't have a few guys in your class who can be trusted, then forget it.

If you do have the men, then create an assembly line for RLP items. Each of you can specialize in various activities, like removing loose threads (IPs), using clear nail polish on button-holes to prevent more IPs, folding, ironing, positioning, bed-making. If you only have to do two of these things, and you do it three times more than any man working only for himself, not only are you going to be ultimately faster, but your end product is going to be much more polished. If each of you does this, specializes, and performs his specialty for all three or four of the group, then preparing for RLP can be significantly easier, faster, and less of a pain in the ass.

But that only works if you can trust your partners absolutely. If there's any question about their reliability or commitment, this will ultimately fail and you'll have to do the re-test prepping by yourself.

Sleep. Sleep is a time-machine. If you want to finish OCS as soon as possible (which you certainly do), then sleep every minute you can. Every minute you sleep is a minute of OCS you don't remember. That means you want to sleep always. You're also going to be a walking zombie, tired from lack of sleep, stress, and malnutrition. You're going to want to sleep anyway.

You're not allowed to sleep unless it's designated sleeping time, but don't let that stop you for a second. Your PT mat is just cozy enough. Put it on the floor and you'll be set for a nap. You'll be tired enough that, in a pinch, you don't even need the mat - any horizontal surface will do. Take advantage of every nap time possible.

When you move halls after Indoc, try very, very hard to get a room somewhere in the center of the hall. This way you have a built-in early warning system. You're often not allowed to close your door, even when you have an hour of free time, so you have to nap in plain view of the hallway. When a Chief or DI enters the hallways, anyone who sees him/her will 'brace the bulkhead' (stand 6" from the wall at strict attention) and scream "Good Morning (insert title here)." Then everyone will be required to rush out of their rooms and do the same. If you're in the middle, chances are that at least one of the 10-15 people between you and either doorway (each end of the hall has one) will see the DI/Chief and announce their presence, thereby waking you up.

A lot of DIs and Chiefs only *require* this greeting if they're seen by someone actually *in* the hallway, meaning that if someone inside his/her room and sees the Chief or DI walking down your hallway, they don't have to announce their presence. Make it a class protocol, for the general benefit of all, to *always* announce the presence of a DI or Chief. Even if they tell you not to do it, continue to announce their presence. You'll never get any more punishment than a quick scolding, and you could save someone in your class (and therefore yourself - because if one person is wrong, everyone's wrong) from a much more in-depth punishment.

Another great time to sleep is "sweepers." Let me be clear: I am not advocating shirking your cleaning responsibilities. What I *am* advocating is only doing your fair share.

"Sweepers" is the time of day after dinner where the entirety of the OCS students clean the barracks. The Candi-Os run it and ultimately get the areas checked off by the Chief or DI on duty. The barracks areas are divided into tasking for each class, and each class divides up the work.

My sweepers crew was always the SpecWar guys and one cool Pilot candidate. We always volunteered for the biggest, worst, job. We always made sure the job size was hugely disproportionate to the number of guys we had. Despite the fact that most of our class didn't like us, nobody could ever say that the SpecWar guys weren't pulling three times our own weight.

The seven or eight of us would do half the class's work in half the time it took the other 75% of the class to do the other half. We would be done with everything we were assigned before other people had really even started. That's the kind of guys who belong at BUD/S - we buckled down and powered through the work, always figuring out ways to complete the work faster and easier. We had it down to a science. The problem was that when we were done, we'd get re-tasked to 'help' finish the jobs other groups had been given. Ultimately we would often end up cleaning 90% of our class's areas.

We quickly realized this was bullshit, and that we should not be expected to pick up everyone else's lazy slack. So we developed a plan. In addition to the worst/biggest job, we also volunteered for the most remote job. Sweeping and dusting an empty barracks hall, for example. This way, when we were done we had a viable excuse for being off on our own.

We would choose a room, close the door, and move the desk in front of it. Then we'd sleep in peace. When our "sweepers captain" came by and knocked on the door, we would just tell him we had to move all the furniture away from the walls in order to thoroughly scrub and re-polish a stain in the floor. We got an epic amount of sleep doing this.

Find time to sleep. It'll make your time go faster and the challenge of sneaking as many naps as possible can give meaning to the most menial tasks. Mostly, though, you'll be tired and naps are awesome.

Find a bed-down location. Similar to the last bit of advice in that it involves sleep, but not the same. Find a place to sleep other than your room. Every day you'll be required to have your room look as though you didn't sleep in it. Some guys wake up very early and make their beds. Other guys sleep on top of their beds under extra blankets and just tighten their beds every day. They'll still have to remake their beds a few times a week because the tightness of the sheets goes away.

The smartest guys don't sleep on their beds at all. They don't sleep on the ground either. The smartest guys sleep in an unoccupied room in their hall. Every hall has a few unoccupied rooms (unless your class is enormous) that are used to store extra chairs and whatnot. The beds still have mattresses though. You can steal some extra blankets from the linen closet and store them in the drawers underneath the bed during the day. At night, you can pull them out, unroll them, and sleep soundly, knowing that you don't have to spend a second fixing your bed in the morning. This, aside from the black market food supply, was probably the single most helpful innovation the guys and I came up with at OCS.

Officer Candidate School: Don't Be That Guy.

Don't be afraid. It takes something tantamount to an act of god to drop you from OCS. The least fit "fatbody" in your class will almost certainly graduate and become an Ensign. Don't be disheartened that the bar is so low, take solace in the fact that goofing around is not going to lose you your commission. Understand that, despite what anyone might say, nobody at OCS talks to any of the Instructors at BUD/S. Not only would the OCS staff not know where to start, but if they *did* find someone to talk to, that person wouldn't care. In fact, if someone from OCS were to call and say that you were not focussing on your studies, and just wanted to work out all the time, that you lied for your buddies, or tried to get away with shenanigans, that would probably make you seem like a *better* SEAL candidate.

I'd jump over hurdles to get that guy in my platoons.

But, realistically, there is zero communication from OCS to BUD/S. In fact, the BUD/S staff always seems surprised when new OCS graduates show up. There is no communication, so don't worry that a bad reputation will precede you. And, as I've said, a bad reputation at OCS would actually commute to a good reputation and BUD/S.

Don't be afraid of the Candi-Os who are running your Indoc either. They're scared to death of the DI and have very specific limitations on what they're allowed to do. They're also only a few weeks ahead of you, even if they act like they know everything.

They can't do a thing to you and they certainly aren't allowed to lay a hand on you. And they don't know a thing despite the images they project.

Don't expect much of your peers. I was shocked at the low caliber of my classmates at OCS. They ran the gambit from your simple emaciated-and-lazy-slob to your entitled-fat-chick to the always lovable borderline-autistic-kid-with-rage-problems. They were, aside from the SpecWar guys and a few Pilots, an impressively unimpressive bunch.

You can't and shouldn't rely on your classmates to do much. It's really not a huge deal, but you can put yourself at a disadvantage if you rely on them to complete much of anything on their own.

Don't touch your eyes. This seems like stupidly-specific advice, but it's not. The grounds at OCS are covered with goose shit. That means that every surface, even the floors inside the barracks, has a nice coat of goose crap tracked onto it. You, by default, will have goose crap on your hands the moment you touch anything. If you get goose crap particles in your eye, you will develop conjunctivitis. Pinkeye, bitches.

Guys get rolled all the time for bad cases of pinkeye. This means a couple extra weeks of OCS. You don't want that any more than you want Chlamydia. Chlamydia might be preferable, actually. So don't touch your face. Seriously.

Don't be a leader. This is counter-intuitive, but it ultimately makes sense. Not only are class leaders required to be more straight-laced than the rest of the class, but more of their time is demanded. You're probably not going to like being the straight-laced enforcer. More importantly, you need to be spending your time sneaking workouts and naps to slow down your physical atrophy. Being charged with any leadership position will take time and focus away from the things you need to do and make you spend time doing stupid things, like ensuring the class sings "Anchors Aweigh" every night and mediating a cat-fight between two fat chicks who are fighting over breeding rights with the sniveling little SWO-candidate they've both managed to browbeat into submission. Forget it. Just be a schmuck if you can and life will be better.

Don't Drink the KoolAid. Remember at all times that "OCS is Gay." This should be readily apparent, but never forget it. And more importantly, watch out for the snakes in your class who *do* drink the KoolAid. They'll probably try to have some form of "Come-to-Jesus" meeting where they reference your irreverence for the institution and your lack of regard for getting the class beat occasionally. The next thing you know, they're anonymously ratting you and your boys out to the Chief every chance they get in order to exert control over you and ingratiate themselves to the instructors.

There are spineless people in every class who will take the preached "Honor, Courage, and Commitment" principles to heart without context. The dangerous thing is that the "honor violation" or "integrity violation" is really the only way you can get kicked out of OCS. It happens only rarely, but it happened to a Pilot candidate in my Chief's previous class:

The class was in their Service Dress Blues inspection, standing in formation in the gym. In the Blues inspection, Officer Candidates inspect one another. It's a way of "showing discipline" and attention to detail. For most people, it's an exercise in balance - you don't want to grade too hard and fail the person, but you don't want to grade so easily that the Chief feels the need to re-grade them (which would likely result in a failed inspection).

A Pilot candidate was inspecting a SWO candidate's uniform, and before the Chief got there to oversee the inspection, he noticed a long, stray hair on her shoulder. Nobody was watching, so he removed the hair. When the Chief got to there to supervise the inspection, she noticed that the hair she'd seen before was gone. She asked the Pilot if he had removed the hair. He said he hadn't. The Chief asked the SWO chick. She said he hadn't touched her. The SWO passed her inspection.

Two days later she came to the Chief, bawling, because she "couldn't live with herself for lying" and told the Chief that the Pilot candidate had, in fact, removed the hair. This chick got rolled for failing the inspection and the Pilot candidate apparently lost his contract and was sent home.

Our chief told us this story with pride, that she had actually instilled the values of honesty, integrity, honor, and courage in this girl. I think most people would look at this differently. This guy risked himself to help his teammate out, but she was so incredibly weak and self-absorbed that she sold him out. She drank the KoolAid so much that she probably would've bled it. I have little doubt that anyone considering being a SEAL officer is going to have enough spine to resist the indoctrination. Those around you, however, will not. There will be glassy-eyed idiots who will do the 'honorable' thing and rat you out for a pat on the head. Watch out for them. They will bring you down.

Don't Get Chicks. Speaking of people bringing you down, don't even *look* at the females. Not all the females at OCS are worthless. Just most of them. There was one really badass chick in our class. She was cute, could PT like mad, was very smart, and never got caught up in the petty cat-fights that abound in a closed social environment like OCS. We found out she was a lesbian when her girlfriend showed up at graduation. There were two more girls in our class who were worthwhile. They weren't studs like the first girl, but they weren't dead weight either.

The rest of the females in my class were a train wreck. Ugly, fat, lazy, entitled, made-up like Hong Kong hookers when possible, and tried to hit on every guy they could. At West Point it's called "Grey Goggles" when your perception of women changes drastically because you've only seen ugly chicks for months. The same thing happens for a lot of guys at OCS and these fat sluts took advantage of it. They go for these worthless, annoying, ugly females they'd never have considered touching before OCS.

And once those guys do the deed, their testicles are almost literally in a vice because all it would take for the chick to get the guys kicked out would be to talk. Fornication is forbidden at OCS, and these chicks were not above fabricating a story of how they were forcibly taken advantage of. So these pathetic guys become their hostages. I am not exaggerating. The moment you whip it out and stick it in is the moment you're no longer free to live your own life at OCS.

A large minority of the females at OCS are pure toxic. No chick is worth the risk. And, statistically speaking, she's probably the kind of ugly you'd never even *consider* on the outside. So stay away. Stay far, far away from the women.

You have a lot to lose, nothing to gain, and you'll probably regret it. No touchy. You'll get plenty of action in San Diego.

Officer Candidate School: Mark's Parting Wisdom.

OCS was, by far, the most miserable I'd ever been. I would rather do Hell Week again than deal with RLP. BUD/S was nowhere near as miserable as OCS. I'm not exaggerating and I'm not alone

In BUD/S you are outside almost all the time. You're outside, on the beach, in San Diego. In OCS you're confined almost exclusively to the indoors of a few dank, monotonous buildings. Despite the fact that you get beat on the beach and immersed in the ocean, you never get as depressed in BUD/S as you do in OCS - fresh air and sunlight do wonders.

In BUD/S you eat well and exercise constantly. Okay, so you could do with a little less exercise than BUD/S. Fair enough. But if given the choice between the horrible sedentary OCS lifestyle and the overly-active life at BUD/S, there's a clear winner.

BUD/S takes a lot of time from you, but you have freedom when you're not working. You can go out in town to get a bite to eat. You have the weekends off (except when you're on the Island in Third Phase) and you can sleep in and get a massage if you want. You're allowed to read, talk on your cell phone, and eat as much as you want. In OCS you're only permitted to read books on the Navy's official reading list, cell phone use is prohibited, and you can't even eat a full meal. There's so much more freedom at BUD/S that OCS feels like prison in comparison.

There is a point to your suffering in BUD/S. Not only does every 'gut-check' evolution at BUD/S have a point in itself, but the whole miserable process serves to thin out the class and harden those who remain. The 'gut-check' evolutions in OCS are pointless, without merit, and miserable more than they are difficult. There is no real honor in their completion, only frustration that you were subjected to them.

Completion of BUD/S is an honorable, respectable, meritorious achievement few will ever experience. Completion of OCS is a foregone conclusion, a dubious and largely unimportant achievement that anyone can realize.

Graduating OCS confirms you have a pulse.

Graduating BUD/S proves you have balls.

In the first few weeks of First Phase my class was enduring a particularly savage beating. We were entering our third hour of the beating and things were ridiculous. We were doing Egyptian Pushups, where your feet and knees are together, your hands form a diamond, and your ass is straight up in the air. You lower your forehead into the diamond formed by your fingers on one count, and fully extend your arms on the next. One. Down. Up. Two. Down. Up. Three. We'd been doing these for so long that the tops of my hands were raw and bleeding from the sand in my hair and on my face rubbing through the skin. (I still have the scars)

The floor of the classroom was slimy, flooded, and grimy from the sand, sweat, saltwater, and urine. Yes, the beating was so violent that guys were pissing themselves as they fought to keep up with the accelerating calls of "backs, bellies, feet, bellies, feet, backs, bellies, backs, bellies, backs, feet." It was so hot and humid in the room that condensation was raining from the soaked ceiling tiles above.

Students are falling over. One guy collapses and shits himself. The instructors are roaring as they sprint from student to student, screaming at him to "stop being such a pussy" as they kick him to the ground. Things were so ridiculous that I had one of those moments where you cease to feel your body. I couldn't feel the pain. The sounds faded down to a hum, and everything slowed down. I turned to my buddy next to me who had been in my OCS class. He was smiling. I realized I was, too.

"Hey man," he said to me in a completely normal voice, "at least we're not in RLP." True. A huge smile broke across his face. I started laughing hysterically because he was right. As bad as this moment was, I could be sitting in my room at OCS folding my perfectly-stenciled tighty-whitey underwear into a perfectly starched and folded 6"x6" square. I was instantly overcome with a feeling of relief that I was finally at BUD/S and would never have to do any of the ridiculous OCS evolutions ever again.

All of this being said, though, OCS is not hard. It sucks. You will hate nearly every minute of your life there. But nothing you will do there is difficult, it's just miserable. If you follow the advice I've offered in this last section, you can take the edge off your time there and monumentally improve your quality of life. Just have some balls, have some fun, get as much sleep as you can, and get through it. Everything after is a party in comparison.

Chapter 7

PTRR: Living In Limbo As A Whiteshirt.

"Most people get ahead during the time that others waste."
- Henry Ford

PTRR stands for Physical Training Rehabilitation and Remediation. There are two groups of BUD/S students in PTRR, white shirt rollbacks and officers waiting to class up. White shirt rollbacks are guys who have gotten rolled upon arrival to BUD/S, during Basic Orientation ("BO" or "Indoc"), or during First Phase prior to the completion of Hell Week. A white shirt rollback can expect to class up with the next class that arrives as long as he's fit for full duty.

An officer arrives in PTRR after he checks in at BUD/S. He can expect to be in PTRR for anywhere between 2 and 14 months depending on the number of officers who checked in before him - there are only a limited number of officers allowed in each class. On average a new officer will spend 6-7 months in PTRR waiting to class up.

PTRR is a good opportunity for enlisted guys to heal and gives officers the chance to learn how BUD/S is run. Officers will learn to run the O-Course, the best soft-sand running techniques, the location of the chow hall, and the proper procedures for inspections and the like. Even things like the proper "BUD/S way" to tie your boots will be important. Having spent some time in PTRR allows officers to teach their class BUD/S culture when they fly out to Great Lakes to meet them.

While in PTRR your day will begin around 7am and go to the early afternoon (days past 2pm are rare). The mornings include a swim and a pt or an O-course and soft-sand run (depending on the day). Most days you'll get off after lunch. The entire PTRR class isn't a real, numbered BUD/S class, but many people in PTRR will be in your BUD/S class when you ultimately class up.

This section is going to be more helpful for officers than enlisted guys because if you're enlisted and end up spending any time in PTRR, you've probably been rolled from a class and thus know the lay of the land already.

PTRR: Key Tasks.

Learn the Ropes. If you're an officer waiting to class up, your primary responsibility will be to learn everything you can about BUD/S so you can set your class up for success when you get to class up. If you're enlisted, you've already been through some portion of BUD/S and your job is to make sure you help prepare the officers to set your class up for success. A good proportion of the guys around you will ultimately class up with you, so take ownership, regardless of your rank, and get ready to crush BUD/S.

Talk to the guys in First, Second, and Third Phases when possible. You can learn a great deal from the things they get beat for. You can get to know the personalities and red-button issues for each instructor, which will help you avoid as many beatings as possible.

Stay Motivated. It's easy to be motivated your first few months in Coronado. The Silver Strand (another name for Coronado) is gorgeous and BUD/S is to be your ultimate proving ground. After a few months, though, it's easy to get discouraged. If you're enlisted you probably won't spend too much time in PTRR and this isn't much of an issue. If you're an officer, however, and you're going to spend months in PTRR, you'll start to see class after class go through Hell Week. When you see a class check in, complete Hell Week, pass Pool Comp, leave for the Island, come back, and graduate and you're still doing the same old O-Course soft-sand run, it's damn hard to stay motivated. Find a way. Find a hobby or three. Read a lot. Chase women. Enjoy San Diego. Don't get discouraged.

Get/Stay Healthy. If you're in PTRR because you got hurt, getting healthy should be your primary goal. If you're serious about recovering, you'll be eating well, getting 8-10 hours of sleep a night, and doing your rehab religiously. You'll be avoiding alcohol and tobacco.

If you're in PTRR because you're waiting to class up, stay healthy. Get plenty of sleep and don't party too hard (even though you can). I know a guy who took a year to finish BUD/S because he kept getting hurt. His weekend binge drinking added months to his time at BUD/S by preventing him from healing, recovering, and avoiding injury in the first place.

Be responsible and keep your mind on your goals.

PTRR: TTPs.

Get away. It's easy to go crazy in PTRR. In fact it's hard *not* to go crazy when you see a class's full cycle from checking in to graduation day, but the big discouragements like that come only rarely. The real danger in PTRR is losing your mind on the daily drudgery.

Your days, when taken individually, aren't bad. You get off early and get to live in San Diego (on Coronado - even better). You get a solid workout most days. You're not trapped inside or made to fold your laundry all night. The PTRR instructor staff is more disinterested than it is cruel. Your inspections are usually only to ensure a general tidiness as opposed to the rigid standards of a BUD/S class. PTRR actually seems like it would be a good deal. But you will slowly go insane.

The schedule every week has little variation and just being in the compound wears you out. Save your sanity by ensuring you get away from the BUD/S compound often. There are dozens of things to do in San Diego and on Coronado. There's a marina across the street from the base where you can rent motorboats, fishing boats, kayaks, and sailboats for reasonable fees. There are restaurants on Orange Ave. in Coronado for every whim. In the summer there are vacationing ladies you might wish to befriend. They come from Arizona, Mexico, Nevada, and other parts of California looking for a fun vacation. You can be fun if you want to,

180

can't you?

Downtown San Diego has a ton to offer, from the San Diego Zoo to Balboa Park to the bar scene of the famous/infamous Gaslamp District and the coed-rich Pacific Beach (PB) area. 30 minutes north is La Jolla, where you can swim off the beach and see hundreds of Leopard Sharks and Garibaldi fish when the season's right (highly recommended). All year round you can swim with the California Sea Lions who live on the rock cliffs at the southern end of La Jolla Cove. It's free and it's a pretty cool way to get a workout.

It doesn't matter what you're into. Find yourself off the base more than you're on it. It might seem odd advice at first, but after a month of PTRR I guarantee you'll feel the truth in my advice.

Live off base. If you're an officer or a married enlisted man, you can live off base and collect BAH. Do it. You'll still have a barracks room on base, but you don't have to live there. You just keep it for the purposes of inspections - which are a lot easier to prepare for if you don't live in the room. The only time you'll be required to sleep on base is First Phase until you've completed Hell Week. Other than those three weeks, you're free to live and sleep in your off-base apartment.

A lot of guys rent houses in PB or Imperial Beach (IB - the small city to the south). Having a place of your own is a fantastic thing - you have room to take care of your gear and a sanctuary from the violent atmosphere of BUD/S.

Some of my friends actually rented a condo in the luxury high-rises directly north of the compound on Coronado. They're called the Coronado Shores. The condo was amazing and surprisingly affordable. These condos rent for $8-12k a month in the Summer but the majority are unoccupied the rest of the year. If you rent them for a year, you'll usually pay around $3500/month for a 3-bedroom. That's amazingly affordable for what you're getting. There are pools and hot tubs (which are a godsend in First Phase - a nice hot tub soak while stretching can really help you stay healthy). You can invite your guys over on the weekends to barbecue and soak. The commute is never any longer than 5 minutes by foot, which is unspeakably valuable - it allows you to go home on a 45-minute break. If you forget something at home, it's no big deal. Every other tenant in your building will be as old as your grandparents, meaning it's quiet and peaceful 24 hours/ day. For what you want when you're in BUD/S. If I could do it all over I would rent a condo in the Shores for the entirety of the pipeline.

Hoard gear. Gear is currency in BUD/S, particularly dive knives and actuators. Get a collection of extra gear (which you don't keep in your barracks room - extra gear is frowned upon). This way you can have an inspection-ready set of gear and gear to use on swims.

Dive knives used in BUD/S are not real dive knives. They're not stainless and they don't keep an edge. The SRK knives issued will literally rust in the 10 minutes it takes to get from the ocean to the fresh water shower. Your guys will lose their knives or forget to sharpen them. Having an extra standing by in your car can save your whole class a beating.

An actuator is a plastic assembly with metal parts on the inside. It bolts onto your UDT life vest and a CO_2 cartridge screws into the bottom. In the instance of an emergency in the water, you can pull the actuator's lever, piercing the CO_2 cartridge which fills the vest with air. The actuator has a number of small metal parts that rust easily. The internal spring rusts easily and wears out quickly.

Dive knives and actuators are inspected during Barracks Inspections as well as Swimmer Inspections (held before each swim). You can never have too many of each prepared. When guys quit or get dropped, get their gear from them. They're required to turn them in, but there's not the slightest punishment if they don't. Get the gear for the good of the boys - it's an advantage of being at BUD/S ahead of the class. Take advantage of it.

Use your car as storage. There are some things you're not allowed to have at BUD/S, like multivitamins or Motrin. There are also some things you simply don't want Instructors tossing on the ground while they inspect your room. Store them in your car. Your room will be thoroughly searched from time to time. I know one guy who even got kicked out for having a Red Bull in his room in PTRR, no shit. There were no amplifying reasons that he got booted for the Red Bull and other people who used Monster Energy Drinks to 'distract' Instructors during PI/BIs didn't.

When you check in at BUD/S you'll sign a document with all the prohibited items on it. At the time I went to BUD/S it included caffeinated products, multivitamins, pain-killers/antiinflammatories and all over-the-counter drugs. Even Zyrtec, my allergy medication, was off limits. So I kept it in my car and took it anyways.

You get punished not for breaking the rules, but for getting caught. So don't get caught. I only every heard about one vehicle search at BUD/S and I never saw one. Have a plan, though, for the occasion they tell your class to drive their vehicles around for inspection. Put all your contraband in a few plastic grocery bags without any evidence to their ownership. If they ask you to pull your vehicles around, just ditch the bags when you go get your car. But your car probably won't be searched.

Gather intelligence. The classes ahead of you can give you some seriously valuable information. They can tell you the most updated information about BUD/S because they're living it. They can tell you about the different instructors and what each man expects. They can tell you that Instructor A will get you wet and sandy if you don't "Hooyah" loud enough, that Instructor B is a stickler for a sharp knife on swim inspections, and that Instructor C craves Sugar-Free Red Bull and Copenhagen Long-Cut.

Know your enemy. Know everything you can about every evolution and every instructor. Use your time well and you'll find it will pay dividends in morale as you rack up small victories you never would've known about if you hadn't done your research.

Work on your weaknesses. In PTRR you'll have the opportunity to work on every timed evolution: runs, swims, O-Courses. Learn the standards for First Phase times. Realize your weakness (mine was always the O-Course) and make it your mission to make that weakness into a strength. The first month I was in PTRR I spent an hour or two on the Balance Logs, the

Dirty Name, and the Rope Swing every weekend. By the time I classed up I had no problem with any of these obstacles because of my extra work. This was my one exception to the "stay away from the compound" rule - ensuring I was ready to crush the evolutions when I classed up.

There is no excuse for a performance roll if you've been in PTRR. You should be able to do the O-Course blindfolded by the time you class up. If you can't, then you should quit. That being said, get your work done and get out of dodge. Don't spend any more time on the base than you have to, but don't spend less than you need to either. If you can pass every Third Phase time, then you're golden and don't need to spend any extra time on anything.

PTRR: Don't Be That Guy.

Stay out of Team Guy bars. There is no official rule about SEAL bars and there's no such thing as an official Team Guy bar. That being said, there is very much an unofficial rule. Specifically, Danny's and McP's on Coronado are off limits to any BUD/S or SQT student. Go there the day you get your trident and not a minute before.

You may not hear about it while you're in the bar, but you will most certainly feel the pain the next day at work. Besides, your instructors drink there. Do you really want a single moment more face-time with them than is required? The answer is no, you don't.

Don't join a Crossfit or MMA gym. You need to avoid the local CrossFit and MMA gyms for multiple reasons. These are both great ways (particularly MMA) to get hurt. You're not at BUD/S to do MMA, you're at BUD/S to become a SEAL. Don't risk your shot because you think MMA will be fun. It will, but it has a decent chance to hurt you. Even a sprained wrist or stitches from face-shot can get you rolled. Don't take that chance.

There is no hiding your identity in San Diego. I can walk down Orange Avenue or any street in San Diego and point out the BUD/S students. So can everyone else. As dumb as it sounds, there are old-school ex-Team Guys who feel like BUD/S is getting soft (it's not) and so harbor resentment toward every BUD/S student they see. There are also current Team Guys who like to harass

BUD/S students. If you go to any CrossFit or MMA gym, chances are that the owners are Team Guys or ex-Team Guys. Not only that, but the majority of the clientele are connected to NSW. While most of these guys will probably respect that you're training on your own, you can almost guarantee there's an old-school douchebag in the crowd who will make a call to his buddy in the Instructor Cadre. He's likely to exaggerate your conversation to put words in your mouth like, "Yeah, I'm training to be a Navy SEAL, but BUD/S is just too easy so I wanted to get an actual workout in on my own."

It doesn't matter what you actually said. The story they get is the story they believe. I implore you to leave these gyms alone. The number of my friends who had similar things happen to them would floor you. Add this very likely outcome to the possibility of getting hurt and you'll see that it doesn't make much sense to join your local CrossFit or MMA gym.

Don't wear BUD/S gear in public. This should go without saying, but it happens every class. You're visible as a BUD/S student. Don't increase your signature more than necessary by wearing BUD/S gear in public. Don't lounge on the beach or surf in UDT shorts. Don't wear a stenciled shirt to dinner. Don't walk around with your fins strapped to your backpack.

The only exception here is the wetsuit. It's a crappy wetsuit, but if it's the only one you have you can get away with using it when you surf or free-dive. The further away you are from the BUD/S compound, the safer you are. I wouldn't surf on Gator Beach (the beach on the northern portion of the base) wearing your BUD/S wetsuit, but if you went free-diving for sharks and sea lions in La Jolla, you probably wouldn't have any problems.

The guiding principle should be visibility. The lower your profile, the better off you are. Most Team Guys won't care, but some will, and that one retired master chief can really fuck your world up.

PTRR: Mark's Parting Wisdom.

PTRR is a good life, but terrible. You really do get to live a comfortable life most of the time, and much of your time is your own. It gives you a great idea of what BUD/S is going to be like and affords you an enviable opportunity to know insider tricks you couldn't otherwise know. By the time you class up you'll have the home field advantage.

Take advantage of all that PTRR offers, but stay sane by staying away from the compound and barracks in your free time. Decompress every day. Relax on the weekends. Find a hobby or two that will help keep your mind off BUD/S when you're not working.

Be ready to class up. Whether you're in PTRR for a month or a year, there's no excuse for not being prepared to class up. Get ready for the real thing. Look forward to First Phase, it's like nothing you've ever done before and it'll make you a man.

Chapter 8

Pre-BUD/S: Getting After It At Great Lakes.

"It is amazing how much crisper the general experience
Of life becomes when your body is given a chance
To develop a little strength."
                    - Frank Duff

Pre-BUD/S, also known as BUD/S Prep, was commissioned in 2008 in response to a national requirement to train more Navy SEALs without lowering standards. At Pre-BUD/S prospective BUD/S students will undergo 4-10 weeks of physical training and mentorship.

There are a handful of active and retired SEALs who run the program at Pre-BUD/S, also held on Great Lakes Naval Base, but the majority of the staff members are former college athletes who the students refer to as "coaches." They're young, friendly, and energetic. Some of the chicks were pretty hot, too - distracting to many, but their presence invariably made some guys put out more on the workouts than they would've had there not been some attractive chicks in the gym.

Upon arrival at BUD/S Prep you'll take the advanced PST (800 yds CSS no fins, pushups, sit-ups, pull-ups, and a 3 mile run). Based on your performance you'll be broken into the Blue (needs work), Grey (middle of the pack), or Red (ready for BUD/S) group. Your workouts will be tailored to your group in order to improve your technique or fitness level in appropriate proportion. Your weeks will usually consist of 5 swim workouts, 3 run workouts, and 2 strength/PT workouts. Each day will also have roughly 2 hours of academic classes on everything from mental toughness to SEAL history to big-navy 'sailorization' classes.

The time at Pre-BUD/S the class will be composed of enlisted men only. The officers will meet their class in Coronado after a lengthy time in PTRR to begin Basic Orientation and, shortly thereafter, First Phase.

When you leave BUD/S Prep, you will be in great shape. You will be able to run farther, swim faster, and do more pushups and sit-ups than you've ever done. Physically, you'll be the man. You'll have every physical tool you need to make it. The only thing Pre-BUD/S won't take care of for you will be the mental strength. That comes from you.

Pre-BUD/S: Key Tasks.

Get fit. This is simple, but the single most important thing you'll do in BUD/S Prep. Get fit. It's easy. Just do everything they tell you to do. You'll get multiple opportunities to work out every day. Capitalize on them.

The hardest part of getting to BUD/S was working out on your own. When you were a civilian training from your home, you could always just blow off the workout. There were probably women you could've spent more time with. There were video games to play and beer to drink. There were friends who undoubtably wanted to hang out more. But you sacrificed, on your own, that time to work out. Not only did you sacrifice time, but you committed yourself to the pursuit of fitness. You were likely the only master of your workouts, deciding for yourself how to work out, what to do each day, for how long, and when to stop. It's a lot harder to drive the car than it is to ride in it.

You're in luck at Pre-BUD/S. The workouts are there for you to do. You don't have to decide what to do or for how long. You don't have the option to skip out on a workout to play video games or chase tail. You have no options in the best way possible. You don't have your freedom taken from you, you have more freedom now because you're on the path to being a Team Guy. All you have to do now is add effort and you're there. Do the workouts. Put out. Get everything you can from every opportunity. Eat well. Sleep and recover. Relax on your days off. Get strong and fast and you can't fail.

Pass the screener. One of the primary ways Pre-BUD/S is improving BUD/S success rates is to do a preliminary screening of candidates. There are people who get dropped from the program in Pre-BUD/S due to integrity issues (theft, etc), but the majority of those who are dropped from the program even before they get out to Coronado are simply unable to pass the exit screener physical test. It happens every class, but not to many guys. The exit standards are as follows:

> 1000 meter swim with fins - 20:00
> 70 push-ups
> 60 sit-ups
> 10 pull-ups
> 4 mile run - 31:00

These are the minimum numbers required to pass. If you've been at Pre-BUD/S for a month and you're unable to meet these numbers, you're wrong. If you put sincere effort into the workouts, these scores are easy to meet or beat.

Keep in mind that these are minimum scores. If you find yourself in a Pre-BUD/S class larger than your BUD/S class will be, they will take the top 300 (or whatever the number they're allowed to send to BUD/S) and the remainder will wait in Pre-BUD/S for the next class. Nobody who passes these minimum standards will be dropped for their performance. If you can't meet these standards after a full cycle of Pre-BUD/S, however, you will be dropped.

If you pay attention to the first bit of guidance, to get fit, passing the screener is a formality. Trust that even a man coming to Boot Camp with a minimum pass on the SEAL Challenge PST can pass the exit standard PST without much stress. All you have to do is take ownership of your training and you'll be in Coronado in the surf in no time.

Pre-BUD/S: TTPs.

Learn to swim with fins. There are two ways to swim the CSS with fins: flutter kick and dolphin kick. Learn them both and decide which one you like better. I am not a big guy and most people wouldn't consider me powerfully-built, so the dolphin-kick was my technique of choice.

The flutter kick requires almost no technique. You know how to do it. You just have to do it powerfully for a long time. If you're an ox and you do ruck-runs with a refrigerator strapped to your back or you're a competitive freestyle swimmer, you may find the flutter kick suits you best.

The dolphin-kick is much more technical. It takes much longer to become proficient, but your efforts are repaid over and over with efficiency. You need to get your timing right so you're kicking once on the breath and once on the pull. The trickiest part of the dolphin-kick is that it's not a kick - it's a full-body undulation. This is the source of its efficiency: where the flutter kick is almost entirely hip flexors and ass, the dolphin-kick uses your entire core to propel you.

When I went to BUD/S Prep they required a flutter kick despite the fact that the BUD/S Instructors in PTRR and Indoc were strong proponents of the dolphin-kick. Learn both if it's an option. If it isn't, prepare yourself to learn the dolphin-kick from the officers when you meet up with them.

* * *

Decompress. Great Lakes base itself is toxic. The base is the epitome of fleet mentality. I was there for two weeks and it got to me in that amount of time. My class was even held up by an MA (Master-at-Arms, or Military Policeman) because a few of us had our hands in our pockets. It was 25 degrees out and he came screaming across a parking lot to yell at us. We only escaped trouble because our OIC (a LTJG) swapped out his stocking cap for a rank-insignia cover before he walked over to tell the MA to leave us alone.

A place like that can sap even the most motivated guy of his spirit despite the high quality of the training regimen. Avoid being sucked dry by making use of your liberty on the weekends. Go into Chicago, get a hotel room with a bunch of friends, and have a good time in the city. Chicago is a fantastic city to visit, so go whenever you can. Catch a sports event if you like baseball or basketball. Go to a movie. Chase women. Partake of the city's plentiful bars if you're over 21, just don't get in trouble. Do whatever you need to do to recharge your batteries. You'll get enough training during the week that you can almost certainly afford to take the weekends off. Decompress every weekend and you'll perform *that* much better during the week.

Move up in groups. The classes are broken into groups based on performance. If you're in a low group, make every effort to move up to a faster group. If you're a Blue swimmer, make it your mission to become a Grey swimmer. If you're a Grey runner, work hard to make the Red runner group. When you feel like you're ready to make the jump, talk to coaches and instructors.

There isn't a single staff member at BUD/S Prep who won't applaud your efforts and desires to improve your standing. If you get blown off, keep trying. Your mom always told you that "the squeaky wheel gets the grease." Deserve the promotion, then demand it. Get into that Red group in every evolution so you can be sure you class up a the soonest opportunity. Not only that, but the quest to move up will add meaning and motivation and a short-term concrete goal to work toward - and goals always help keep your mind on the prize. Get some.

* * *

Stretch. The workouts in Pre-BUD/S are great. You won't have to run, swim, or lift on your own time. Your level of fitness will be taken care of for you as long as you participate. You can maximize your workouts, however, and recover faster by stretching on your own time.

Your day will end at 5 or 6 in the evening and you'll have plenty of time to yourself. Get in the habit of stretching on your own. Make a commitment to an extensive stretching routine (you can read or listen to music while you stretch) and you'll see fewer injuries and better performance. It costs you nothing and gains you a great deal. Why not do it?

Pre-BUD/S: Don't Be That Guy.

Don't expect friendliness at BUD/S. When you're in Pre-BUD/S it's easy to grow accustomed to snacks every afternoon and regular naps. It's easy get comfortable with encouraging workouts and supportive coaches. That hot chick teaching the class on the proper form for squats can really make your afternoon.

There are no hot chicks in BUD/S. There is no encouragement, there are no smiling Instructors, and there is no comfort. BUD/S is violent and cruel. The transition from Pre-BUD/S to BUD/S can be shocking to some - they are shocked, then scared, and then they quit.

Remember this. In fact I'd go so far as to never be friendly with the coaches. It's too easy to fall into the habit of civility and too hard to break yourself of it. Don't treat them rudely. Treat them with reserved respect, but don't be friendly. Keep your distance. Don't ogle the chicks, as hard as that will be. When you do that, you give into them and you lose power. Pay just enough attention to them that you know what the workout is, then put your focus and effort into the workout. This will make the transition to BUD/S significantly less shocking.

Don't get cocky. If you're the best athlete, concentrate on getting better and helping your classmates improve themselves. If you're a stud, don't be cocky. Remember that while physical fitness is a good indicator of success at BUD/S, it isn't everything.

Dick Couch wrote in *The Warrior Elite* that Tom Norris was the bottom of his BUD/S class, physically. Tom Norris went on to win the Medal of Honor. A guy in your class who just barely passes his PSTs and the exit standard probably won't be the Honorman, but he might be. Even if he isn't, he can still be a fantastic SEAL.

Conversely, the best athletes in your BUD/S class will probably quit. It doesn't *always* happen, but does happen more often than not. The top guys will often be among the first to quit - having never really encountered hardship up to that point, and the guys at the bottom will often make excellent SEALs - having to fight tooth and nail for every inch of ground they make the entire pipeline.

Don't be cocky if you're at the top and don't be discouraged if you aren't. As long as you get to the next step, you're good to go. The top graduate of your SQT class will be called the Honorman.

Do you know what they call the guy who graduates at the bottom if the class?

A SEAL.

Pre-BUD/S: Mark's Parting Wisdom.

Get ready. This is your last chance to get some deep breaths in before you get kicked in the nuts. BUD/S Prep affords you an amazing opportunity to tune yourself up physically and mentally. You will be given amazing workouts to do with almost zero side tasks. You have the amazing luxury of time and opportunity. Focus during the week. Relax on the weekends.

Read as much as you can. Stretch. Relax. Get plenty of sleep. Stay out of trouble. Set yourself up for success and use every opportunity to further temper your body and mind. You'll get strong and fit and you'll be ready for BUD/S when you get there.

BUD/S Prep is a wonderful program if you make use of it. Keep everything in perspective and you'll be golden.

Chapter 9

BUD/S Orientation: The Block Formerly Known as Indoc.

Bibamus, moriendum est.
"Drink up, Death is near."
                                    - Seneca the Elder

Basic Orientation (BO) is the new name for Indoc (short for Indoctrination). Back in the day the Instructors used to be able to beat Indoc classes. Now Indoc's sole form of punishment is the 'chit,' a piece of paper detailing your deficiency. The chits don't mean a thing, really, and can be ignored for the most part.

Because of these changes, the Instructors often refer to BO as "Gay-doc." That being said, the hardest PT sessions we had in the entire pipeline were in BO. Most PT sessions in First, Second, and Third Phase quickly degenerate into beatings or surf torture. In BO, however, PT sessions can last a while and be quite taxing. You won't get a legitimate BUD/S beating until First Phase, but you and your classmates will still gain an intimate familiarity with the surf zone.

BO is also your class's first exposure to BUD/S as a class. Being able to quickly pass information, or "word," and being able to get an accurate boat crew muster, or headcount, will make your time in BO (and the rest of BUD/S, for that matter) a little less uncomfortable. Your class will start out performing like a bag of dead kittens, but by the end of BO you'll be a functioning BUD/S class ready for the crucible of First Phase.

There are often a good number of students who quit in BO before they even get to First Phase. There is nothing even close to Hell Week in BO, but you will get the first real taste of BUD/S and that taste does a lot of guys in. You'll do a Land Portage ("Boats on Heads") familiarization, where you run up and down the beach on soft sand and in the water carrying the IBS (Inflatable Boat, Small) on your head. It's only a few hours, but it's a taste of daily life at BUD/S until after Hell Week. Some guys just can't take it, they're physically weak. Most guys can take it, but get psyched out and quit because they're anticipating pain. This is mental weakness. The worst part of every evolution is that minute you're "standing by," waiting for the instructors, and your mind is running wild with the possibilities. The worst part of Hell Week is when you're sitting in the tents, probably covered in Vaseline, waiting for Breakout to start. No part of Hell Week is as bad as waiting for Hell Week to finally start. BO is pure anticipation of BUD/S, and in this way it can get the better of a lot of students.

When you're going through BO, keep this always in mind. Don't let your imagination run wild with phantasmagoric visions of Instructors tearing your intestines out or killing you. They won't. BO is actually pretty weak. The Instructors talk a big game to get as many guys psyched out as possible. Don't let them win.

BO: Key Tasks.

Learn a "Sense of Urgency." This is your best weapon against the Instructor staff. If you lack a sense of urgency, you'll see just how fast your instructors can go from cuddly chipmunk to rabid wolverine (0.3 seconds if you were wondering). In BUD/S (and the Teams for that matter) your sense of urgency is everything - it will be your saving grace and your downfall. You will run from evolution to evolution. When you get to the next evolution you'll have an ungodly small amount of time allotted to change out into the proper uniform (you'll even develop an ultra-efficient buddy system to get in and out of wet wetsuits in a matter of seconds). When the Instructors see that you're, in fact, not going *quite* as fast as they'd like, you'll feel their displeasure. Then, when you're done getting beat, you start over again.

Miss the timeline again and you'll enjoy a "Chilly Dip," which is when your entire class has to get completely wet in uniform within a small period of time. Usually around 10 seconds. The only way to make this happen is to drop down right on the edge of the pool, rotating and grabbing the edge of the pool as you fall so the moment you're submerged you can bounce yourself right out and clear the deck for the classmate behind you waiting for his turn to chilly dip. Chilly dips might be welcome during the hot months of summer, but you'll find they don't happen often in the summer. You will, however, enjoy a regular chilly dip on colder, overcast days of winter.

Didn't make the time on the chilly dip? Stand by, faggots. Everything, from getting in line at chow to changing out to cleaning the barracks to tying your boots will be watched. If you ever lack a sense of urgency it will be taught to you through pain. Trust me when I say it's better to develop it on your own than it is to have it taught.

Wet and sandy. In BO you'll be taught the proper way to get wet and sandy: completely. When you're told to get wet and sandy, you'll move with alacrity - that sense of urgency we just talked about, to the surf zone. You'll throw yourself into the surf and get entirely wet. Get to your feet and sprint to the sand berm. If your destination is on the beach, then the ocean-facing side of the berm will work. If you're running back to the grinder, you're better off running over the top and rolling down the backside. After you've rolled down, sit and take handfuls of sand and purr them over your head. Take another handful and make sure your face is covered. If one guy has a single patch of uniform or skin without sand on it, you'll do it again with an even shorter timeline.

Prepare uniforms. Two good inspection uniforms can get you through BUD/S. Why two? Because even if you pass you'll probably end up getting wet and sandy in your inspection uniform. This ruins it and you'll need one standing by for the next inspection. The good news is that the worst part of preparing a uniform cannot be destroyed.

Hitting the surf in a uniform means it needs to be cleaned, starched, and pressed again. It doesn't, however, make IPs (Irish Pendants - loose threads) reappear. You'll have plenty of time to prep your uniforms, going over every stitch with clear nail polish and clipping every stray thread with nail clippers. Check every seam. Even clip stray threads from inside pockets - these can and will be checked. Take the time in BO to fully prepare these uniforms.

Don't neglect your boots, either. You will have a pair of Bates boots for work and a pair for inspection. Your work boots will have to be blackened with polish every night (about 30 seconds of work per boot) to keep them supple and keep the instructors off your back. Your inspection boots should shine. The top of the toe is particularly important. Put in the work in BO so you can just maintain your equipment during First Phase.

Gear Preparation. In addition to preparing your inspection uniforms, you'll also have to prepare all of your issued gear. Everything will be stenciled with your last name in white ink. You get the proper stencil from the supply office, where they have stiff cardboard strips and a stencil-punching machine. Get two or three stencils because one will inevitably be ruined and you don't want to be short a good stencil at 2am before an inspection. You'll find washer-safe laundry pens at the Surf Mart on base. Every piece of gear will be stenciled in a specific place. Hats under the brim. Canteen pouches centered on the outside. Wetsuits in a number of specific places. White T-shirts centered and aligned with the level of your armpits, perfectly horizontal.

Someone will inevitably forget a stencil or put it in the wrong place or misspell his own name, resulting in a solid beating when the instructors discover the inconsistency. This serves a number of purposes beyond being an excuse to beat you. One, it evaluates and develops your ability to follow simple, ultra-specific instructions. Two, it evaluates your officers' ability to lead and accomplish tasks. Three, it teaches the importance of a certain level of uniformity: if every wetsuit is stenciled in the same place, you only need to look in one place to find the name instead of searching the whole wetsuit and wasting time. Remember, it's all about efficiency and the sense of urgency. Similarly, platoons will usually require a med pack to be kept in a specific pocket or pouch on your kit so that every person knows where to find his unconscious buddy's tourniquet. Everything in BUD/S has a purpose, no matter how dumb it might seem at the time.

Learn to do call-outs. In BUD/S you'll be waiting for the instructors for every evolution. When the instructors show up, you'll do a "call out." Two designated students who know the instructors faces (usually a rollback for this reason), will call the instructors out by rank. Senior man first, down to the junior instructor. They'll yell a name, "Instructor FLANNIGAN!" and the class will respond with a roaring "Hooyah Instructor Flannigan!" If the callout is loud (almost violent) and together, you're good to go for the moment. Mess up a callout by not yelling in unison, get the order wrong, or forget an instructor's name and you'll pay.

Learn Swim procedures. In BO you'll do a few bay swims. Once you phase up you'll be doing all of your swims in the ocean. Before every swim you'll have a Swimmer Inspection. The purpose of the inspection is to ensure your gear is in good shape, you put it on correctly, and your class is squared away.

The gear you'll be wearing is as follows. You'll have on the khaki UDT Shorts and your stenciled white t-shirt. Over this you'll be wearing your wetsuit and wetsuit booties. Your wetsuit hood will be on and tucked into your wetsuit neck without wrinkles or folds. Over your wetsuit you wear your UDT life-vest. The straps are even and flat (no rolls or folds), and each side is secured with a half-hitch to prevent the straps from sliding from the rings. The vest itself is clean, rust free, and deflated entirely. The neural nut (on the oral inflation tube) should be open, allowing the instructor to feel the smooth operation of the inflation tube. Your actuator (the black plastic device that your CO_2 canister screw into) should be attached to the vest with the stainless steel nut. The actuator should operate smoothly and close fully on its own. There should be no evidence of rust or sand in the movement of the lever. Also over your wetsuit you will wear a green web belt with a knife sheath on one side. Your fins will be propped up at your feet, leaning against one another to form a vertical triangle, like a ladder or the Eiffel Tower. Your dive mask will be on top of the fins. When standing at attention for the inspection your upper arms will be down with your elbows against your ribs, but your elbows are bent to 90 degrees holding your dive knife, blade toward you, in the right hand and your CO_2 cartridge in your left hand. The CO_2 cartridge should be clean and rust-free. The knife should have a razor-edge and should be rust-free. Instructors will always test the blade. Some will fail you if the blade doesn't shave their arm-hair off. Always be able to shave your arm hair off.

You'll be standing in a line facing your swim buddy with enough room between you for the instructors to walk. When they arrive you'll do callouts. They'll tell you to stand by for inspection and you'll draw your knife and stand at attention. The instructors will disperse and do their inspections. If you pass you put your knife away, screw your CO_2 into your actuator, close your neural nut, and wait for the inspection to finish. If you fail you'll be dropped down and do pushups or bear crawls or whatever punishment until you're relieved at the end. Once the class has been inspected you'll line up with your buddy on the beach until it's time to enter the water and join a swimmer pool at the start point.

From the swimmer pool you and your buddy will get ready to go as the instructors have you count off by swim pair. You'll count off "swim pair 1," "swim pair 2," "swim pair 3" until the end. Pay attention during the count-off because if you mess up because you weren't paying attention, the whole class will pay afterwards. And your class will probably have something to say about getting them beat because you're stupid or lazy or inattentive.

The instructors will start the swim with the customary "Three, Two, One, Bust 'em" and you and your partner will swim to the turnaround point (usually a jet ski or kayak or buoy). As you round the turnaround point, you'll sound off with your swim pair number and wait to be checked off by the instructor. When you get the okay, head back to the start point. The Instructor at the end will give you your time as you sound off. You'll do a "bottom sample" by diving to the bottom of the ocean/bay beneath you and returning with a handful of sand from the bottom and putting it on your head. You get style points by grabbing a lobster or crab from the bottom instead - it's been done to great effect in the past. After your bottom sample you swim in to check in with your swim pair number and time. After they record your time, you face the ocean, knock out 20 pushups, "Hooyah Ocean/Bay Swim!" and recover.

Before all this took place, though, your class will have rolled the jet skis (ocean swims) or carried the kayaks (bay swims) to the water's edge and placed in them the laminated swim pair lists. The swim pair lists are made by the Admin Officer of your class. They're laminated (for the lists in kayaks/jet skis), legible, and accurate. They're on clipboards with grease pencils (for laminated sheets) and pens/sharpies for the non-laminated shore-bound copies. After the swim is over the class has to recover the jet skis/ kayaks and run to get ready for the next evolution.

Learn PI/BI procedures. The Personnel Inspection/Barracks Inspection begins with the Personnel Inspection. Your class lines up in columns, each boat crew in its own column, senior man (boat crew leader) in front. You'll be wearing your cover in BO (your helmet replaces the cammie cover during Phases). After you call out the instructors, they'll begin inspecting. Pre-determined recorders - students who carry the clipboard for each instructor and write down Pass or Fail as they're told - run out to meet the instructors and begin recording.

Instructors look at everything from haircuts and shave to uniform preparation to whether you're wearing the correct belt buckle in the correct orientation and whether your polish job is good enough. You'll fail a good majority of these inspection for inexplicable reasons and then pass the next one with a worse uniform. These inspections are as much a test of your ability to endure arbitrary punishment as much as your ability to prepare a uniform. If you fail your inspection, your helmet/cover will be tossed on the ground. If you pass, you'll be given your cover back. Your cover will not usually be given back to you.

Once the PI is done, you'll go to the barracks and stand by for your room inspection. One person will stand outside the door, waiting for the instructors to inspect. The other students are in the room standing by. Instead of standing by, though, it's a good opportunity to do a last-minute wipe-down of the room, ready to spring to attention at any moment when the man outside clears his throat or coughs or says a loud "Good Morning Chief Howser!"

Your room usually involves your instructors dumping a handful of sand on your floor and then failing you for having a sandy floor. One time I had an instructor come into our room to take a crap (some of the barracks buildings have a restroom attached to them). After he took the crap, he walked out and started to inspect our room. We were going to pass when he discovered that he'd failed to flush the toilet: we failed because there was a floater. Fair? Nope. Funny? Yup.

After your room inspection, it's time to pay up. If you failed both inspections you're fucked. If you failed the room inspection but passed the uniform inspection, you get to change out of your inspection uniform before getting beat wet and sandy. If you failed the personnel inspection but passed the room inspection, you might as well have failed everything because you're getting beat in your inspection uniform. If you passed everything by some stroke of luck or bribery, you can change out and go stand by (out of sight, for sure) for the class to finish getting beat and change out.

Establish a Height Line. Boat crews are assigned by height, which makes sense because you want everyone in your boat crew to be as close to the same size as possible to evenly distribute the weight of the boat when it's on your heads. The problem is that people will quit so often that your boat crews will often change multiple time every day until the end of Hell Week. In order to make this go smoothly, your OIC (Officer in Charge) will need to have a laminated height-line in his pocket at all times. When people quit or get dropped he can just look at the list and re-allocate people to the correct boat crews. Making this line is a pain-in-the-ass, particularly when it's done at a muster on Saturday or at the end of a long day, but it's necessary. Not only should your OIC have a copy of the height line, but your LPO and a few boat crew leaders (the more senior guys) should also have copies in case the OIC quits or gets dropped.

Establish Boat Crew Muster procedures. Head counts are one of the single most important things you do in BUD/S. When you're in the Teams, even in a hot extract, you will not take off in that helo until you're 100% you have every man. For this very reason, the importance of an immediate and accurate head count will be beaten into your soul from the very moment you arrive at BUD/S.

Here's the thing: it's impossible for one man to count 40 people fast enough, not to mention the 300+ your class will start with. When it's time to get a boat crew muster every boat crew leader will get his own head count. If you're up, you're down. That means that if you have every man accounted for, you take a knee with the rest of your boat crew. If you're down a man, you remain on your feet holding out a finger with the number of guys you're missing. When the OIC arrives at you, you tell him the names of the guys you're missing. This way he can simply subtract the number of guys he's missing from his headcount and get a solid headcount almost immediately. In order to do this quickly, everyone has to do his part. Boat crew members need to line up on their boat crew leader immediately, take a knee, and shut the fuck up. Boat crew leaders need to be able to look at their crew and, in a second, know who he's missing, and the OIC has to keep his cool while boat crews work out their kinks. In the beginning of BO, a head count will take minutes. By the time you phase up, your head count should take 5-10 seconds. By the end of Third Phase, your head count will take 2-3 seconds.

At the beginning of BO it will pay dividends to practice getting head-counts a few times. If you have the inevitable 300+ students in your class, you might find it helps the OIC to have another level of hierarchy. A 300 person class can have 40 boat crews. That's still too many to make a quick count, so having 8 squads of 4 boat crews can make getting a count *that* much easier and faster. Remember, a few practice musters can save your whole class a great deal of ass pain.

Mask Appreciation. Any evolution with the word "appreciation" in it is going to suck - just wait for "Wetsuit Appreciation" in Hell Week. It's a sick sort of humor you find only at BUD/S. Mask Appreciation is one of the main BO evolutions that guys quit during, and it's all about being comfortable in the water. If you're not comfortable in the water, you'll find yourself panicking during this evolution. Some guys panic so violently they quit before they even know what's going on and they instantly regret it.

Again, the worst part of Mask Appreciation is the build-up. The instructors brief it like they're going to open your abdomen and pull out your intestines *Braveheart*-style. Then they make half the class sit up the in the classroom and listen to the first half as guys scream and make dramatic drowning sounds. Here's what's really happening.

The first part of the evolution takes place on the pool deck, where you lay with your head hanging over the water and your feet pointed away. You lean back, dunking your head in the water at *just* the right angle to force water to surge into your nose. While your head's underwater in this disconcerting position, you fill your dive mask with water and put it on. This way your eyes and nose are constantly filled with pool water. Then you lift your head out of the water with your mask holding water against your face, and you do flutter-kicks while singing stupid songs. If your mask mysteriously empties (because you either scrunched up one side of your face or quickly exhaled through your nose and thereby broke the seal), you'll fill the mask up again and continue.

After you're done on the pool deck, you get in the pool in a circle and tread water with a full mask. Then you tread water with both hands above the water and pass dive bricks and beach balls around the circle. With a full mask. The very worst part of this drill is that you can't see well at all, and so it's hard to find your classmates next to you to pass the stuff to. Invariably the circle will start to break up because guys panic/drown. That makes your job harder, because you have to swim back and forth, hands out of the water, keeping a beach ball or dive brick out of the water while trying to locate your panicked classmates. On top of all this, you have water pushing its way down your nose into your throat. If you try to breath normally, the water can really make it hard to breath and cause panic. If instead you hold your breath, then blow it out quickly and suck it back in just as quickly, you'll find the high velocity of the air minimizes the amount of water you end up breathing in. As long as you do this calmly, you'll be much better off than your classmates.

That's really all there is to the evolution. Keep your calm and remember all the preparation you did to be more comfortable in the water (you *did* do it, right?). Keep in mind that few people are going to be as comfortable as you in the water. The guys who didn't prepare themselves are the guys you hear screaming and hacking up pool water.

You're better than they are, so don't sweat it.

Land Portage Familiarization. Boats on heads. Oh my. Your land portage familiarization is planned to scare the crap out of you. The boat isn't that heavy. Until it's filled with water and sand.

And you have to run on soft sand with it on your head. And someone in your boat crew is ducking boat (it had better not be you).

Boats on heads will be a part of your life until you finish Hell Week. During Hell Week it'll be the *entirety* of your life. A standard IBS will have a boat crew of 7 men. The two guys in front are called "ones", the two in the middle are "twos", the guys at the back are the "threes", and the coxswain (pronounced "cox-in") is in the very back between the 3-spots.

The hardest, toughest guys in your boat crew go in the 2 spot, but they can't stay there the whole time. The 2 spot carries the most weight because the boat sags in the middle, and limits the length of your stride because it has people both in front and behind.

The faster guys go in the 1 spot and pull the boat forward, both by a grip on the boat and (mostly) by the outside hand's grip on the handle. If your 1 man isn't pulling forward on that handle, he's not doing his job.

Land Portage Familiarization will make some guys quit. It sucks, but it's not pain in the moment that will make guys quit - it's the realization that this is the next month of their lives. When you've got a boat on your head and you're running up a hill in soft sand, you either attack or you quit. The guys who don't attack become victims of the pain; seconds feel like hours. Realizing the pain's never going to end, they buckle. Guys who respond to the pain and stress with violence stand a good chance of success at BUD/ S. Attack the pain of land portage and you'll find yourself at the head of your class and - a nice side effect of the extra energy put in - you'll finish better and get beat less in the end.

Remember: it pays to be a winner.

BO: TTPs.

Have multiple inspection uniforms. The ideal situation in BUD/S is never to hit the surf in your inspection uniform. That won't happen, so let's live in the real world. Because you never know when you're going to hit the surf in (and thus ruin) an inspection uniform, you should always have a backup inspection uniform. If you get beat in your inspection uniform Monday and then need to stand inspection Tuesday, you'll feel the heat if you don't take this advice.

Prep of an inspection uniform is simple: start by getting rid of all loose threads. Clean up every seam that can possibly be touched with the uniform remaining on your body. The bottoms of pockets and the internal seams of sleeves 6" up from your wrist are not out of play, so be thorough. Trim threads with fingernail clippers and secure all stitching (particularly on buttons and on the stitching around button holes) with a small amount of super glue. It dries clear and hard, isn't ruined by saltwater, and is easy to use. Just be sure to avoid excessive clumping and you'll be good to go. Give the same treatment to your two inspection covers ("cover" is the navy word for "hat").

Once all threads are secured, take the uniforms and covers to AB Brites, a dry-cleaners a few miles down the Strand in Imperial Beach (IB). Tell them you want a light starch. A full starch from AB Brites will let your uniform stand on its own without you inside it. It looks kinda ridiculous and it's not very comfortable. Getting beat in that uniform hurts. Light starch is more than sufficient. They'll also starch/shape your cover for inspection and affix any rank insignia you might need. Sure, you could do an okay job with the uniform on your own, but next to an AB Brites uniform your self-starched uniform will look like dogs' balls. It's worth the little bit of money to get the uniforms done right. It's worth it for the sleep gained alone.

Once you get your uniform items back from the cleaners, make sure all your seams and buttons are still good to go. Don't skimp on this. Pay attention to detail here and you'll be set. If they're good after AB Brites, you'll probably not have to do much more to them the rest of BUD/S.

Now stencil your uniform items. The white tape on your chest and ass need your last name on them in black ink. Buy one of those roll-tipped laundry pens with the rubber pump on the back. They suck to write with, but the ink lasts forever and doesn't bleed. (The alternative is a "laundry safe" Sharpie, but these don't last and they tend to bleed. You might think you've found a shortcut, but they really never hold up to BUD/S. Do it right the first time and you'll be set.")

To get the laundry pen started, pump the bulb on the top a few dozen times and then continue pumping while trying to write on a board of cardboard. The friction from the cardboard should loosen up the ball and start the ink flowing. Much of the uniform stenciling is simple as tracing the pattern you cut to stencil the white name tapes.

The white T-shirt is a different story. The cotton stretches and makes stenciling difficult. You *will* be failed in inspections for a shitty stencil. If your stencil is bad enough, you'll get beat all day for it. Here's the secret: the stencil should be centered and in line with the bottom of the armpits of the shirt. Stretch the shirt out over a piece of cardboard or wood (to give you a sold backing for stenciling) and note the correct position for the stencil. Hold down the cardboard stencil in the right place, and repeatedly stab/dab the laundry pen into the shirt, moving as areas in the stencil fill. It takes a while and you'll have to develop the right touch, but once you get it down, your stencils will be great. Doing it this way prevents the crappy/stretchy shirt from moving and causing your stencil to end up angled, crooked, or wavy. You'll see the marked difference between your shirts and the guys who didn't do this right. Do a dozen shirts at once. You'll get better this way and won't have to stencil a new shirt every night. You can never have too many clean whiteshirts, and you'll be able to use any extras to polish your boots with after you get your brown shirt. Save the best two stencil-jobs for inspections.

Make sure you get the right belt for inspections (with extra buckles - you'll need a brand new 10-minutes-out-of-the-box buckle for every inspection) and the belt is a different material than your normal belt. Make sure you cut it down so there are only 2-4 inches of extra belt wrapping under when you're wearing it. Make sure you put it on the right direction (the man's belt orientation vs. the woman's belt orientation: a man has the brass-tipped "bitter end" of the belt on the left side of the buckle as you're wearing it). Make sure your military ID is in your upper left breast pocket, facing out, sitting vertically. Make sure that every button on your entire uniform is fastened. I failed my first inspection at the last minute when the instructor saw that I hadn't buttoned the back pockets of my pants. You only get 3 "hits." Don't waste them on stupid stuff. Your haircut, shave, and boots should also be good. We'll get to those in a moment here.

Front-load this prep work on your first few week nights/weekends in Coronado (instead of going out or watching movies, etc) and you'll find you're getting a lot more sleep than your classmates. It's possible to get 7-9 hours of sleep almost every night of First Phase if you're smart like this. (Not so with Second or Third Phase though, so live it up in First Phase).

Shave your head. They say that you shouldn't shave your head until you start First Phase. I say bullshit. Do it. Especially if you show up with a shaved head - how would they know it's not your regular haircut anyhow. I know you'll look stupid, but you're in BUD/S to become a SEAL - not to pick up women in the Gaslamp District on the weekends. If you shave your head and keep it shaved, you'll never have to worry about your haircut. That's one thing less you have to do every weekend. That's an extra hour of sleep. That's money in the fucking bank.

If you're too pretty to shave your head, make sure you get a fresh haircut every weekend. Crown Barber on Orange Ave in Coronado is the most popular place to go for a reason. They have a good military rate, you can tell them "BUD/S Inspection Haircut" and they'll give you exactly what you need (including a hot shave on the neckline and around the ears), and you'll still look human. Get a Navy Regulation haircut on base and you'll look like a fat-calved sailor or marine. That's worse than a shaved head.

Shave Every Day. And shave well. At any point an Instructor might be looking for a reason to beat your class. A bad shave, a single missed hair under your chin, is reason enough. Make sure you shave every day. I shaved every night before bed, but I can get away with that because I don't grow much facial hair. If you're a hairy Wookie like some guys in my class, you may be shaving at lunch, too. It doesn't matter if you shaved that morning - if a grumpy Master Chief from one of the Teams walks by and sees what appears to be an unsatisfactory shave, he'll make a phone call. That phone call sucks. It won't matter that you shaved that morning - it will only matter that someone perceived that you hadn't. End of story, game over. So don't give them the chance.

Polish Inspection Boots. Your inspection boots should be shiny, the toes in particular. Use Parade Gloss polish, not regular black polish. Get a good solid layer brushed on, then move onto using hot water and an old T-shirt to really shine up the toe. Another option is to use the boot shop on Orange Ave. For around $30, they can do an amazing job on an initial polish job. The polish they use is silicon-based, so much of the shine will even last hitting the surf. After you get the boots back from them, all you need to do is use the Parade Gloss on the toe of the boot and you'll be solid.

Kiwi also makes a Shine Sponge that adds a last-minute bit of shine to boost you into the next level of squared-away. You can brush the sponge over your boots at the last minute before inspection and they'll glow for the next 30 minutes. That's all you need. Get a few and pass them around. You'll be worshiped and copied next inspection. Just be sure you hide the sponge before the Instructors show. There's also a product called Instant Spitshine that some guys had a lot of success with. You basically paint on a shiny layer that looks like you spent hours on your boots.

Stencil Your Gear. BUD/S is chaos. There will be times when all of your class's gear get tossed into one huge pile. Often this pile is underwater. Sometimes it's in the sand. For this reason it's incredibly important to have your gear labelled. And it all should be labelled in the same place. Most of the gear is easy to stencil and your class will have a standard location for each stencil. Wetsuits just take persistence. They tend to soak up the ink and your name fades quickly, so keep stenciling until it's good enough.

The one stencil that needs to be redone every week is your fins. You have to label them with white laundry pens, but the ink doesn't stick to rubber well, it gets wet, sand rubs it off, and the flexing rubber cracks it. Here's the secret to a good fin stencil: Start by roughing up the area you're going to stencil. Use sandpaper to really scour it. Then be sure to wash it off well, getting rid of all the rubber shavings. Once it's clean, dry, and roughed up, do a solid, thick stencil. This might take a few coats to get a really solid stencil. When the paint is dry and you're satisfied with the stencil, get some clear nail polish and paint over the stencil. Don't just cover the letters, cover the entire area the stencil covers. This makes it harder for the paint to chip off. If you don't want to get nail polish, you can do a similar procedure with rubber cement. Either way, your stencil will be substantially better than most - making your life easier when you're looking for your gear in a pile while Instructors swarm with bullhorns and a hose. And you'll probably have to redo them a lot less than everyone else.

Dive Knife Tips. The knife you get issued in BUD/S is the SRK Cold Steel. It is, in no way, a dive knife. That's why they give it to you for a dive knife. It rusts in a second and doesn't hold a great edge through the corrosive saltwater. When you get your gear issue, they'll usually issue you an old piece of shit - a rusty strip of metal - and call it a knife. Return it and insist on being issued a decent knife. Get a new one if you can. If you have trouble with the supply staff (you probably will), talk to your boat crew leader. For some reason (they're from the fleet in most cases) they respond significantly differently to an officer than they do to an enlisted BUD/S student. The new knives come with a crappy plastic sheath. Try to get a nylon cloth one if you can. The plastic one has a lot more metal on it (rusts), it tends to break (sometimes mid-swim), it rusts your *knife* faster, and it's less comfortable on the swim. The nylon sheath looks more ghetto, but it's significantly more functional.

Go in with your boat crew and buy an electric knife sharpener - like the kind they use for kitchen knives. I bought a ChefMate brand sharpener at Target. The first time you use the sharpener, it'll take almost an hour to get a good edge because the sharpener grinds a sharper angle than comes on your SRK. That's fine. Just keep running the knife through the coarse grinder until you see the grind getting the edge of the blade. At that point move the knife to the middle and then the fine grind. If you've done it right, your knife will now cut the hair off your forearm. That, you'll recall, is the standard for a good knife. If you can shave your arm hair, you pass. If you can't, your knife often gets spiked into the sand. After the initial sharpening ordeal, you'll be set. While your classmates spend 30-90 minutes (depending on skill and knife use) every day on their knives, your knife will take 4-5 passes through the sharpener and be good to go again. Again, success at BUD/S all about front-loading the work so you can do very little work the rest of your time there. Keep in mind that you don't want to store the sharpener in your barracks room. You can either keep it in your car or your boat crew leader's off-base housing. In fact if your boat crew leader is a decent guy, he can just sharpen your knife for you every night at his place. It's not cheating, it's smart teamwork. A good boat crew leader would be happy to do this.

If you got the nylon sheath, you only have one metal piece to worry about - the button. If you got the plastic sheath, you have a few more screws to contend with. The ocean water is not kind to metal. Protect your metal by initially sanding any corrosion off, wiping it down, and painting over the metal with black fingernail polish. Then paint over the black nail polish with rubber cement to keep it looking black. Again, a little extra work up front will prevent you from having to worry too much about your sheath the rest of BUD/S.

Another thing you can do to combat the fast corrosion of the knife (the silver parts of the blade will rust in minutes) is to use petroleum jelly (like Vaseline, A&D lotion, or Chapstick). You can't have it on the blade for the inspection, though, so this takes a little prep. If you're using Chapstick, just keep the tube in the sleeve of your wetsuit. If you're using A&D or Vaseline, take a gob of it before you form up for the inspection and put it inside your fin. That way you can reach down after you pass your inspection, get it on your fingers, and wipe a thin coat over every silver surface of the blade. It's not expressly forbidden, but do it subtly anyhow. It's never really a good idea to attract attention at BUD/S. If you get caught, you can simply repeat the common BUD/S maxim: "take care of your gear, and your gear will take care of you." Most instructors will simply say "okay" and move on. You'll never get in any real trouble taking extra-good care of your equipment, so feel safe saving your blade. Just be careful of the sharp cutting edge when you're putting the jelly/Chapstick/ointment on it - it's sharp enough to shave with so it's sharp enough to cut you pretty badly.

Sandpaper. Get some fine grit sandpaper and keep it on hand before swims to take care of any last-minute rust. You only need a very small piece at any time - a few square inches will suffice. But you'll need it. No matter how well you take care of your gear, no matter how long you let it air-dry, no matter how meticulously you fresh-water rinse it, something is going to end up mysteriously rusty. You could put an immaculate knife in your bag in the morning and pull it out for the swim 2 hours later to find it covered in rust. If you have the sandpaper handy, it's not a big deal. If you don't have the paper, you can use actual *sand*, but it takes longer and the result isn't quite as good or uniform.

UDT Vest Care. Your UDT vest is a grey rubber life vest you'll wear every swim. It's also inspected during your Barracks Inspections. When inspected your vest will be hanging on your rack (bed), and the actuator (the little black box with the red pull-cord that you screw the CO_2 cartridge into) is disassembled on your desk to show that it's in good condition and isn't rusted or sandy.

It helps to have a few extra actuators. Sometimes the springs inside them go bad, which means they won't close all the way on their own. Sometimes when you're taking them apart (using a tool called a "scribe"), you lose one of the many small pieces. Sometimes you don't have time to take one apart or clean it before an inspection. In any of these cases a spare actuator will be a godsend. If you don't run into one of these situations, surely someone in your class will. And you'll be able to save his ass. That's good feeling - a feeling at the heart of being a good Team Guy - helping out one of your boys.

You might choose to have an extra inspection actuator, but it's not that important because they're pretty easy to take care of. When you get out of the saltwater and go to the freshwater decontamination showers, or "*the decon,*" take the CO_2 cartridge out and run a stream of water into the actuator while you pull the lever up and down a dozen times. This expels the saltwater and sand that inevitably end up in there and allows you the luxury of leaving it alone until you're done for the day. While you're rinsing, be sure to rinse your CO_2 cartridge and dive knife too.

For inspection, fully disassemble the actuator on your desk and hang your vest on your rack. The vest should have no water in it. When you're swimming, small amounts of water leak in and build up. Shake your vest and you'll feel the water sloshing. Position the threaded nipple (where you attach your actuator, down and squeeze the whole vest rapidly, forcing the air out toward the ground at high velocity. Follow this up by rolling the vest like you're trying to squeeze out the last dab of toothpaste. Then blow it up and expel all the air toward the ground again. After that, your vest is probably dry enough for an inspection. Just hang it with the nipple down so any water that does accumulate drips right out.

A word of warning about CLR. CLR (Calcium, Lime, Rust) cleaner does get rid of rust, but you don't want to use it. The moment you use CLR, the shiny anti-rust coating on most of your equipment is dissolved. The places where the rust ate the metal are now pits and will happily play host to more rust as soon as possible. Use CLR on the innards of an actuator and I guarantee that even an immediate freshwater rinse won't prevent the actuator from being ruined. Avoid CLR. It gets your stuff clean immediately, but makes it inoperable thereafter.

Stay out of sight. This is self-explanatory, but I'm going to talk about it a minute anyhow. Instructors are SEALs. The majority of them don't want to be at BUD/S. Your instructor wants to be in a platoon. He wants to go to war. And he thinks you're a piece of shit, a worthless weakling who's trying to get into his fraternity and dilute the quality of men in the Teams. Usually he's right. Most guys in your class would be worthless in a platoon. His BUD/S class was the last hard class and he's not allowed to be as hard on you as he remembers his instructors being on him. If he sees you it's nothing to him but an opportunity to make you quit.

So don't let him see you except when you have to. Stay out of sight. There are places to hide, and they move depending on what the rules are and what construction is happening. They have nicknames like The Pit, The Batcave, The Beach, The Junkyard, etc. Here you can catch a peaceful 5 minute nap on some clean cement. It may not seem like much from outside, but there's nothing better when you're running from place to place, putting boats on heads, and getting wet and sandy. Your whiteshirt rollbacks know where these sanctuaries are.

Stay in step. Soft sand runs will rape your soul. That sounds overly dramatic, but it's only a slight overstatement. Even without a boat on your head. My Indoc (now called BO) Proctor told my class that the sand on Coronado was the softest sand in the world. When you're trying to keep up with one of the instructors, you'll feel what he meant. Good running technique for the hardball surfaces doesn't count for shit in the soft sand.

Here's what works: land on flat feet. The greater the surface area you're putting your weight on, the better. Think of snowshoes. It's the same principle. For that very same reason, step in the exact footprints of the man in front of you. He's already flattened the surface for you. That's less energy expended and wasted per step. Every footfall you put in the footprint of the man in front of you, you're saving energy. It doesn't matter whether his stride is longer or shorter than your traditional stride. Make it work. Lengthen or shorten your stride to match the footprints. You'll feel the difference and be able to get into a rhythm - the increased effort required to do this more than pays for itself. If you don't step in his footprints, you'll run yourself down until you're face down in the sand, gasping for your life, head spinning, and instructors screaming at you to stop being such a pussy. Goon squad for you, son.

Crush the solo swim. There is one swim in BO that matters. That's the solo swim. During the solo swim your time will dictate where you fall in the swim pair list. The top two swimmers will become swim pair #1. The third and fourth swimmers will become swim pair #2. If you do well in the solo swim, you will be in a fast pair. If you perform poorly, you'll be in a slow pair. You want to be in as fast a pair as possible because, as we've already discussed, the further from the pass/fail threshold you are, the better your quality of life. Do well in the solo swim, you won't worry about being drug to a failure by a weak swim buddy.

You've already mastered the combat sidestroke. You've done it on your SEAL Challenge PST. You've done it in BUD/S Prep. You'll live it in BUD/S. Learn the dolphin kick or get absurdly strong in your flutter kick.

More important than swimming fast is swimming straight. If you swim twice as far, you have to swim twice as fast in order to finish in the same place. Swimming in the pool it's easy to swim straight. There's a line on the bottom. There's a lane line. There is no line on the bottom of San Diego Bay; there are no lane lines in the Pacific Ocean. It's harder to swim straight in the open water than you'd think. The trick is to pick out two points, one more distant than the other, that you can line up behind one another to make sure you're staying in a straight line. If they stay lined up as you swim toward them, you'll know you're going straight at them. If, on the other hand, they diverge, you're not traveling directly at them. If the one nearest you appears to be drifting to the right, you're moving off course left. If the landmark nearest you looks like it's sliding left, you're moving off course to the right. Look up every stroke at first, then every few strokes, to ensure you're traveling straight. By the time you finish BUD/S, you'll probably be looking every 5-6 strokes, but you'll have to work up to that.

Use these tools to crush the solo swim and you'll be set up for success.

Swim pair lists. The instructors need swim pair lists. One paper list on a clipboard with a pen attached for each truck - usually one and the start/end and one truck that will shadow the swim onshore. Each jet-ski/kayak will also need a laminated list with a grease pencil attached to the clipboard. These should always be ready beforehand - don't give the instructors any reason to beat the class. Each list should also include a black sharpie.

Changes will have to made at the last minute. People will quit. People will go to medical. Make the changes in a red or green sharpie so the instructors can't make errant changes and blame them on you. Your changes are in black. Anything they do to fuck with the lists to generate a reason to beat you and the class will be in the color marker they have on their clipboard. Trust me when I say they'll take advantage of you if you give them the opportunity.

Practice change-outs. Pants, socks, boots. This will be your mantra and another thing you'll want to learn before the instructors take it upon themselves to teach you. When changing from UDT shorts back into uniform, pants first, then socks, then your boots. Always in that order and quickly.

I know it seems dumb, but your class will need to practice changing out on a weekend before you start. Practicing a couple of times will save you a world of wet and sandy pain the first few weeks in BUD/S. Like I've said before - you don't need any extra BUD/S. Sacrifice an hour or two one Sunday before you class up and it will repay your investment a dozen times over.

BO: Learning the Obstacle Course.

The Obstacle Course at BUD/S is one of the most visible evolutions at BUD/S. The 50-foot Cargo Net towers over Silver Strand Blvd and the Slide For Life can be seen from over a mile down the beach. The O-Course also bears the distinction of the most unpredictable timed evolution. If you normally run the 4-mile run in 28 minutes, you can expect to run it in 29 on a bad day or in 27 on a good day. The same can be said for swims: a bad day is unlikely to result in failure.

The O-Course, on the other hand, can reach up and bite you on any given day. If you fail any single obstacle three times, you fail the evolution entirely. It doesn't matter if you ran the entire O-Course in 6 minutes. Three failures on one obstacle is a total failure. You can, fail 3 obstacles 2 times each and, although your time would suffer, you wouldn't fail by default as long as you succeeded on the third try.

A sprained ankle will slow your run and inhibit your swim, but you can push through. That same ankle can make navigating the Balance Logs impossible. You can swim and run with bruised ribs, but you're going to have a hard time getting over the Dirty Name. Each obstacle relies on another aspect of your physical condition, many of which you simply cannot compensate for, making the O-Course both easy (in good health) and treacherous (in poor health).

You'll run the course in pairs. There is a left side and a right side of the course up to the Dirty Name, by which time most pairs are no longer together. You'll start 30 seconds after the pair in front of you and you'll be followed 30 seconds later by the next pair. Before you have a baseline time, there is a lot of waiting for slow people in front of you. The gymnast freaks will fly past you. If your Admin officer isn't worthless, the second time you run the O-Course will be stratified by times: fast guys first, slow guys last. This can alleviate bunching and, by the time you've run the course a handful of times, the whole class will have sorted itself out. Guys that got caught behind a crowd the first few times and therefore posted slower times will before long, get a few fair runs and everything will work itself out. The first few times, however, be prepared for lines, bunching, swearing, and frustration.

Here's a sequential rundown of the obstacles you'll encounter (you may want to check out a few YouTube videos of the O-course so these tips make sense to you):

Parallel Bars. The Parallel Bars are a set of sloped dip-bars. You have to get from one side to the other without your feet contacting the ground beneath. Most BUD/S students traverse the bars by walking their hands forward, bearing their weight on locked-out arms. Some, the more agile gymnast-type guys, prefer to hop along the bars, essentially throwing themselves forward, catching their weight, and repeating. The hop method can be significantly faster and is used by almost every guy who runs the O-Course in under 7 minutes, but requires more practice and upper body strength.

Tires. The tires usually get you when you're tired (they're a bitch in Hell Week), but the smaller ones also tend to snag on boots over size 10. You're required to step in each tire of the two parallel rows, like a sadistic hopscotch, while you run with your hands clasped on top of your head. The tires also serve to slow you down, because running through them tends to trip guys up. Most guys tend to slow down on the tires and step in on their toes to reduce the chances of snagging a tire and earning a trip back to the beginning of the tires.

* * *

Low Wall. The Low Wall favors the brave. Rather, it frowns on timidity. The approach to the wall is a set of incrementally-higher vertical logs. They're essentially steps large enough for only one foot. You'll run up the two steps and leap to the top edge of the wall, catching your elbows (or, if you're the gymnast freak, your waist) over the top of the wall. The top of the wooden wall is padded in rubber, making grip easy. From here you'll swing your body over the wall and drop down on the other side. The trick here is to get a good, high leap onto the wall and use your momentum to get over the wall. Guys who try to be methodical tend to wear themselves out prematurely. Guys who don't attack the wall with enough aggression can't get over it.

High Wall. The High Wall is, as its name suggests, taller than the Low Wall. Instead of logs to assist you over the wall, there are ropes suspended from the top of the wall. You'll run up to the wall, grab the ropes as high as you can, and form a rigid "L" with your body as you walk up the wall while gripping the rope. The temptation, upon reaching the top, is to hook your elbow over the top of the wall and swing yourself over. You can do this, but it's significantly harder and slower than you want. Instead of grasping the top of the wall at the earliest possible time, keep walking up the wall until one of your feet can reach the wooden lip 8" from the top. The moment you can use this as a foothold, you can press yourself right onto the top of the wall using your legs. This little bit of patience lets you save your arms and use your legs - and it's an easy move. From there, spin around and lower yourself to fully-extended arms, and then drop. Don't bother with the rope on the descent - it's easier, faster, and safer to simply lower yourself from the top of the wall and drop. The High Wall obstacle varies in difficulty depending on the weather (and whether the people who went before you had recently been in the surf). A wet rope and slippery wall can make the climb substantially more taxing than when both are dry - friction is your friend here.

Low Crawl. The Low Crawl is a shallow pit over which a series of logs (telephone poles, really) wrapped in barbed wire are laid to force students to crawl as flat as possible. The Low Crawl is one of the most variable obstacles because the whole obstacle depends on how deep the crawl-area is dug out. Sometimes an industrious class and an unobservant (or uncaring) instructor cadre can make this obstacle so easy you can practically do the limbo through it. Other times, more often than it being dug out, the low crawl has been freshly filled. One time my class ran the O-Course the Low Crawl was filled so high that people were getting stuck. Guys were literally burrowing out of it and dragging barbed wire and telephone poles by their shoulder blades. The first guys through bore the brunt of the pain, but everyone in the class got beat when guys failed. In BUD/S there is no excuse for failure; reasons don't matter. Failure is failure regardless of circumstances.

Cargo Net. The Cargo Net is one of the easiest obstacles despite its daunting size. All you have to do is climb up and over and back down. I'm moderately afraid of heights (even still) and the height never bothered me because only concentrated on the ropes in front of me. The tighter the net has been stretched, the easier the climb is, and the net is always tighter near the edges. As you approach the net move as far outside as you can. Grip the vertically-oriented ropes with your hands, facilitating more efficient change of grip as you get faster, and step on horizontally-oriented ropes. Keep your hips (and thereby your weight) as close to the net as possible. Only use your hands to keep you on the net. All vertical movement should come from your legs. Not your arms or shoulders or hands. Trust me when I tell you to preserve your upper-body for later. When you reach the top it's easy to keep three points of contact as you reach an arm to the other side and then swing a leg over. Climbing down is as easy as lowering yourself a few rungs at a time. The key to speed on the Cargo Net is climbing rhythmically. Keep a steady pace and, after a little practice, you'll be flying past your classmates on the net.

Balance Logs. The Balance Logs are a series of logs that roll freely on a 4x4 beam. There are two north-south-oriented start logs, one for each side, and both connect to different ends of the same east-west-oriented log. The goal is to run along one of the start logs, change direction onto the log perpendicular, then transfer to the third (and final) log which is oriented the same direction as the start logs (north-south) and run off the far end. Three logs, two 90-degree changes in direction. The logs get slick when wet and behave differently depending on the amount of sand on the cross-beams they roll on. If there's no sand or rocks, the logs roll in a smooth, fast, predictable manner. If there's a little sand/debris on the beams, then the logs might only roll one direction easily or might behave sporadically. If the beams happen to have conveniently developed small, closely spaced piles of sand and rocks, the logs might only display the slightest tendency to roll. Wink wink, nudge nudge.

The biggest hazard on the logs are your classmates because there are two parallel start logs but only one cross-log and one finish log. You might have waited for your classmate on the other side to reach the cross-log to start your run, but if he's taking his time on the cross-log you might find yourself out of luck. It's a great deal easier to run (or at least move quickly) than it is to stop, and if you're on the same log as another guy, you both fail, so running into another classmate can really ruin your day. Add a light rain to slick those logs up, a small amount of debris on the cross-beams to introduce chaotic log motion, and what starts off as a solid run can quickly spiral into a triple-failure.

Hooyah Logs. Hooyah Logs are a "gimme" obstacle. They're basically a bound pile of logs. You step up each and down each log as you run with your hands on your head and yell "Hooyah Logs." Just be sure to hit each log on the way down and you're golden.

Rope Transfer. The rope transfer involves climbing up a 12 foot rope, swinging to another rope by way of a metal ring in between, and then descending. Some guys have difficulty climbing the rope, but they really have no excuse. There's a right way to climb a rope called a foot lock that makes it so easy you can stop half-way up and take both of your hands off without falling down. You can certainly climb a rope other ways, but you're not training for

CrossFit rope climbs, you're training to be able to climb a rope with kit, weapons, and a rucksack. Your BO instructors will show you how to use the foot lock. Do it the way they teach you and you'll be set for your career. Do it your own way and you'll feel the pain time and time again until you come around.

Dirty Name. The Dirty Name gets its name from all the socially unacceptable things it makes people say. It's a set of uneven bars made with telephone poles. The first poles are shoulder height. You jump onto it, cradling the pole in your bent waist, and then stand up on it. Then you jump from the first pole to the second, where you roll over the top and drop to the ground below.

When I got my O-Course intro from one of the PTRR instructors, he would literally say "This is the XXXX. Just fucking do it. This is the XXXX. Just fucking do it." When he got to the Dirty Name he said "This is the Dirty Fucking Name. Just fucking get the fuck over it. Just fucking hit it hard and get the fuck over it." Needless to say I was offended by his choice of words. Not his profanity, though, his advice: I ran hard and jumped hard, but my jump wasn't high enough. I took the telephone pole across my ribcage and fell to the ground like I got hit with a train. I couldn't breathe. I didn't want to risk any attention, so I gasped my way through the rest of the obstacles in a record slow time.

After two days of not being able to breathe, I went to a civilian doctor. I was afraid BUD/S medical would roll me into the next class before we even classed up. I wasn't going to let that happen, so I paid for X-rays out of pocket. Three cracked ribs. I went into BUD/S medical, downplayed the ribs, and convinced the doctor not to look further into them. Behind closed doors, I convinced him to put me on Light Limited Duty (LLD) for the three weeks before we flew out to meet our class at Great Lakes. My ribs wouldn't be healed by then, but there's no O-Course at Great Lakes and I'd probably be healed by the time we got back. He was persuaded and that's how I broke my ribs but still managed to class up on time.

The Weaver. The Weaver is easy to complete, but difficult to master. A gradual slope up and then down formed by parallel metal pipe, you navigate the Weaver by weaving over and under alternating pipes. The idea is to swing over one and use the momentum to swing yourself under the next and right onto the one after that. Doing this obstacle properly means moving fast. Learning to do it properly means your forearms are going to get the skin ripped off them the first few times.

Burma Bridge. The Burma Bridge is another easy obstacle. You climb up a rope (which you should be quite proficient at), walk across a rope bridge, and then climb down another rope. The only complications come in when you have too many people on the rope at one time. There are allowed to be three guys on the bridge at one time, but the walking surface of the bridge is, literally, just a rope. If you have two other guys on it at one time, it's exceedingly difficult to get your footing. That being said, I've never heard of a single person failing the Burma Bridge even once.

Hooyah Logs. More hooyah in case you weren't motivated. These logs are usually one log taller than the other Hooyah Logs. No dramas. Just hit them all on the way down and you're good.

Slide for Life. The Slide for Life is my least favorite obstacle. The full obstacle is a series of four wooden platforms you climb up, a long rope affixed to the top that you slide down, and a bar on the ground you have to touch before dismounting the ropes.

There are three different ways you'll do the obstacle depending on what phase you're in. You'll start off doing the "Low" Slide for Life. When you're in First Phase you graduate to the "High" Slide for Life. After you pass Pool Comp, you do the "High" Slide for Life by doing the "commando crawl" or "Ranger crawl" method.

The "Low" Slide for Life uses only the lowest platform. From the low platform you grab ahold of and hang underneath a rope that runs parallel to the ground about 4 feet off the sand. You start with the low rope because you won't get hurt if you fall. The downside, however, is that the low rope is notable harder than the high rope because it sags. The high rope sags too, but the angle is steep enough that you're always sliding down. Gravity is your friend on the high rope. The low rope is parallel to the ground, so sagging means that you're trying to slide up the last half of the rope traverse. If you make it all the way across your first time, you probably won't be able to grip your canteen when you're done. Your forearms and hands will be entirely, completely, and ridiculously expended. The best advice I can offer for the low rope is that you want to cross your boots over the rope so that you slide the back of your boots, not your calves or pants, on the rope. Go as fast as you can while staying smooth. I would recommend a regular grip workout prior to arriving, even something as simple as a bar hang, to make this obstacle easier.

The "High" Slide for Life is better than the "Low" because the rope, regardless of sag, is angled downward. The trade-off is that you have to climb up the outside each of the three lower platforms to reach the "glory hole" in the top platform. Climb through the hole onto the top and you're good to go. Some guys do a pull-up on the edge of each platform and pull themselves over the edge, but smart students use biomechanics to their advantage. Standing on the lowest platform facing out, reach your arms onto the top surface of the platform above you. Your upper arms will be straight up and your forearms will be pointing behind you. Reach as deep into the platform as you can - the deeper you can grip the better your leverage will be. Get a good hold on a slat and lift your feet using your abs, swinging your feet over your head and onto the platform above. Keep pulling and you can get your whole body onto the platform. The whole maneuver looks like a flip, or a backwards somersault, but takes almost no energy and is safer than trying to do a full body pull-up on the outside of each platform. Do this one more time and you'll reach the hole in the top platform. Put your hands on either side of the hole and jump. When you're at the top of your jump, lock your arms and pull your legs up. You're on the top platform. Hang under the rope and slide to the bottom.

After Pool Comp you'll stop sliding underneath the rope. Instead, you pull yourself down, riding on top of the rope. This is referred to as the "Ranger crawl" or "commando crawl." From the top platform you reach out off the platform and try to lie flat on the rope. Swing your right knee over the rope, catching your ankle on the rope. Your right knee is on the right side of the rope pointing downwards, your right toe is on the left side of the rope also pointing down. Make sure the rope is centered on your chest, and start pulling. As you leave the platform your left leg is hanging straight down and the rope is running down your chest, past your waist, between your legs, and its last contact with your body is in the crook of your right ankle. A combination of pulling hands and pushing with your right foot propels you down the rope with a refreshing quickness. The only hard part of the whole process is getting on the rope initially, because in order to swing your knee over the rope the rest of your body pretty much has to be hanging off the platform, holding onto the rope as your only source of stability. Once you get your knee over, however, you'll find that you're surprisingly stable. Moreover, the commando crawl gets you off the platform onto solid ground so quickly that it's worth the risk.

Rope Swing. The Rope Swing would be easy if it weren't after the Slide for Life. All you have to do is grab the rope mid-stride and use your momentum to swing you up onto a horizontal beam 4ft above the sand. You've got to land with enough control to stay on the beam. If you fall, you've got to try again. It takes a little practice to get it down the first few times, but once you learn not to slow down or jump as you grab the rope, everything falls into place. Once you have the Rope Swing down, however, you're only a fraction of the way there. Your forearms are going to be so burned-up from the Low Slide for Life that the first time you do the Rope Swing, you're going to try to grip the rope by clamping your wrists on the rope. This obviously won't work, which is why the Rope Swing is the obstacle everyone fails at first.

Monkey Bars. From the beam you land on after the Rope Swing, you run down a static balance log to a set of monkey bars. The balance beam is solid and therefore not an issue. The monkey bars aren't any different than you'd see on a playground, but after the Slide for Life and the Rope Swing, just keeping your grip on the bars can be impossible. What's more: if you fall off the balance log or the monkey bars, you start back at the rope swing again. If your grip was insufficient to finish the monkey bars, you're not getting back up the Rope Swing. Fail.

Tires. After you get through the monkey bars, you're more than happy to slow down for the tires. Get 'em done and get to the incline wall.

Incline Wall. The Incline Wall is nothing more than a slick platform at a 45-degree angle to the ground. You approach from the high side. You can just dive over the top and grab the top edge as you start to slide down the back side. Grabbing the top edge as you slide down the back side rotates your body so your feet end up underneath you. You'll be tired enough by this time that you'll end up throwing yourself over the wall. No big deal. Just get over it, slide down the back, and land on your feet.

Spider Wall. If your technique on the Spider Wall is poor, you'll quickly become a hilarious spectacle for everyone else. The Spider Wall is a wooden wall with horizontal grips for your hands and lips for your boots. They're essentially rock-climbing grips and they're placed close enough on top of one another that it's tempting to grasp the top of the wall instead of the grip. Touching the top of the wall will fail the obstacle. You start on one edge and have to edge your way to the other side of the wall. The grips make two changes in elevation to further complicate your movement. If you've ever done any rock climbing, you'll know the secret to the Spider Wall: keep your hips against the wall and use your legs to climb. If you don't, you'll end up sand-darting from the top of the wall. The thud of guys falling off the Spider Wall is unmistakable and hilarious. Failure to keep your weight against the wall puts all your weight on your grip. After the Slide for Life, Rope Swing, and Monkey Bars, you don't have the grip strength to spare. Good technique on the Spider Wall preceded by good technique on the other forearm-intensive obstacles, however, can make this a fast and easy obstacle.

Vaults. The Vaults are the final obstacle and are composed of a series of horizontal telephone poles at waist-height. The only stipulations are that you have to get over the logs with only your hands touching them. If anything other than your hands touches the logs, you have to start over.

By the end of the O-Course you're so smoked that you can easily drag a boot across a log on accident. You might be able to get away with it, but don't risk it - it's not worth it. There have been multiple instances where a student has grazed the log with his foot and, not thinking anyone had seen, continued as though nothing happened. The Instructor who saw it waited until the entire class was done and formed up ready to leave. The beating lasted almost two hours, the student got individual attention from the Instructors every day after work for the remainder of Second Phase, and his classmates still don't like him.

There are two basic techniques to finish the Vaults, hurdling and rotating.

Hurdling requires more technique and athleticism and is only the slightest bit faster than rotating. The only guys who hurdle the vaults are the guys who haven't figured out the rotate technique and the guys at the front of the class fighting to shave off seconds in order to get their times under 6 minutes. Hurdling is just what it sounds like: as you hit the log your arms are flexed, ready to help propel you up and over. You simultaneously hop and straighten out your arms and tuck your legs up as you jump over the log. You land facing the same direction you took off, and repeat for the next log. The biggest disadvantage is that it's extremely easy to catch your foot on the logs if you don't put enough energy into each hurdle.

The rotating technique is only a fraction of a second slower and, although it makes you pretty dizzy, gets you through the obstacle with very little risk of dragging a foot on the logs. Approaching the log with locked-out arms, put your hands on the far left side of the log. Using the momentum of your run against your locked-out arms, your feet will rise off the ground with minimal effort. Because your whole body is rotating over the top of the log, you only have to get your right foot over the log. As your right foot clears, your weight will be over the log and, as you fall over the other side, a left leg stuck straight out (parallel to the log you're going over) will rotate over as it follows your right leg. You'll end up backwards, facing the log you just rotated over. Just carry the spinning momentum from going over the log into an about-face and repeat. You'll essentially be spinning a full rotation for every vault you get over, a small price to pay for an easy and low-risk way to clear the last obstacle.

Over the last three Vaults you will sound off with (yell) your rate/ rank and last name for the graders. After you've cleared the last vault all that remains is a 15m sprint to the finish, during which you continue to repeat your last name. When you finish you do some pushups (facing the ocean, always), yell "Hooyah O-Course," and jog a few cool-down laps.

BO: Don't Be That Guy.

Don't be late to muster. Ever. Don't ever, ever make someone in your class barge in your room and drag you out of bed. Be a man. Be responsible for yourself. Only shitbags are late to muster. Enough said.

Don't show up without gear. Bring the right gear to every evolution. Make sure the gear has been properly taken care of and fully assembled. There is no excuse for bringing only one fin to a swim. Yes, this happened in my class. There is no excuse for installing your actuator upside down. Same guy. There is no excuse for a rusty knife. Where's your sandpaper? There will not be, and there should not be, any mercy on someone so incapable of taking care of himself that he can't do these few, simple things.

People in your class will always be willing to help you get your gear in the right condition provided you're willing to learn and work hard yourself. If you're not self sufficient and you're content to lean on your classmates, you'll find your whole class engaged in an effort to get you quit or hurt. It happens to those who deserve it. Don't earn that shame and you won't get it. Put out, take care of yourself, help your buddies, and you'll be the guy your classmates lean on for support.

Don't cheat on boat crews. When you're in the initial height line, there's often a great deal of chicken-shit jostling to line up next to this guy and to avoid that guy. Fuck that. Be a man. BUD/S sucks regardless of who's in your boat crew. Sure, it might suck a touch more with a shitty boat crew, but it won't be the difference between becoming a SEAL and not. Remember that the hardships are the things that will separate you from the regular men you'll spend much of your life with.

What? This coming from the guy who climbed out of a window after an inspection? Climbing out of that window didn't take advantage of a single one of my classmates. Nobody lost. Certainly, I would've lost had I been caught, but nobody else lost. Loading your boat crew fucks over everyone else in your class.

A good man is hurt and med-dropped every class because pieces of shit above and below him load their boat crews, leaving him with weaklings and boat duckers. Don't fuck him out of his dream because you wanted to get secured from drag races 5 minutes earlier.

There are platoon OICs at my SEAL Team right now who stacked their boat crews. I didn't go to BUD/S with them, but I know. People talk. When you get to a Team you're going to find that the community is small enough that you know someone everywhere you go, even right out of BUD/S. Your reputation travels. The cardinal sin for a Team Guy is looking out for yourself before your buddies and will earn you the nicknames IGM ("I got mine") and Blue Falcon ("Buddy Fucker"). Stacking your boat crew at the expense of the rest of your class doesn't work out for anyone in the end.

Don't sweat chits. In BO they give chits when you fail something. You get a chit if you fail a run, fail an inspection, have a bad haircut, or just end up in the wrong place at the wrong time. Chits don't count for shit.

Let me repeat that.

Chits don't count for shit.

Nobody looks at them. Nobody counts them. Nobody gives a fuck.

There is a block at the bottom of the chit to respond and sign. Just sign. Do not respond. Responding is the single way you can get in trouble when it comes to chits. Take the bullshit. Suck it up. Submit to the gayness. It honestly doesn't matter.

Don't buy "BUD/S kits." The ACE Hardware on Orange Ave. in Coronado sells BUD/S kits. Don't buy them. They're a waste of time. Buy a scribe, some fine grain sandpaper, a tub of Vaseline, and you'll be good to go. The rest of the shit in the kit (wire brushes, tool boxes, etc) is a waste of time and money. Get only what you need and save yourself some cash for a beer or two on the weekends.

BO: Mark's Parting Wisdom.

Every phase of BUD/S your class will have a proctor. Your proctor is your class's connection to the rest of the instructors. He helps the class leadership understand what they need to prepare for. He is the class's voice to the instructor staff and the staff's voice to the class. His goal is to set the class up for success. He won't make anything easier, but he'll make sure the class is as ready as it should be for what's coming.

My class's BO instructor was a smart man who didn't speak much. He could run and we heard rumors about black-ops heroics he'd performed on the battlefield. Some proctors play the double agent and will sell you out to the instructor staff to get you beat more. Our BO instructor was not that man.

The Friday before we started First Phase he took us on a beach run. We ran out of the grinder toward the ocean. Once we hit the beach, we turned south and headed toward Tijuana. The sun was getting low, golden froth rode on the surf, and the salt breeze held strings of seabirds overhead. A day of chaos, stress, and pain culminated in this almost meditative sunset jog. The silent footfalls of the men around compacted the wet sand and the swishing of cargo pant legs made the only sound I could hear over my breath, the waves, and the gulls above.

This.

This is the fucking life.

Work out all day. Sunset runs on a private beach in southern California.

Hell, the barracks rooms we live in would sell for seven figures even in a shitty market.

This will do.

We approach the end of the Navy beach and the beginning of Silver Strand State Park. Our turnaround point. We turn inland and move onto the soft sand as we head back north toward the compound. Halfway there our proctor turns and runs toward the ocean. He stops on the berm above the beach and turns around, a silhouette of a man against an ever-darkening red sky. He straightens his cover and puts his hands in his pocket. We stand in formation, 5 men wide and over 40 deep, watching. He touches each man in the first row on the shoulder as he speaks. The class is silent. Even the gulls held their breaths while he spoke.

"BUD/S is a right of passage. We won't make it easy on you because it can't be easy. We would cheat you and we would cheat ourselves. It is not personal; it is a grim necessity that we make you push you past your limits and back. Some of you will break. Many of you will find you are not made of the right stuff for this life.

"This is no game. This is Navy SEAL training. This is serious business for serious men. But if you find it within you to stay and fight while others around you drop like flies, I can promise you this: being a SEAL is a good life. The best life. You will never find brotherhood like you will find in the SEAL Teams."

He looked away from us, out to sea, and continue to speak. "For those of you who don't know if you can do these things we demand of you: *there*," as he steps aside and, with a sweeping gesture, frames the grey silhouette of a guided missile frigate on the water, "*There* is the alternative, gents. You can go there. Or you can stay here."

The class erupted in a boisterous "Hooyah" and our proctor immediately took off sprinting north on the soft sand path.

Fuck.

Anyone who doesn't finish with him is going to get beat.

Fucking run, gents.

Chapter 10

First Phase: The Real Deal.

"We should remember that one man is much the same as another,
and that he is best who is trained in the severest school."

- Thucydides

In the days leading up to First Phase, all you can think about is "phasing up." You'll be busy preparing your helmet, making sure your gear is stenciled, and cleaning your barracks room. The party animals in your class will be hitting the town. The fastidious among you will be setting aside a new white shirt for every day, stenciled and ready for action. Your class has to move from 618 (the PTRR and post-Hellweek barracks) to 602 where you'll live until you've completed Hell Week (or - more likely - quit).

You can feel the anticipation. The floors of 602 feel like they've been designed for beatings. The walls are made to be hosed down. You're within whispering distance of the grinder and the First Phase office. You know that instructors have a habit of occasionally dropping by in the dead of night, yanking a class out of bed, and beating them. You never realized the luxury it was to live in 618 away from the instructors. 602 is a microscope, you're an ant, and the sun is bright.

It's hard to eat a full meal here. Sleep becomes fitful. First Phase used to take center stage in your dreams. Now that dream transforms into a nightmare. The anxiety is debilitating, suffocating.

At the very same time, you realize you've arrived. You're finally in the position to walk the walk. There's no more question. You're in the doorway and you're ready to jump. Now you get to find out what you're made of. Now you get to test your mettle against the hardest training the country has to offer. Your hard work has gotten you here and you know what you've got to do. When this realization washes over you, it's possible to breath deep despite the butterflies in your throat.

This is your chance, finally, to prove to yourself that you have what it takes; this is your opportunity to show every person who doubted you what you're made of.

Walk that walk.

Carry that boat.

Hit that surf.

Do those pushups.

Get your ass to Hell Week.

Don't be a pussy.

Get your brown shirt.

Get some.

Author's Note on Changes in the BUD/S Pipeline.

BUD/S is constantly changing. By the time you read this book, chances are that a few things have changed. If you've read Dick Couch's book "The Warrior Elite," which you absolutely should, you'll find that a great deal has changed since he was there.

Recently BUD/S moved from 26 weeks, or a full six months, to 21 weeks, or 7 weeks per phase. Did that change make it easier? Ask the Instructors: I'd wager they're making sure it's not any easier. The chow hall also moved from across the street to right on the beach, and while the 6-miles-per-day chow hall runs might not be happening, you'll find the relative calm, remote location of the public chow hall across the street might have been worth running 6 miles every day. With a BUD/S-only chow hall, you're not as safe from the Instructors as you used to be. And the ocean - your best friend in the whole wide world - happens to be right there.

So when you get there and you hear from old-timers (or the class in front of you) that you have it easy - that they, in fact, were the last hard BUD/S class, feel free to ignore them. One evolution might be easier, the next one will probably be harder.

An example: when I was in Second Phase, a Master Chief showed us old video footage of his class's Pool Comp (if you don't know what Pool Comp is, see the chapter on Second Phase). There were two striking differences we all saw:

(1) His Pool Comp was incredibly violent. We got our heads

smashed into the pool deck and tossed around, sure. But his Instructors were throwing elbows, punching, throwing knees, and altogether beating the living crap out of the students. Point: Master Chief.

(2) His Pool Comp seemed to have no rules or required procedures. They were allowed to do absolutely anything other than surface. Our Pool Comp was governed by a hyper-rigid set of rules. Deviate slightly from the rules one time (like tracing a hose too quickly or not thoroughly enough), and you fail immediately. We would have killed to take a knee to the gut in order to gain a little leniency from immediate failure. Point: Without a doubt, my class.

But these changes are superficial. BUD/S is still BUD/S and will remain BUD/S as long as it's run by SEALs. Nobody in the community can afford to let the standards drop: our lives are, quite literally, on the line. BUD/S is one of biggest reason the SEAL Teams are so elite: making it easier would diminish who we are, and we've worked too hard to get here.

So take pride in your BUD/S experience. Prepare for it fully, embrace the suck, own it, suffer a little while with a couple dozen of your closest friends, and step out of the fire a Team Guy.

First Phase: The First Morning.

The morning of First Phase, Day One is designed to make you quit. It's as though the instructors had been handcuffed before and, this morning, they took a bunch of meth and chewed through the handcuffs. They don't seem to have rules or limits. Their violence and cruelty is unfathomable. They want you to suffer deeply. You can see this much in their eyes and hear it in their voices. They truly hate you today. And they want to scare you. They want you to think they can do anything. They want you to think that it never ends.

First Phase, despite the appearance of chaos, is anything but. Every action is planned, every evolution choreographed. The instructors hold their duty as the "keepers of the Trident" sacred, as they should. They would rather die than let someone unfit wear the Trident. That is no joke. But they are not demons. They can't kill you (unless you're a *complete* douche). But they want you to quit and they sense weakness.

They are masters of Psychological Operations. First Phase *is* Psy-Ops and the instructors are consummate professionals. No one evolution makes a man quit. Anticipation of things to come is what makes a man quit.

There were two petty officers in my class, an E-4 and an E-5 who were both on their second shot at BUD/S. They had both only made it to the first day of First Phase the first time they went through. They, like so many others, quit the morning of First Phase. They said that it hadn't been the beating that had made them quit - they could handle that beating. It had been the realization that this sort of pain would be their daily life for six months. So they bolted.

They spent some time in the fleet, worked out together, and came back prepared. They were excellent on the O-Course throughout Indoc, solid runners, and good swimmers. They helped guys prepare gear and kept their wits about them during Indoc inspections when a lot of other guys panicked. They were solid and I knew I'd be graduating BUD/S with them.

The morning of Day One starts with a "Grinder PT." It was common knowledge, however, that this almost immediately degenerated into a beating and surf torture. It's a shock-and-awe morning. Everyone knows this going in, which took the edge off for me. I knew what to expect. Everyone did. The morning was going to suck, but I'd only have to do it once. And once it was done, it was done. I was ready to start working through BUD/S.

We formed up in the "Pit" behind the 602 and got ready to run out to the grinder in formation. Everyone was settling into position and preparing for pain. I saw one of the two petty officers running around franticly. His face was white - actually white, his eyes were wide. He was in full panic. He was looking for his friend. Just then we heard the bell ring twice. *That's* where his friend was. His eyes widened all the way, said "Oh Shit!" and ran to the grinder despite our best efforts to restrain him. 30 seconds later the bell rang twice more. We never saw them again.

These guys were strong and confident. A lot of guys looked up to them. And they had just quit, literally *as* the class started to step off to its first of many violent beatings. Fuck it. Guess we misjudged those guys. They weren't going to stop me. Cadence was called and we screamed the responses as we pridefully marched to our demise.

"To my left!"
"Hey!"
"To my left!"
"Hey!"
"Hooyah."

"Hey!"
"Hooyah."
"Hey!"
"Hooyah."
"Hey, hey, hey!"
"Two!"
"TWO!"
"Six One!"
"SIX ONE!"
"Two!"
"TWO!"
"Six One!"
"SIX ONE!"
"Fired Up!"
"Fired Up!"
"Motivated."
"Motivated."
"Fired Up!"
"Fired Up!"
"Dedicated."
"Dedicated."
"Hooyah!"
"Hooyah!"
"Ah-Ha!"
"Ah-Ha!"
"Hooyah!"

"HOOOOOOOOOYYYYAAAAAAAHHHHH!!!!!!" We screamed as we sprinted through the grinder to stand on a pair of freshly painted, evenly spaced foot-prints. We put our canteens down to the left as we'd rehearsed. As long as everyone was the same, we'd be safe.

Front and center, poised on an elevated wood platform, was one of the instructors. No instructors were nice, but some were easier on us than others. The instructor on the podium, as luck would have it, was not one of the kinder instructors. He had a megaphone slung over his shoulder, one hand on his hip, and the other held the microphone for the megaphone. He was already displeased with our performance.

"Hit the fucking surf. You have 30 seconds. Bust 'em."

"HOOOYAH!" There is no way in hell a class of 200 is going to get all the way to the beach, climb over the berm, run down to the low-tide, get completely wet, get out of the water, run back up and over the berm, all the way back to the grinder, and fall in in formation in 30 seconds. One man, sprinting there and back completely naked could barely make the time. He knew we wouldn't come close. So did we. But we sure tried, because not trying would bring the wrath of god upon us, and rightfully so.

More than one ancient battle has been won by a drastically outnumbered force that refused to quit, whose soldiers elected to "sell their lives dearly" instead of surrendering. This single-minded hardness and aggression is something we, as fat, lazy American civilians, lack. Our lives are largely too soft to breed anything like this attitude. That's why there's BUD/S. BUD/S will change the way you look at the world.

A normal person backed into a corner by a man holding a knife will give up his wallet when told to. It just makes sense.

A Team Guy in the same situation is just as likely to spit on the ground, crack his neck, flex his hands into loose fists, and growl "Come and get it, motherfucker." This is the same attitude it takes to run toward someone who is shooting at you. This is the same attitude required for success in our kind of combat.

BUD/S transforms you like this and it starts on Day One as you fight that voice inside you that tells you to stop trying because the game is rigged and the goal is impossible.

Fuck that, you have to tell yourself. I dare you: get to the surf and back in 30 seconds. Show that instructor that he can't beat you. Show him that if he gives you an impossible task, you hate him so much you're going to complete it just to say "fuck you" to him.

The PT session quickly devolved into hitting the surf, which soon further devolved into surf torture - or "surf immersion" as the instructors like to call it. "You faggots are taking up so much time running back and forth to the surf zone that you might as well stay out there." Surf torture claimed a handful more weak-minded men and boys who made the mistake of evaluating their lot in life while in the surf zone. They had just been beat and now they were shivering violently in the unfeeling Pacific as sand filled their eyelids. And it wasn't even dawn of Day One, yet. That was enough for them.

No more than 3 minutes after the last quitter rang out, the evolution was secured and we ran off the beach to decon, change, and stand by for the Week One PI/BI.

Things to Remember:

As in all things, anticipation is worse than the actual event. The two petty officers were among the strongest physical performers in the class. They had the most experience and the respect of the class. But they never even gave BUD/S a chance. Both times they quit, they didn't make it through the morning of Day One. There is only one reason: fear. They were scared. They anticipated how bad things were going to get and that was enough. Don't do this. And remember that the worst part of every evolution is the anticipation of how bad it's going to be.

You're making progress. The whole time you were in DEP, Boot Camp, BUD/S Prep, and BO, First Phase loomed large on the horizon. It got larger as it got closer. Not on Day One. On Day One, BUD/S officially starts to get shorter. Every surf torture and every beating brings you that much closer to being done with BUD/S. Each moment endured is one less minute you'll ever have to do, one less minute between you and becoming a Navy SEAL. This day, for the first time ever, BUD/S is shrinking in front of you you. It's exciting and empowering. Embrace it and never forget that you're on the offensive now. Conquer it one evolution at a time.

First Phase: Surf Immersion.

Surf Immersion has a lot of other names. Students more accurately call it "surf torture." Instructors officially refer to it as "surf immersion." The more sadistic instructors call it "playing in the water" or "enjoying the beautiful Pacific." A rose by any other name smells as sweet, and surf torture by any other name still sucks a dick.

You know it's coming when you're lined up shoulder to shoulder, back to surf, and an ambulance (called the "amboo" - really just a Suburban with big, soft off-road tires to handle the soft sand) creeps over the crest of the berm. Usually it's a bit of a surprise. You're busy putting out for some evolution, you see the amboo, you see a small crowd of instructors sitting on top of the berm drinking Monsters and Red Bull with big lips full of Copenhagen and bigger smiles, and one instructor walking toward you with a megaphone who says "shoulder to shoulder." You repeat it loudly - like you do every command in BUD/S, and comply.

Then he reads you a list of your sins and tells you to "about face."

"About Face!" The whole class turns and looks at that cold, ugly ocean and shivers.

"Lock arms!"

"Lock arms!" Every man interlocks his arms with his neighbors.

"Forward march."

"Forward March!" And the class wades into the bracing ocean. This walk is way longer than you'd think. They send you out there pretty deep because they know the waves are just going to wash the phalanx of students back up onto the sand anyhow. And it sucks more if it's deeper.

"Stop."

"Stop!"

"Take seats."

"Take Seats!" Every man shudders as he sits down, submerged to his armpits, and then lays back as the sand and saltwater wash over his face. Sometimes you'll be surf tortured with your feet toward the ocean and head toward the beach. This is preferable. Sometimes you'll get a last minute "about face" before you "take seats." That's when you know life is going to suck.

With your feet toward the ocean you can see and feel the waves coming. And the waves that do ride over your body deposit most of their sand on your clothes. As the chain of interlocked students gets pushed onto the beach, your head is also the first thing to rise out of the surf due to the angle of the beach.

WIth your feet toward land you don't see a thing. You can't feel the waves coming so you don't know when to close your eyes tight or when to hold your breath. Because of this you end up inhaling a great deal of salt water. And the bulk of the sand in those shallow waves ends up in your eyes. Your eyes get so full of sand that you can't see or move your eyes. As the waves push you and your classmates onto the beach, your feet are elevated by the incline of the sand, pushing your head even further under.

As the waves push your class onto the beach, some sections of students will get pushed significantly farther ashore than others. What started as a straight line of linked students ends up a kinked mess. You're supposed to keep your arms locked with the men next to you, but invariably someone will stop trying and expect you to hold onto his limp arm. That's a buddy fucker right there because it's impossible to lock arms with a noodle, and if you don't hold onto him, you both get in trouble. So you keep trying.

At some predetermined time, you're called to your feet and told to walk in to shore. You'll foolishly hope this is the last time and you're about to be secured (in BUD/S "secured" means the end of an evolution), but you know it's just a med check. Some guys aren't able to get to their feet on their own because their hip flexors are completely locked up. Toward the end of Hell Week I had to have guys lift me to my feet to get out of the surf zone: I was simply unable to bend my legs at the hips. (My hips are still in terrible shape almost a decade later). You hobble in and shiver in a line as a corpsman (medic) checks you for signs of hypothermia. He checks your pupil dilation with a flashlight and cognitive function with a stupid question.

"Mr. Xavier, how to you spell water?"

"C-O-L-D." I made a point to answer his stupid questions with stupid answers. What was he going to do? Surf torture me?

As you're waiting for everyone to get checked, your arms are away from your body, your hands are above your head, and even your fingers are spread apart. Every square inch of your skin is exposed to the air, freezing you to the quick. Until the first time I experienced this, I had never imagined a world where putting my fingers together or resting my elbows against my ribs was a forbidden luxury. They take everything from you at BUD/S.

After the med checks, you turn right back around and do it again. This time it's usually a little shorter, but immersion times vary based on the day's water temperature. There is an exposure chart the staff uses as a limit for duration and repetitions in the surf, so remember that, despite appearances, the whole evolution is stringently controlled.

Surf torture is, more than anything, demoralizing. It sucks beyond belief and you can't do a thing about it other than lie there and take it. The instructors say bend over, you bend over, and the ocean rapes you. The best way to combat the demoralizing effects is to sing. Your whole class will sing. You're supposed to sing frogman songs (there are actually quite a few old-school frogman drinking songs), SEAL cadences, or a patriotic song. My class didn't dig that. We sang Lady Gaga, Journey, and other gay pop songs. It seriously, seriously pissed off the instructors but we didn't care. That's the really beautiful thing about surf torture: you, for once, have nothing to lose. They'll talk about beating you or freezing you to death, but they're already doing their worst. You're already so cold you pee your pants to thaw your legs and there's so much misery around you that guys lose control of their bowels and, literally, shit themselves.

The other shitty thing about surf torture involves Coronado's proximity to Tijuana (or "TJ"). You see, when it rains, TJ's sewage system simply can't handle the volume. It backs up. It dumps tons (literally) of shit (also literally) into the ocean. You may find yourself lucky enough to experience this firsthand during a surf torture. During Hell Week my class got to spend some quality time in the surf on Wednesday night. We didn't call this time "surf torture," it was "sewage torture." We were laying right in the middle of a thick, gooey plume of TJ's shit. A full turd washed up on my shoulder. The sewage was so thick and ripe that the shore was covered in hundreds of fish flopping around on the sand, preferring the sand and death to the sewage water. So here we are, arms locked, hip flexors locked up, it smells like the inside of a port-a-potty, there are fish flipping themselves over the sand, guys are throwing up, and we're bathing in shit.

Every time you enjoy a little surf immersion, remember this: at least it's water and not shit. And if it's shit, then, well, that sucks.

First Phase: Inspections.

Personnel and Barracks Inspections (PI/BI) are one of the worst parts of BUD/S. Not because the beatings are so much worse than anything else (although they can be pretty bad) but because you and your roommates can potentially waste all weekend cleaning and still fail. My roommates and I quickly realized that avoiding a 1 hour beating and another 1 hour on uniform/boot prep wasn't worth 12 hours of cleaning a barracks room. So we came up with a plan:

1 hour beating + 1 hour uniform prep + 1 hour for pain and suffering = 3 hours of cleaning. We never exceeded 3 hours preparing for a PI/BI, but for those three hours, we all worked hard. We didn't pass every inspection, but neither did the guys who sacrificed their whole Sundays to clean. The guys who passed every inspection had usually cleaned even less than we did.

PI/BIs change drastically for First Phase from BO. Beatings take the place of chits. Instructors get violent. As you stand by your room waiting to be inspected, you can hear instructors screaming and your classmates doing 8-count body builders (a horrific exercise). Sometimes if you look down the hall, you'll see the occasional chair come crashing out the door and into the wall. You'll see plumes of paper fluttering to the ground. It's like the Tasmanian Devil from Looney Toons is in there. Other times instructors favor the stoic professional route, where they walk in, calmly tick off three failings like a metronome, and leave while the bewildered grader, your classmate, gives you a sympathetic look and a shrug that says "he's done that in every room" before he rushes out to grade the next failed room.

Eventually the graders will get brave and savvy enough to fudge the scores a bit. Guys who fail will sometimes not fail if the instructor is too amped (roided?) up to notice. But not yet, and not often. It's not usually worth the risk. The fallout from an instructor catching a fudged score would be sweeping and cataclysmic - the kind of beating that would make you cry tears of blood before it's over. It's better to just take your licks.

There are better ways, though, to effect a good outcome when it comes to PI/BIs. In the Personnel Inspection there's actually not much you can do. Make sure your haircut and shave are sharp. Make sure your boots are as shiny as possible, particularly on the toe. Make sure you put the belt on the right way (as opposed to the direction females wear them). Past that, there's not really much you can do to defend against an instructor failing you because your cammies "don't look quite right" or because you "look like a faggot." There's literally nothing you can do about that. Some of us, apparently, just look like "faggots." I got that one a lot, go figure.

The BI, however, is a different story. Here you have a fighting chance to derail instructors on the prowl. You can short-circuit the tantrum they were planning to throw. These are the strategies used to great effect; by a classmate of mine named Ben. Ben didn't fail a single BI the entirety of BUD/S because he had mastered the first impression and then quickly distracted the instructors.

Shiny floors. A visibly shiny floor is a good idea. Note what time of day the inspections are going to be and look at your room from the doorway, see where the reflections from the windows are going to bounce the strongest. Spend the majority of your time on those spots. Mop 'n' Glo is popular, but probably only because the Surf Mart (Navy Exchange Minimart by the BUD/S barracks) sells it.

Tight Racks. You have to sleep on your rack (bed), but not in it. The best thing to do in order to maintain a perfect rack with tight

259

sheets is to make it once. Make it once and use a uniform item called "shirt stays" to hold the sheets down. Shirt stays are elastic bands with alligator clips on each end. If you make your bed and then secure two opposing sides with shirt stays on the underside of the mattress, your sheets will stay taught and crisp, even if you sleep on top of them. Now, go and buy a cheap ($30) sleeping bag to sleep in on top of your mattress. Now you never have to do a single thing to your bed and it will look immaculate 10 seconds after you wake up. That's more sleep time and a perfectly made bed every morning.

Pleasant smells. If it smells clean, it is clean. Use strongly-scented cleaners like Pine-Sol to clean your room's horizontal surfaces. Sure, a damp rag will get it just as clean, but it certainly won't make it smell as clean. Your barracks is right on the beach, where the air is impregnated with fine sand. If you leave a freshly cleaned horizontal surface alone for 10 minutes, it's going to end up dusty. When your room is standing by for its turn to be inspected, everyone inside the room can be cleaning. The instructors will walk in and absentmindedly run their hands along the surface of the desk. If they feel even a little bit of sand, that's a hit. So when you're in that last minute scramble to clean, get that desk. And get it with the strongest smelling cleaner so the scent is heavy in the air. Hell, take a rag soaked with the stuff and wipe the inside of the doorframe with the solution so it hits them stronger and faster when they walk in.

The most brazen example of the pleasant smell was also the most successful. Ben bought a coffee maker. When it was time to head out for the PI, he'd start a pot brewing. By the time his room was to be inspected, there would be a fresh pot of hot coffee ready. The smell made his room heavenly. And there were coffee cups ready for instructors to partake of.

After you dazzle, distract. Ben was an even better distractor than he was a dazzler. Not only did he have a pot of fresh coffee brewed with cups and coffee accoutrements (sugar, cream, etc) set out, but he also had a box of donuts and other goodies in wait.

Ben's refrigerator was fully stocked with Gatorade, Monster, Red Bull (sugar-free), and various tins of chewing tobacco.

"Seaman Ben, are you trying to bribe your way out of an inspection?"

"Negative Instructor Smith."

"Well, good. That would be wrong. Your room passes."

"Hooyah Instructor Smith."

"Now, put on another pot of coffee and next time don't forget a can of Copenhagen Long-Cut."

"Hooyah Instructor Smith."

As the Instructors congregated in Ben's room for refreshments, there was more for their entertainment. Ben had an epic collection of pornographic magazines. Every week he'd cut out a display for the inside of all the lockers in the room. Between the erotica and the refreshments, there wasn't a single instructor who so much as looked at Ben's room, which he'd spent a total of 40 minutes cleaning. By the end of BUD/S, the beginning of a BI was marked by a beeline of instructors walking past every other room to fill up on goodies from Ben's room before starting their inspection of everyone else. It was almost as though Ben's room didn't count. It was the break room they hit before getting back to work.

Ben was smart. He took the instructors out of instructor mode and put them into lounging mode. They hung out in his room and enjoyed the caffeine or nicotine (or both) of their choice while looking at naked women before being forced back to work.

Not only was Ben the proprietor of the best break room ever, but, had the instructors ever objectively looked at what he was doing (there's no evidence they ever did), they still would have approved. To this day, I can only admire that Ben took a lose/lose situation and won. BIs are, by definition, defensive. You set up and then you wait to be attacked. Those are the rules. Ben said "forget the rules" and went on the offensive. He engaged in a well-executed Psy-Ops campaign and he won because of it. He took a no-win situation and came out on top every week. He was proactive and aggressive and had balls and, had the instructors ever thought about this while they were ogling tits and downing Red Bulls, they would've liked him even more.

Now I simply could not have pulled off the crazy shit that Ben did. I'm not even sure how *Ben* did. But you can take bits and pieces from his winning strategy to make life a little easier and take a little edge off PI/BI days.

First Phase: Drown Proofing.

Drown proofing is an evolution designed to ensure all potential SEAL operators have the ability to remain calm in the water. When on combat diving missions, even in training, panic is deadly. And the ability to remain calm in stressful training situations does, in fact, indicate your ability to remain calm under fire.

Drown proofing itself involves having your hands tied behind your back and your feet bound together while doing a number of activities in the water including bobbing from surface to the bottom of the pool, floating in place, swimming the width of the pool and back, and retrieving your dive mask in your teeth.

Drown proofing is an easy pass for most people. Unless you have so little fat and so much dense muscle that you look like you're wearing a Batman suit when you take your shirt off, you really won't have any physical problems. If you spend enough time in the water that you're comfortable with it, you won't have any mental problems either.

You might even like it.

I loved drown-proofing because it's quiet underwater. You can't hear the Instructors and you can just relax. Everything done in drown-proofing is made easier by being calm and smooth, so there's real motivation to get yourself into an almost meditative state. Drown proofing was my excuse to relax in the middle of a hectic, violent day.

In BO you'll have a few opportunities to practice drown-proofing techniques, usually just holding your hands behind your back (i.e. not tied up). If you're in PTRR for any length of time, you'll probably do these practices a dozen times before you get to First Phase. Play these practice times for real. They're almost exactly like the real thing - maybe a little harder - because in the real evolution you don't even have to think about keeping your hands and feet together. Being actually tied up makes it easier.

The evolution begins with you sitting on the pool deck with two lengths of rope. You tie your own ankles together before putting your hands behind your back for your buddy to tie. In both instances get the ropes/knots as tight as you possibly can without undue pain. They stretch and the knots slip underwater. And yes, you will probably fail if your ropes come off - even if it's not your fault. When you put your hands behind your back, face your palms away from your body and cross at the wrists. This is the most comfortable position that allows the rope to remain tight and steady and allows your body all the flexibility you'll want for the evolution. The buddy who tied your wrists is your buddy for the rest of the evolution. He'll be giving you the visual signals to move from one activity to the other as well as tossing your mask to you when you get to the end.

Bobbing. Now you're assigned a square, a designated space created by the crossing lane lines, that you'll do the majority of the evolution in. When the Instructors tell you to "enter the water," you'll slip into the pool and get in your square. Now you turn around to face your buddy and start to bob.

Bobbing is bouncing from the bottom of the 12ft Combat Training Tank (CTT - the pool) to the surface and back while staying in your square. I recommend you take a breath every time you surface. Guys who take their breath at the bottom don't do so well.

Keep an eye out for classmates who are too focused on breathing to realize they're moving all around the pool. You don't usually fail for leaving your box while bobbing, but you can. You're a buddy fucker if you bob into someone else. A number of guys in my class failed their first try because other students bobbed right into them, or right on top of them, and either forced them to free their hands or to panic. Stay in your fucking box and watch out for the inconsiderate incompetents who don't stay in theirs.

There's a balance to find on your descent with how much air you take in and how much you hold in your lungs. The balance is based around your body's natural buoyancy. I'm an abnormally buoyant person, meaning that my body likes to float. When I took my breath I had to let almost all of it out immediately. If I didn't, I'd end up floating. Floating is not bobbing, so I would very gradually increase the size of breath I took until I almost (but not quite) stopped as I descended to the bottom. Each successful breath was a balancing act: I'd start sinking quickly and slow down as the air in my lungs expanded and increased my relative buoyancy until, at a certain depth, the water pressure from above me would overcome the upward force and I'd accelerate to the bottom of the pool. But no one breath is going to make you fail. If you take too large a breath and stall on the way down, you can just release a little air. If you take too small a breath, you can just push to the surface faster and make up for it with a good, deep breath the next bob. You can do the entire evolution without finding a comfortable balance, but it's more comfortable and much easier if you experiment to find a good balance.

My best friend in BUD/S was obscenely, shockingly negative in the water and sank like a missile. Even with a full breath he'd sink to the bottom, so he could take most of a lungful to the bottom and still bob effectively. His density was nice for the bobbing, but almost ended his BUD/S career in the float that comes after bobbing.

Floating. After an Instructor is satisfied that you're calm and controlled, he'll tell your buddy to have you float. Your buddy will give you the signal and you'll start to float. The float is, for most students, the hardest part of drown proofing. The requirements are threefold:

- Stay on the surface.
- Stay in your square.
- Stay calm.

Guys with large torsos in relation to their legs have the easiest time because all they need to do is take a deep breath and lean forward in the water by digging their heads as deep as possible while remaining on the surface, curving their backs as much as possible with the intention of keeping their spine and ribcage a little out of the water, using the air in their lungs as flotation. Guys who can do this just hold their breaths and quickly dart their heads out of the water to gasp a lungful of air before returning to their shrimp-shaped body position.

My gangly body is 2/3 legs by weight, so this didn't really work for me. Regardless of how hard I bent my back and buried my head in the water, I'd find myself slipping down and out of position, pulled by my heavy legs. So I had to add a slight dolphin kick, just enough to keep myself on the surface. I never really moved anywhere, but I kept my eyes on the square of lane lines beneath me and occasionally turned my body so I would stay within the bounds.

My best friend in training, the 200lb Batman-suit body builder, could take that full breath with him to the bottom of the pool. Floating nearly did him in. He wasn't panicking or uncomfortable - he was just physically unable to float. He was ultimately rolled for drown proofing, but passed with the subsequent class. What he had to resort to was a circular spin. He actually looked like a flea on the surface of the water because in order to remain in his square he did a dolphin kick on his side, body bent in half to ensure his circle stayed within bounds. He was essentially doing spastic 360s on his side the whole time. It wasn't pretty and it wasn't easy, but he's a team guy now and this evolution was the only thing he ever had trouble with.

And when he got rolled, he practiced drown proofing for hours a day, every day. Weekends included. That very physical attribute that got him dozens of women at the beach, his freakish physique, almost took his dream from him. But he beat it by working harder than anyone and not giving up.

But even if you think you're in the same boat he was, you're probably not. He was the (physically) densest student the instructor staff had ever seen. Guys who thought they were negative in the water looked like helium balloons next to Batman.

For everyone else the float isn't a big deal. And if it is, practice until it isn't a factor anymore. If Batman could do it, you can too.

Traverse. After floating for the allotted time period, your buddy will indicate that it's time to swim. You won't be able to see him very well while floating (especially if you're doing the water-flea technique), so you'll probably end up floating a lot longer than you need to. Look at your buddy as often as possible. When he tells you to traverse, you turn toward a designated end of the pool and swim there. It doesn't matter how you get there, but most guys do a full-body dolphin kick and breathe like they're doing the butterfly or breast stroke. Once you get to the edge (but don't touch it - that's instant failure), turn around, somehow survive the crush of other students swimming to your same turnaround point, and return to the spot indicated by your buddy. You'll be out of breath, so you get to bob three or four times as your recovery.

Retrieve. As you bob and catch your breath, your buddy will hold up your dive mask. You nod your head "yes" and he tosses your mask. You hope it lands in your square because it's easier that way, but you don't fail if it goes outside your square. Once the mask hits the bottom of the pool, you locate it (your buddy can help you spot it by pointing), dive down, pick it up in your mouth (remember, your hands and feet are still tied), surface, and swim it to the edge of the pool, where you climb out and report yourself as a "Pass" to the recording Instructor.

Sometimes it takes a dive or two to find your mask, sometimes it takes a few tries to get a good bite on your mask, and sometimes you have to use your head and face to flip it over so you have something to bite onto, but everyone passes once they get to the mask retrieval. The only ways you can fail are to remove the ropes from your wrists (which, by this point, you're probably holding onto to prevent them from falling off) or to quit.

Keep the ropes around your wrists and don't be a pussy and drown proofing is an easy day. Honestly the worst part about drown proofing is the violently burning eyes after the evolution is over. The CTT's water is heavily chlorinated - probably beyond any legal civilian limit - because of the sheer volume of disgusting swimmers who get in that pool (every BUD/S class) and because some of the evolutions later in BUD/S make guys shit their pants underwater, literally. Deal with the burning eyes, stay calm, keep your ropes on, and relax in your underwater break from screaming instructors.

When you pass, you can show your friends and family what you did. There are dozens of "drown-proofing" videos on YouTube. Even though it's easy, it looks impressive to the uninitiated.

First Phase: 50m Underwater Swim.

The 50m underwater swim is another evolution that is widely dreaded without good reason. Most classes will have everyone pass, many on the first try. If you fail the underwater swim you'll enjoy some remedial training (a beating and then some coaching) and then, a few days later, get another chance to pass. If you fail that retest (you shouldn't), you'll be rolled. If you've already been rolled for the underwater swim, then two more failures will result in you being dropped. But I've never heard of anyone even being rolled for the swim. It's easy, you just have to *want* it enough. And if you for some reason can't get it down, you simply don't have what it takes to be a SEAL.

The first time you do an underwater swim is in BO when you do a 35m swim to practice, but it doesn't count for anything. The only underwater swim that matters is the 50m in First Phase, during which you'll swim the 25m width of the CTT from one side to the other and back again to your starting point.

The evolution starts with you sitting on the pool deck facing away from the pool while groups of 6-8 start their swims. You can hear them jump in, followed by silence, followed by the gasping of students as they re-emerge victorious. Occasionally you'll hear the jeering of the instructors as a student surfaces and gasps as he doggy-paddles to the edge of the pool. Every once in a while you'll hear an instructor cursing out an unconscious student as he drags the student to the surface and to the pool deck. Like every other evolution in BUD/S, the wait is the worst part. Guys get nervous and psych themselves out. That makes their hearts pump rapidly and causes their muscles to tense up, using more Oxygen and making it more difficult for them to successfully complete their swims.

As you wait on the pool deck, remember your Arousal Control breathing (4, 4 for 4). Visualize a calm, peaceful, gliding stroke. Stay calm and collected.

When it's your turn you'll stand up and walk to the edge of the pool with your group. Out in front of you float the safety-swimmer instructors. They're wearing wetsuits, fins, dive masks, and snorkels. When you're swimming, they'll be shadowing you on the surface to ensure your safety. If you pass out, they'll bring you to the surface. If you pass out after having touched the wall at 50m you still pass. One guy in my class passed out about 4 feet from the edge of the pool, but unconsciously glided head-first into the wall. He passed. The instructor drug him to the surface, he regained consciousness after a minute or so, he reported his "Pass," and then he got beat for failing to thank his instructor. But he passed.

On a signal from the instructors, you'll jump from the edge of the pool into the water, feet first. Once you hit the water, you do a forward flip underwater (not having taken a breath since you jumped in) and start your swim. You are not permitted to push off the wall on entry, so you will start swimming in open water.

Swim as deep as you can, just above the bottom of the pool, to take advantage of physics. If you swim deep you won't have to expend any energy fighting to stay under. The water pressure above you keeps you down, letting you relax your whole body except the muscles used for your stroke. Compare that to the amount of energy require to stay underwater if you're only swimming a few feet below the surface. Try both and you'll quickly see that it's worth swimming deep.

Additionally, and perhaps more importantly, it's easier to hold your breath the deeper you are due to differing partial pressures of the Oxygen (O_2) and Carbon Dioxide (CO_2) in your lungs. Contrary to popular belief, the reason you feel that need to take another breath is not that your lungs are out of O2. You actually have plenty of Oxygen left. What you're feeling is an increase in the proportion of CO_2 to Oxygen. It's the CO_2 buildup that makes you need to take another breath. But Oxygen and Carbon Dioxide compress under pressure at different rates. When you dive deep, the CO_2 compresses more than the O2, effectively increasing the ratio of O2 to CO_2 (by volume) your body feels. That means you can actually use more of the O2 in your lungs before you feel that pulling at your chest that tells you it's time to breath. You can hold your breath longer in comfort the deeper you swim.

So swim deep. And when you get to depth, stay there. Relax your whole body other than the necessary muscles for your stroke. For example, relax your neck. There's zero need for you to look straight ahead of you. You can swim across the pool just as effectively by looking down at the lane lines you pass. (You might even want to close your eyes for most of the time to help you stay more relaxed.) Not only does this head position keep your neck and back relaxed (thereby reducing O2 use), but it also keeps your body more streamlined. When you're swimming take long, smooth strokes and glide after each stroke. Glide until you nearly stop. Then do it again. Get the most distance out of every stroke. Stay loose and long in the water.

Touch the far wall right where it intersects the bottom of the pool. A lot of guys will see the wall, which is only the half-way Mark, and automatically swim up 6 feet to touch the wall above the viewing windows (used by instructors during Pool Comp and other pool evolutions). Don't do that. It's stupid. Stay deep. Touch that wall at the bottom.

Rotate your body around smoothly by curling into a ball. Plant your feet on the wall, and push off firmly. This push-off can make the evolution for you. Make sure you're in a perfectly streamlined position: arms over your head with hands clasped, upper arms pressed into your ears, back straight, toes pointed. You can get more than half-way back to the finish with a good push-off. If you don't get a good push, you can certainly still complete the evolution, it's just a bit harder.

When I did my swim I got so keyed up after I touched the wall that I accidentally drifted away from the wall as I rotated. I tried to push off and found that I'd just wasted all my energy kicking off a wall of water. But there are no excuses in BUD/S, so I simply swam my way back just like I did the way out. It was a bit harder and I definitely enjoyed that fresh air after I finished, but it's doable either way.

After you push off and glide, continue your deep strokes until you hit the wall. Again, hit the wall where it meets the bottom of the pool. If you pass out at this depth you have a much better chance of gliding into the wall. The shallower you are, the more your body will tend to surface instead of continuing forward.

Additionally, you might feel the urge to swim shallower so you can get your breath sooner. You're wrong. If you swim along the bottom and touch the wall at the bottom, you can plant your feet underneath you and rocket yourself to the surface. Staying deep makes it easier to keep holding your breath, increases your chances of passing, and gets you a lungful of fresh air sooner. You can't lose if you go deep.

That's what she said.

Some guys will practice breath holds in preparation for the 50m underwater swim. You certainly can do this, but it's not worth your time. You're already going to be in excellent cardiac shape. Your natural mammalian dive reflex (it happens when your face hits colder water) will help you by automatically decreasing your body's circulation and therefore it's need for fresh O2. You can dive deep to gain the advantage of partial pressure and the benefits of neutral flotation. And you can leverage all of these factors for an evolution that never takes longer than 90 seconds. Most guys are done in less time than that. Don't practice breath holds and don't hyperventilate (the former is unnecessary, the latter is dangerous). The swim is largely a mental evolution. Can you overcome your body's most basic of needs - the desire to breathe? Can you do something you've never done before? Can you force yourself out of your comfort zone and succeed? These are mental questions, not physical challenges.

If you got to the underwater swim, I guaranteed you've got the abilities you need to finish the evolution with little or no problem. The only question is whether you've got the mental ability to push through. Don't be a pussy and you'll be just fine here.

First Phase: Lifesaving.

The purpose of the Lifesaving evolution is not to teach you how to save drowning victims. It's to judge your aggression, physicality, and determination. Instructors will test your ability to learn procedures and then use them in less than ideal circumstances. The instructors will teach you 3-4 different techniques used in different scenarios. None of these is complicated. You'll practice the techniques on each other throughout BO so you're familiar with them.

When it comes time for the real evolution, you'll be 'saving' your instructors. Your instructors don't particularly want to be saved. Each round starts with an instructor in the water acting out a scenario. You decide what to do, go out there, save his life, drag him to the edge of the pool, and pull him onto the deck. Done. Get back in line and wait for your turn at the next scenario. They start easy and get harder. By the end the scenario degenerates into an all-out brawl. Your instructors are strong as fuck and they hate you. You will not have an easy time the last round.

Some instructors will bear-hug you and drag you under. Others will dive straight to the bottom the moment you touch them. Fight to complete the technique. Some instructors ease up when they realize you're not shaken and you're still trying to complete the procedures. Others are out for blood. There was one instructor in my lifesaving evolution who could only be tamed by pain. He tried to squirm and thrash, so when I looped my arm around his chest, I grabbed a good handful of his armpit hair and pulled. He went from rabid wolverine to cuddly chipmunk in 0.3 seconds and I 'saved' him without much trouble.

Another time I had to spin my instructor around as I pulled him out and onto the deck, but he kept spreading his legs apart so far that I couldn't rotate him. So I dunked him under for about 15 seconds to let him know I was going to drown him if he didn't give in. He spread his legs again. I dunked him again, this time for about 45 seconds. He got the message and stopped fucking with me. I caught some heat for that, but I won and I passed.

Lifesaving's a pretty fun evolution, but it does get some guys. One guy in my class even screamed "save me, save me!" because he thought the instructor was going to drown him. It took that guy until SQT until we stopped telling him to quit on a daily basis. Don't be that guy.

I don't recommend the book for much else, but there's a great description of Lifesaving in the book *Suffer in Silence*. Most of the book is barely-repressed jaded bitterness about having quit, but the author certainly nailed the Lifesaving scenes.

First Phase: Knot-Tying.

Underwater knot tying is another one of the oft-feared baseline evolutions of First Phase that rarely, if ever, causes problems for students. The evolution starts as you tread water in front of your instructor in the deep end of the CTT. Beneath you just above the bottom of the pool is a rope, held down by dive weights. In your hand is a length of synthetic rope, usually 12-18 inches. You've taped the ends closed and burned the bitter ends together for durability. You've carried this length of rope around since you checked in. It's been girth-hitched to your canteen so you have been able to take it off the canteen at any point in order to practice your knots.

You initially learned the knots in BUD/S Prep: the Bowline, the Square Knot, the Clove Hitch, the Right Angle, and Beckett's Bend. When you checked in at BUD/S you got a refresher from the rollbacks in your class. You know these knots cold. You can do them behind your back at this point.

You look at your instructor, sound off with your rank, name, and the knot you're going to tie on this breath. Most of the time he'll say "Bullshit, you're going to tie the Bowline *and* Beckett's Bend." You sound off again with your rank, name, and the two knots you're going to tie on this breath. He says "okay." You give him the 'thumbs down' signal - you're ready to go down and tie. He returns the signal - get some.

You swim down and squeeze your knees on the diving brick or lay the weight belt over the back of your calves so you don't have to worry about floating away from the rope (the only major concern in this evolution). You tie your first knot, paying special attention to making it neat and tight. Your instructor will fail you for a sloppy knot. When you're done, you give the "okay" signal to your instructor, who checks your knot. He really only needs a few seconds to make sure it's right, but will take 30 seconds to waste time on your breath hold. When he returns the 'okay' signal, you're free to untie the knot. If you need to breathe, you give him the 'thumbs up' signal - I need to go to the surface. He'll return the signal - fine, surface. You'll surface with your hand over your head and start the process over again. If you stayed down, you simply tie the next knot, get it approved, and repeat until you need to surface.

If you really want some street cred, tie all the knots on one breath. There's nothing funnier than your instructor having to go to the surface for a breath three times while you're still on your first. Do that and you'll notice the instructors don't talk quite so much shit as they did in the beginning. They'll still fuck your world up from time to time, but you can count getting five knots in one breath as a victory.

You are officially allowed one breath per knot. If you try to do two on one breath and can't get it, untie your rope and request to surface. You'll get chewed out for being a pussy, but you won't fail. If you need it you can take a breath for each knot. But you probably won't need it.

First Phase: Timed Runs.

The four-mile timed run is the cornerstone of a Monday morning in BUD/S. You can expect a four-mile timed run every single Monday throughout all Phases except during Hell Week. The runs usually happen around 4:30 in the morning when it's dark and cold and the beaches are nearly deserted. Having already slipped the recording sheets into the ambulance and instructor trucks, the class stands by in formation on the beach with two students perched on the berm to call the instructors out. The class is wearing T-shirts tucked into their cammie pants, and boots (Bates - which are well-suited to the amount of running required in BUD/s).

When the trucks roll into view the lookouts yell "stand by!" and the class tightens up. The lookouts call the instructors out, the class responds, and the instructors tell the class to line up. They position the ambulance behind the class - it will trail the last runner the entire run - and yell "Bust 'em!" The run starts in a major clusterfuck but quickly spreads out as fast runners pull away in front and the big guys grind it out in the back.

The class stretches out as it moves north toward the turn-around point, running on the thin strip of hard-pack sand between the water and the soft sand. The route takes the class past the Coronado Shores luxury condominium complex to the Hotel Del Coronado, the Island's most distinguishing landmark. At the rocks (the same ones used for Rock Portage) in front of the Hotel Del you're forced to run inland into the soft sand until you get around the rocks. On rare occasions the tide is low enough that it's possible to run in ankle-deep water around the western side of the rocks - a risk that will reward you with 10 or 15 seconds chopped off your total time if it works out for you. On all other days you'll find an old retaining wall just inland of the rocks provides the firmest footing as you skirt the huge boulders and angle back toward the hard-pack sand. The run continues north, nearly to the fence denoting the southern boundary of Naval Air Station North Island.

At 'exactly' 2 miles, a pickup with instructors in it will be waiting. As you approach you rip your shirt off and toss it in the bed of the truck as you round it and start heading back south toward the start. This not only makes you look cool (sun's out, guns out, right?), but makes it impossible to cheat the run. As you approach the finish the first finishers will be yelling out times. When you finish you report the time that was yelled for you to the recorder and then fall into formation to stretch or do a cool-down jog in a circle.

Run failures - the losers, or goon squad - will hit the surf as they finish and enjoy a solid beating while the rest of the class, winners, stretch and jog. Sometimes even guys who pass will have to hit the surf and get beat because they didn't improve their time from the week prior. This comparison doesn't happen every time, but you never know when it will. To further complicate the situation, you're not allowed to wear a watch on the run. They don't want you pacing yourself or gaming the evolution - the instructors want you putting out a full effort every time.

In First Phase you are required to complete the 4 Mile Timed Run in 32 minutes. That's an 8 minute mile. In Second Phase you're required to run the 4 miles in 31 minutes. In Third Phase the times drop to 30 minutes - a 7 minute 30 second mile pace. These times aren't overly fast, but you have to put it in context. You'll already be running constantly. Every day. Everywhere. Running.

If you don't have a substantial running base to begin with, this can take a toll on your legs. Shin splints can lead to stress fractures which either lead to medical rolls or performance problems. And you're tired because when you're not doing a timed run you're getting beat, running with a boat on your head, swimming, bear crawling backwards up sand berms, doing pushups, and getting wet and sandy. All of this can wear you down and hinder your running performance. Fail two runs in any phase and you get performance rolled to the next class. Do it again and you're looking at a performance drop.

So get that good running base in before you head to BUD/S and you'll have a much easier time with the Timed Runs (and the rest of BUD/S) than you would otherwise. This is why it's important, once you get your SEAL Challenge Contract, to begin running more and more. The more solid a base you have before you get to BUD/S, the faster and more durable you'll be. The guys who had the easiest time with BUD/S tended to be excellent runners. The guys who struggled were often subpar runners.

First Phase: Timed Swims.

Timed swims in First Phase (and for the remainder of BUD/S for that matter) are very similar to the swims in BO, but they're in the ocean instead of San Diego Bay. The swim starts offshore of the beach entrance to the grinder (seen from further away by the landmark of the barracks and the rope-climb tower on the beach-side of the fence. The swim heads 1 nautical mile north, past the rocks at the Hotel Del Coronado, where an instructor awaits on a jet ski next to a huge orange buoy. He's got waterproofed swim pair list. As you round the buoy, sound off with your swim pair number and wait for him to check you off before continuing.

"Swim pair 2!"

"2, go."

Then you head back south to the start point (where another jet ski awaits). As you start to head back south, you'll have to keep your head up to watch out for collisions as pairs swim in behind you toward the jet ski. Angling a few degrees further out to sea will quickly get you out of the collision zone because pairs tend to swim too close to shore and have to turn out away from the shore to reach the jet ski.

When you reach (and pass) the instructor at the finish buoy, you'll hear your time yelled out. The instructor will tell you to get a 'bottom sample' before you go in, so you and your buddy will dive down to the sandy bottom of the ocean beneath you (usually somewhere between 15 and 25 feet deep), grab a handful of sand from the bottom (or, if you're lucky, a lobster), return to the surface with it, and place it on your head. When the instructor sees that you and your buddy both got a good *bottom sample*, he'll send you into the beach.

When you reach the beach, you'll check in with the instructor sitting in the Suburban. You'll tell him your swim pair number, names, and swim time. Then you'll face the ocean, knock out your pushups (numbered based on what phase you are in), and go hit the *decon* to freshwater rinse all of your gear.

The main differences between the Bay Swims of BO and the Ocean Swims of the Phases are the length - all regular timed ocean swims are 2 nautical miles, the water temperature - you can count on the ocean to be notably colder than the bay, and waves - there aren't any waves in the bay, but the waves in the ocean can really throw off your guiding if you're not careful. On the upside most students find the longer swims easier because you're no longer climbing over your classmates in the water like salmon fighting upstream. The extra room afforded by the longer course (and the Pacific Ocean) gives each pair a lot more room to move.

The waves are a non-issue as long as you stay outside of where they break. If you're too close to the break, the waves will start to push you ashore. Not only will this throw off your guiding, but will force you to expend energy fighting the push. Avoid this waste of energy by keeping your line far enough offshore to avoid all but the biggest swells.

Your swim buddy is the most important factor in any swim. If he's not putting out or he's a slow swimmer or a bad guide, you'll fail your swim. If, on the other hand, he's a good swimmer and he can guide well, you can trade off guiding with him.

My swim buddy and I divided our swims into four parts and rotated for each. Because you aren't allowed to swim further from your buddy than 6 feet, you have to swim facing one another. The swimmer who is guiding (navigating, steering, whatever you want to call it) is usually half a body length in front and his partner is staring at his belt underwater to maintain his distance and speed. This works great, but it can get tiring to swim on the same side the whole way. The fastest, smartest swim pair switch sides at least once to increase their endurance. Halfway through the route north, I would switch from being closer to shore (and looking out to sea) to being further out to sea (but looking toward shore). When we hit the turnaround, we'd switch again. Halfway through the return leg we'd switch one final time. Not only did this system save our bodies from swimming on the same side the whole time, but rotated who was guiding - the man facing the shore would always guide. Guiding takes a lot more energy than simply holding on and matching your buddy's speed and heading, so it's good to switch off if both you and your swim buddy are capable.

In order to do well in these swims, you have to do well predictably. That means making sure your gear fits right. Your wet suit should be tight, but loose enough that it takes little effort to stretch your arms straight overhead. If they don't let you get streamlined easily, you need the next size up. A poor streamlined position will wear you out sooner, slow you down, and cause you to swim in big loops (instead of straight to the buoy). Your neoprene booties should fit snugly and the fins should fit snugly over them. If they're too loose or too tight, you'll get rubbed raw. Raw spots take a long time to heal when you can't "lay off" of them at all, your skin is constantly wet and sandy. Best avoid the situation altogether with properly fitting gear.

When you've got your fins adjusted right where you want them, be sure you tape the buckles and straps that hold them in position. A half-strip of rigger's (duct) tape wrapped around the buckle will ensure your fins don't loosen during a swim. Losing a fin during a swim will not only slow you down considerably, but also result in an amazing beating (sometimes of the entire class) as you spend hours in the surf "looking for that shitbag's lost gear."

If you have problems with the wetsuit chafing your armpits or between your thighs, you can either use a small film of petroleum jelly (Vaseline) or use a purpose-made product like Body Glide.

The main health problems guys get from swims are ear and skin infections. The water is polluted with sewage from Tijuana. Guys have found open hypodermic needles and full, used diapers on swims. That's how bad it can be. When guys start swimming with open chafing and cuts, the resulting infections (MRSA, staph infections, flesh-eating bacteria, etc) can get guys rolled. To decrease your chances of being rolled for any of these problems, hygiene and prevention are both important.

You're going to swim with open wounds/sores. It's a fact of life in BUD/S. But you can minimize your chances of infection by rinsing them off as soon as you get out of the water. When you're in the decon, be sure to rinse out your ears. Find a single stream of warm water coming out of the shower head and angle your head to flush out your ears. The idea is that you want to get every drop of sea/bay water out of your ears. At night in the shower wash your whole body, particularly any open wounds, with the Hibiclens soap they provide in the barracks showers. You'll also want to rinse out your ears again. This time use the hot shower water to loosen up all the particles stuck in your earwax. Once you feel they're pretty cleaned out, finish them up with a hydrogen peroxide rinse. The bubbling in your ear can feel a little odd, but the benefits are worth tickled eardrums.

If your instructors ever give you the option of swimming without a wetsuit hood, do not take it. They'll say that the water is really warm, so if your class can agree to swim without hoods, you'll be more comfortable.

It's a trick. Don't fall for it.

If you swim the 2 miles without a hood, you're probably going to get vertigo from the temperature differential between your surface and submerged ears. The swim will feel nice and your neck won't chafe and it'll be easy to guide, but the joy and novelty will wear off. After a few minutes, you'll feel like you're spinning around underwater. You'll start swimming in violent, drunken zigzags. And once you realize it's the temperature difference between your ears, you'll end up switching sides every other stroke, which will completely destroy your momentum. Or, better yet, you can make sure you always do the swims with hoods and you won't have to deal with the vertigo.

Passing swim times start at 95 minutes. By the time you're in Third Phase you'll be expected to swim the 2 nautical miles in under 75 minutes. At various points in BUD/S you'll also be expected to swim a few longer swims - maxing out at 5.5nm. This swim takes hours and you'll have PowerBars, etc at the halfway Mark. These swims, however, are pass/fail. If you finish, ever, then you pass. The only way to fail these longer swims is to drown or quit.

First Phase: Land Portage.

"Land Portage" is often referred to as "Boat on Heads" or "Holy Fuck, Boats on Fucking Heads" in student-speak. Land portage is a repeated and varied evolution in First Phase; in Hell Week, "boats on heads" is the only way you get anywhere. After Hell Week, unless your class seriously fucks up, your only exposure to the boats will be watching junior classes put them on their heads and being unspeakably, incandescently happy that it's not you under that boat anymore.

The boats are called IBS - Inflatable Boat, Small - and are designed to suck. They're not used for any other purpose in the military other than inflicting pain during First Phase. They're heavy, awkward, don't hold air well or long (nothing makes "boats on heads" worse than a limp boat), and they tend to fill up with water and sand, multiplying the weight crushing your skull and cervical vertebrae. The evolution itself involves traveling long distances on unsure footing and at great speeds with the boat on your head. Sometimes the evolution will weave back and forth, moving from knee-high surf to the beach to a soft-sand berm to sand moguls to a pillowy-soft sand path and back and forth for hours. Sometimes the evolution will be a dead sprint in the dead of night until a few students end up dead.

The shortest boats-on-heads evolution my class ever experienced was after Night Rock Portage. We were all formed up at the rocks waiting for the instructors to head back to the grinder to clean boats, when we saw two instructors take off sprinting to the south toward the BUD/S compound. The instructors in the trucks laughed as one leaned out the window and said in the violent monotone voice they love so well, "Catch them. You don't want to lose this one."

"Oh fuck" was on the lips of every student. It wasn't that easy though, because IBS are not maneuverable and we were lined up facing the water, meaning that only one boat had a clear shot at the beach to the south of the rocks. Every other boat would have to try to wheel around the boats to their south to pass them. The gap in the rocks was only wide enough for a boat crew or two to go through at a time, so it became a crushing mass of flailing BUD/S students with tangled legs and boats piling up like a train wreck. The profanity was deafening. After what seemed like minutes but was probably only 30 seconds, the boats broke through and flew after the instructors - who by now had opened up into a full-bore sprint and were rapidly gapping us.

Boat crews sprinted as fast as they could pull their slowest guys while instructors converged on them from all sides, materializing out of the darkness to scream and threaten. I could see instructors grabbing boat duckers out from beneath the IBS mid-stride, ripping them straight into the ground, where the guys behind them would trip over them and the whole boat would go down right on top of the tangled students. Shit always gets bad when the sun goes down. It was sheer chaos. It was dark, so I could barely even see the ground. The only lights were the distant buildings and the chemlites attached to each boat, so instructors seemed to materialize out of the black and disappear back into the black. I could see them flying to and from each boat, and occasionally we'd run past a wrecked boat on top of dazed students while an instructor was about to eat his boat-ducking prey alive. Instructors were leaping on top of boats like the Velociraptors in Jurassic Park - literally from the ground into the boats that were on the students' heads.

The race was pure, unadulterated chaos. The winners got off the beach immediately. The middle pack endured a few minutes of 'remediation'. The goon squad paid the man. But the guys who had it the worst were the guys who were ducking boat. The instructors knew who they were and you can be damn sure the class had already painted targets on their backs.

The moment the class catches wind that you're a boat ducker, you're done. You may even find yourself taken behind a sand berm with a few angry students while the instructors look the other way. We have no time for guys who don't do their part. Boat duckers, by definition, do not pull their own weight. When they don't pull it, someone else has to. The best guys in the class are going to pull as much weight as they can, all the time. If they have to pull too much weight (yours, for instance) too often, they get hurt. They get medically rolled and they get medically dropped. Ducking boat is a mortal sin of such gravity that you cannot truly understand how heinous a crime it is until you experience a boat ducker in your crew. Boat duckers go away. One way or another they go away.

As long as your class did a good height line, your boat crew will be made of similarly-sized guys, evenly distributing the weight of the boat among all 7 heads. 7 men is the ideal size, but sometimes crews will dwindle to 6 men. The positions under the boat are given numbers. The two guys in the front are in the "1" spot. The guys in the middle are in the "2" spot. The guys at the back are in the "3" spot. In a crew of 7, the boat crew leader (usually an officer, but not always) will be the coxswain position between the 3s. From this position he can see all the other positions and change guys out as they tire. Because the IBS bows under it's own weight (as it constantly deflates) and the weight of any sand and water in it, the 2 spot is the heaviest. Few guys can handle the 2 for more than a few moments without starting to duck boat, though, even if a guy says he can handle it, the coxswain would be smart to constantly rotate everyone through the 2 spot.

Ideally your 1s would be fast runners because they're really the source of speed for a boat crew. Not only do they put their heads under the boat, but they push forward constantly on the nylon webbing hand-holds, pulling the boat forward. The 2s would be the shortest, hardest guys (because that would most evenly distribute the force of a sagging boat. The 3s would be the most powerful, because they end up pushing the boat up each berm. The 3s would also be the tallest members of the boat crew because they're the last ones to get in the boat when you transition from the land to the ocean, meaning they can push the boat farther out before having to climb aboard.

But ideal only lasts a short while because the short guys can't be in the 2 spot the entire time. They would break in days or sooner. So everyone takes a turn at the 2 spot, coxswain included.

The boats-on-heads evolutions vary widely, from a few dark minutes to a few hours or the entirety of Hell Week. The paths taken, following an instructor, vary from hard-pack sand to soft berms to knee-deep water to sand so soft it's like quicksand. Regardless of terrain, boats on heads sucks and survival depends on whether you want it enough.

Finishing the evolution with the respect of your boat crew is more important than just finishing, and to do that you have to understand that everyone is in pain. You're not a special case. You don't hurt more than anyone else. You aren't the only one pulling your weight (probably). The weakest members of your boat crew will often be the only ones complaining that they can't go to the 2 spot because they did it yesterday. They also tend to think they're the only ones who are hurting. Guess what. Everyone runs the 2 and everyone hurts.

To minimize your pain, however, you can follow some basic guidelines.

Run smoothly. You can't run like you do on timed runs. With a boat on your head, your body simply can't bounce like that. You'll end up taking shorter, heel-toe rolling steps. Like you would if you wanted to run with a full cup of hot coffee or an egg resting on a spoon. Your steps will also have to be short because a regular stride would have you clipping the heels of the men in front of you and the shins of those behind. One too-long stride is all it takes to get your legs wrapped up and send your boat crashing down on your heads. Nothing calls for extra instructor love like a dropped boat. Your boat crew will hate you too. It sometimes helps to even synchronize your steps with the people in front of and behind you to allow longer strides, but it's not usually worth the extra effort.

You also want to ensure you get a good boat. A stiff/rigid boat is a good boat for both boats-on-heads and surf passage. The stiffer the better. That's what she said. Every boat can be pumped up well, but not every boat can hold its air for more than an hour or two. Nothing will fuck you faster than a flaccid boat. The additional awkwardness feels like it doubles your boat's weight. So get out there and find the stiffest boat you can when you're choosing boats. It will pay dividends.

The last thing you should do during boats-on-heads evolutions is call out the boat duckers. Nobody wants a boat ducker in his boat crew, BUD/S class, or SEAL platoon. Call them out violently. Hurt them if they don't go away on their own. If they're bad enough, get your class's E-6 mafia to take the boat ducker into the decontamination showers for a minute to convince them to perform or leave. If you really want to make a statement, kick that boat ducker out from under your boat mid-evolution. If you have 7, put 6 heads under and use violent force to keep that man out from under the boat. The instructors will immediately see he's been rejected and that man probably won't survive. Even if they make you put him back under, the statement will be made. Usually, though, they'll just make him carry the paddles. Running alongside a boat while carrying a stack of oars is harder than it looks and demoralizing beyond measure. If you really want a man gone, that's the way to do it. The instructors will sometimes force you to let him back in again and tell you never to kick him out again, but they'll note it. The next evolution where you have an opportunity, do the same thing again. Give the fucker the boot. When the instructors yell at you, just spit on the ground, look at the boat ducker with all the hate you have the right to feel toward him, and call him a "fucking boat ducker." There is no surer way to get rid of a guy.

Instructors don't want boat duckers any more than you do.

First Phase: Surf Passage.

Surf passage can be fun at times, but it's also a bit like playing Russian Roulette. Sometimes guys are unlucky and get hurt so badly through no fault of their own they get dropped. For that reason I was always somewhat serious about doing surf passage right: doing it wrong can get you or a member of your boat crew hurt.

Surf passage is, at its core, a simple evolution. Row your boat out past where the waves are breaking (known as *the surf zone*), empty your boat of any water by turning it upside-down and then righting it(called *dumping boat*), and return back through the surf zone to the beach, where you tidy your boat in a prescribed manner and stand at attention. Even if you're the first boat to hit the sand, you might lose the race if another boat can get its boat in order faster. Like every evolution in BUD/S, there are numerous ways to lose and only one way to win.

But surf passage is never that simple. Common additions to each race (and it's always a race) include movement on the water, movement on the land, exercises, and complications. A typical surf passage race might sound like this: "get out past the surf zone, dump boat, row north to the red truck, come in on the red truck, do two laps around the truck with the boat at extended arm, set the boat down, flip it upside down, carry it over the berm and back, paddle out past the surf zone with the boat upside down still, flip the boat back over, row south to the white truck, come in on the white truck, do boats-on-heads lunges back to the red truck, knock out 50 pushups each, square away your boat, and report to me. Bust 'em."

One of the most chaotic parts of this whole evolution is that these comedically complicated races aren't briefed to the whole class. An instructor whispers them to the boat crew leaders, who then sprint back to their boats and begin the race. Some races begin on land; some begin in the surf. Heads-up boat crew leaders will yell to their crews "surf!" or "land!" as they run back, so their crews can get ready and begin the race the moment they get to the boat. That only lasts so long, though, because the smartest boat crew leaders quickly realize that yelling completely negates any advantage they might have over other crews.

Remember, it's always a race. The smartest boat crews work out a code word for each. For example, if my boat crew hears me yell "Nighthawk!" they know to rig for sea; if I yell "Dragon!" they know to rig for land. But nobody else knows, so we have a 5 second head start. When the boats are lined up on the sand facing the ocean, but the race starts with carrying the boat north on the beach before entering the water, that 5 second advantage puts your boat crew at the front. Everyone has to fall in behind you and they have to go further than you do to enter the water.

Having a stiff boat is as important for surf passage as it is for land portage. The first time a wave folds your floppy boat in half as you paddle up it, you'll truly appreciate the value of a rigid boat. Not only will they crest much steeper waves, but they're faster on the water, easier to dump, tend to take on less water, easier to get out of the water, and much lighter to carry in foot races.

Once you've got your stiff boat, the next order of business should be allocating positions in the boat. During land portage you really do have to rotate constantly. Surf passage is different. You're rarely running more than a few minutes at a time, and having the same role every time makes your boat work better. For instance, dumping boat is a real bitch the first time you try to do it.

In order to dump boat, everyone exits the boat over the sides. The right side (make it the same side every time to increase speed as your crew gets proficient) grabs the handles of the opposite side and enters the water feet first, facing the boat, while holding on to the handles. Essentially their legs are hanging in the water and their waists bend over the pylon their side of the boat as they try to pull the left side over on top of them. At the same time, the crew from the left side is treading water and pushing that side of the boat up and out of the water, helping to flip the boat. The moment the boat's momentum starts to pull it over, the guys who were pushing up should hold on, allowing the flipping boat to pull them on top of it as it goes upside down. This dumps the water out from inside the boat. Then the guys on top of the upside down boat pull back toward them as the guys in the water push up, righting the boat. As the boat rights, the guys who were in the water use the momentum of the flipping boat to help pull themselves back in the boat, then quickly pull everyone else into the boat.

The process is complicated, but, if done correctly, can take less than 10 seconds. Done poorly, dumping boat can take minutes. A race can be won or lost by dumping boat well or poorly. Sticking in the same positions in the boat allows each man to get good at his roll. Timing the momentum of the boat to swing you back on top or back in can take practice, so staying consistent can be a huge help.

You can also make up a huge amount of time in transition from land to sea and from sea to land. The important thing when going to from land to sea is the order guys enter the boat. You'll all start pushing the boat out, but once the guys in front get to waist-deep water, they need to get in and start paddling. Then the twos get in, followed by the threes. The coxswain is last in and often needs to be pulled in after he gives the boat one last shove. The faster and more fluid your boat crew can do this, the more likely it is that your boat will remain straight, which is the key to staying in the boat when a wave hits. If your boat hits a wave straight-on, it will probably be fine. But if a wave catches your boat at an angle, you'll get pushed back into shore as the boat capsizes and launches your whole crew back into the water.

The transition from sea to land is no less important. When you get out of the water, it is important to dump boat on land. Even if some crews aren't, still do it. You never know how long you're going to be running on land (sometimes races change from surf passage to land portage mid-evolution) and you really don't want to carry an extra 100 lbs of water on your head if you don't have to. You'll notice that extra water on your third step in the soft sand. And every step after that third step you'll be cursing yourself for not dumping boat when you had the chance.

The key to good boat movement in the water is keeping the boat straight. If every rower puts out equally (that means no duckers), it's easy for the coxswain to keep the boat straight by steering with his oar hanging off the back of the boat like a rudder. If someone's not putting out and the coxswain has to fight to keep the boat straight, you're not only going to move slowly, but you're significantly more likely to be overturned in the surf zone. In order to crest a wave or surf the wave back onto shore, your boat must be completely straight. Any small amount of angle will cause your boat to spin out, ride up on the wave, and crush your soul in a swirl of boat, men, flying paddles, white surf, and undertow. This is made all the more difficult by the IBS itself, which was not made to go straight like a canoe or to be controllable like a whitewater raft. No, the IBS was designed to suck in the water. That's why they use them at BUD/S. These are not military craft and they're used nowhere else other than BUD/S. They're heavy, unwieldy, and slow. So keep them straight or you'll regret it.

The innately shitty character of the IBS makes teamwork all the more important. Rowing should be coordinated by the coxswain's calling "stroke, stroke, stroke," and rowers should put out as hard as they can while keeping with the cadence. It's the coxswain/boat crew leader's job to determine who the weak and strong rowers are and position them accordingly to balance out the power of the boat. And that rowing can't stop as you're nearing the peak of a wave about to crest. Many boat crews have suffered nasty wipeouts - many leading to drop-causing injuries - because they stopped rowing at the crest of the wave. They fight all the way to the top, but give up when two more strokes would've put them over the top. No doubt, it feels weird to lean forward in a near-vertical boat and keep rowing, but it's what has to be done to avoid that painful, spectacular wipeout the instructors love to see.

When (not if) you end up in a wipeout situation, do everything you can to keep control of your paddle. Not only will the instructors beat the crap out of you for every paddle that washes up on shore after your wipeout, but those stray paddles are the primary cause of injuries during surf passage. Also, be sure to keep your feet free from any cross-beams or crevices as you crest a wave. It's tempting to lock your feet in between the bottom of the boat and the pylons on the side, but if you do that and the boat turns upside down violently, you're going to break an ankle, snap a tibia, dislocate a knee, or at least sprain something. BUD/S is hard enough without having to deal with traumatic injuries.

Overall, however, surf passage is not as bad as either land portage or log pt. It's fun sometimes, and every time you're out on the water you're away from the instructors. They're still watching, but you can't hear them yelling at you - and sometimes in BUD/S that's enough.

First Phase: Rock Portage.

You can expect to do boats-on-heads a few times a week. The same for Log PT. And timed evolutions come regularly every week. But Rock Portage doesn't happen as often. Most classes will do rock portage once in the day and twice at night each during First Phase. Rock portage tests your ability to approach danger with aggression and precision. And it sucks, but in a fun way.

The evolution usually begins with a nice, relaxing paddle north from the BUD/S compound to the large stand of rocks on beach of the Hotel Del Coronado. Herein enters the most peculiar part of the evolution: because it's on a beach open to the public, you will have a large crowd gathered to watch. People love to see Navy SEAL training, and vacationers at the Hotel Del eat it up. Before the evolution starts, the Public Affairs Officer (PAO) for the Naval Special Warfare Center (NSWC), which is the training unit BUD/S falls under, will have the area directly around the rocks roped off to the public and he'll be there taking questions while you get your ass kicked. It's actually pretty rewarding to get your ass handed to you while people watch because they're all bundled up drinking coffee and shaking their heads thinking "I could never do that. Ever." And there you are: doing it. Now. The best people to watch are actually the 18-30 year-old men there with their girlfriends/ wives, because they'll be all puffed up to show that they're still men, despite the hundred superior specimens their girlfriends/

wives are watching. They may not even know they're doing it, but you'll see them puff. They wish they had the balls to be you.

Rock portage, at its base level, is the process of landing your IBS on the rocks, disembarking, and safely carrying the boat over the rocks. You start off in a boat pool offshore and try to get your quota of runs in (usually 3-4, depending on your class size) so you can rest longer after it's over. There are multiple instructors in the rocks, each with a lane he'll be calling boats into. You have to be prepared for when the run starts because if you're not ready, some other boat will jump in front of you and take your turn and you'll be behind the rest of the class. This is harder than it seems, though, because of your boat's proximity to the surf zone. You can't just easily sit in a good position because the waves will push you into the rocks before you're ready. And if you're too far out some enterprising boat crew will cut you off and take your run. Too close, you're out of a control; too far, you're out of the game. And you can't just hover on the brink by paddling in reverse either, because the signal that you're ready to go is raising all your oars in the air. If you're hovering right on the edge of the surf, the moment you raise your oars you get washed sideways in the surf and another boat crew will take your spot. That means you have to constantly be jockeying for position and fighting for runs by constantly moving and anticipating instructors and other boat crews alike.

Once you successfully start your run, your boat crew paddles as hard as it can and the coxswain steers the boat for the best spot in the instructor's lane to land. Usually the instructor will help guide. Rock portage is probably one of the most dangerous evolutions in BUD/S (except some of the stupid shit you end up doing on the Island), so it's important to be completely focused. Not that focus is usually an issue - 6-10ft waves crashing you into a large mound of sharp rocks usually focuses everyone pretty effectively.

When the boat slams into the rocks, the first man jumps out with the bowline - a rope attached to the bow of the boat - and scrambles as high into the rocks as he can, where he wraps the line around his waist and sits back putting the line under extreme tension and pulling it into the rocks. Because getting the bowline man out and set is so important and the rocks he'll be climbing over are slippery and sharp, it pays to choose an agile guy to perform this job.

Then the rest of the boat crew gets out, mindful of the sharp and slippery rocks as well as the incoming waves behind them. They lift and shove the boat as high and as far out of the water as they can, then the bowline man scrambles higher, sets himself, and the crew again hoists and shoves and grunts the boat higher. Because the bowline man is the only member of the crew looking toward this water, it's his job to yell "Water!" when a wave is about to hit the crew/boat. This gives the crew a fighting chance to brace themselves against the wave. Eventually the crew gets its boat up and over the rocks and onto the sand. When your boat reaches the sand, your instructor (who's been yelling at you the whole time) will tell you to rig for land (arrange the boat in a particular way, with the paddles secured inside it) and stand by for inspection. Then you get beat a bit, debriefed on how you did, beat a little more, and recycled back into the water for your next run.

The single biggest thing you can do to save yourself from getting hurt during Rock Portage is to make sure your body is *never, ever between the boat and the rocks*. At any point a wave can sneak up and slam the boat into the rocks it happens constantly. If you're in between them, you'll be in the ambulance headed for the emergency room. No questions. And you'll be dropped from BUD/S (at least rolled, but probably dropped - those waves aren't playing around and the boat is heavy and those rocks are hard).

In a similar vein, be careful of where you step. Your boots can easily get wedged between the rocks and you'll be helpless as a rogue wave sneaks up on you and cracks your tibia, sprains your ankle, or dislocates your knee. These things have all happened and will continue to. Just make sure they don't happen to you.

The larger lesson at work here in this evolution is situational awareness, or "SA" as your instructors will call it. Having good SA is one of the most important skills in a SEAL and you'll develop it at BUD/S through pain, both inflicted by your instructors and by your own stupidity. Rock portage is a particularly poor time to fuck up because you can get seriously hurt.

Also, there are lots of hot girls watching (sometimes in bikinis for the daytime rock portage) and you don't want to look like a fag in front of them, now do you?

First Phase: Log PT.

Aside from Hell Week, Log PT is probably the single most dreaded evolutions of all First Phase. The secret to Log PT's horror is the sheer variety of pain it can bring to the table in one evolution. You can be surf tortured holding the log at extended arm - that brings the pain of cold and the pain of static muscle fatigue. You can be made to do lunges for hours on end, which brings the pain of overheating, dire thirst, and extreme muscle fatigue. As the evolution goes on your skin gets rubbed raw by the sand picked up by the wet log. That sand not only rubs your skin off, but makes it harder to grip the log which in turn increases muscle fatigue. Other types of pain can include bludgeoning from a poorly-handled log and pain from ligament tears from pushing through extreme fatigue with poor form or posture. And let's not forget the pain of shame and defeat that gets everyone during Log PT. That's sometimes the worst - and certainly the type of pain that causes most Log PT quitters to ring that bell.

Log PT is composed of a number of different exercises. Many exercises involve moving from position to position on the instructor's count. For example, the eight-counts is an exercise that moves the log from the right-hand starting position (the log on the sand at your right feet with your hands on the log ready to lift it) to the right-hand shoulder position to extended arm (log straight overhead) to the left-hand shoulder position to the left-hand starting position and back. Each step has a number, with a total of eight. When a boat-crew has gone through all eight-counts, they yell the number they're on. 1-2-3-4-5-6-7-8. ONE! 1-2-3-4-5-6-7-8. TWO!

But the wonderful thing about eight-counts is that you'll never just go through all the numbers. An instructor can create untold pain by counting backwards (1-2-3-4-5-6-**5-4-3-2**-3-4-5-6-7-8), by alternating numbers back and forth (1-2-3-4-**3-4-3-4-3-4-3-4-3-4** - which would mean going from left-shoulder position to extended arm repeatedly), or simply stopping in the middle (1-2-3...) which leaves the log at extended arm, the most tiring position in which to carry a log).

Another position often used is the chest carry, where the boat crew stands shoulder to shoulder and carries the log like a bicep-curl with the log touching their chests. The chest carry rapidly deteriorates into the waist carry, which will be immediately and violently corrected. The majority of the time in chest carry involves the log slipping down to your waist, somebody counting to get everyone to lift it in unison, the lift, the moment where you try to rest it on your deltoids like you're doing a power clean, and the inevitable slide back to the waist carry. This position is used for races, where you run on the soft sand as a boat crew, and lunges, another favorite of instructors.

Lunges are a four-count affair. On "one" the right foot goes forward and you bend in the knees and drop your body until your left knee is just above the sand. On "two" your right foot steps back and you stand up. On "three" your left leg goes forward into the lunge. On "four" you return to standing. Lunges are one of the worst exercises under the log. Some classes get a very special evolution of Log PT. The classes call it "forever lunges." You do walking-lunges down the soft-sand running path for an hour straight. Then your boat crew gets to drink water, but only one person in the boat crew gets to drink at a time while the rest of the boat crew holds its log at extended arm. You're torn between extreme thirst and a strong desire to prevent your crew from having to carry your weight for you. At this turnaround point ("hydration and recovery stop") I blacked out and nearly went unconscious. I was the boat crew leader, but one of my boys noticed that I was incoherent and unresponsive, so he moved me off the heavy side of the log into the middle to recover my wits. If he hadn't noticed my sorry state, I probably would've collapsed under the log and brought the log down with me. (A side note - that heads-up boat crew member ended up being my stellar dive buddy in SQT and is now a great SEAL. Be that heads-up guy.)

After the "rest" the evolution turns back north. As always in BUD/S, the evolution is a race. If the boat crew in front of you is failing, with guys screaming at each other or guys collapsing on top of the log in exhaustion, you have to get around them. Staying up with the front group of logs is hard. It seems impossible, even. But the reward of finishing the evolution at the front is not being in the goon squad. And it's always easier to keep up than to catch up. After two hours straight lunging, you don't want to do a single extra chest-carry footrace around the O-course.

The footrace around the perimeter of the O-course is how most Log PT evolutions conclude. The winning crew puts its log away and the rest of the class does another race. This goes on until there are only a few crews left. They make something even more painful up for the goon squad, who often leave the beach wet and sandy and more than a little pissed off at each other.

One of the most ridiculous Log PTs I ever did (aside from the Forever Lunges) was in Hell Week. It was called the Circle of Death. The PT started off like a normal evolution of Log PT (except that it was 2 or 3 in the morning right after breakout), but quickly turned to a constant run over the berm (the large hill of sand between the O-course and the beach), around a truck, and back over the berm. Essentially we were running in a huge oval laid over an enormous hill of soft sand. We put out and, because we were constantly lapping every other boat crew, got a significant amount of rest. Because we were more rested, we continued to lap the boat crews who'd not gotten a rest more and more rapidly. The moral of the story is that it pays to be a winner, and once you have a winner's momentum, you have the advantage. Win early and win often.

The single most important key to success in Log PT evolutions (aside from the obvious "put out" and "don't be a pussy") is getting your boat crew to work in unison. If your whole crew is lunging together, you're carrying only a fraction of the weight of the log. A manageable fraction. If you're not working in unison, you're going to be lifting when other guys are resting. Then it's heavier. And then one side goes up faster than the other, which makes the whole log unsteady, which takes more energy to gain control of again. Move together and you'll find Log PT isn't nearly as bad as it can be.

Your crew should also be aware that not all logs are evenly balanced. Some of them are notably heavier on one side than the other. For that reason, rotate the weaker or more tired. It's better to rotate than to smoke a guy entirely, because there's no place on a log for a guy who's used up. Even if he carried more than his fair share for the first half of the evolution, if he's not able to recover during the evolution, your crew will suffer.

The corollary is also true: do not coddle the weak. If a guy is not pulling his weight, crush him. Guys who don't put out aren't obvious in a lot of evolutions; in Log PT they stick out as they lay on top of the log you're lifting. Kick their asses off your log. The moment they start to bend over the log and rest on it during the "down" portion of lunge, you'll be (literally) carrying their weight (and *them*). When you're struggling to get up, they'll be resting on the log and riding your strength back to standing. Fuck that. The moment you see that, kick that guy off your log it it'll lighten right up. It's the same as the "strap hanger" under an IBS, who's not only not carrying the boat, but actually adding to its weight as he uses the strap to hold himself up. Crush the weak. Eat them alive.

Ignore the instructors' taunts. If they call you out, they're probably watching someone else next to you fail and they're just trying to get you to question yourself. I did once. We were doing lunges and they were kicking my ass. I was putting out as hard as I fucking could. I was working so hard I couldn't breathe and the world was twirling. Three instructors swarmed me, yelling "You don't have what it takes to be a SEAL, sir!" and "Just quit now, sir, you can't cut it." And I wasn't cutting it. Obviously I was failing. Then I looked to my left and saw the problem.

The faggot foreign O next to me on the very end was laying on the log. He was bent over it and I was lifting his whole body. I held the log with one hand, kicked him off of the log with a boot to the side, and as he whined in the sand, the whole crew shifted down, the log got lighter, and the Instructors were sated. They had been calling me out, but the whole time were watching the crew carry the foreign O. They wanted to see what I'd do under pressure. (I figured it out.) They wanted to see what the foreign O would do. (He didn't give a shit.)

The instructors want to see you put out a maximum effort. They're looking for violent effort in the face of certain defeat. Be that guy. There used to be an award at the end of BUD/S called the "Fire in the Gut" award. They don't give it anymore, but pretend they do. Get it. Have that fire and success will follow.

First Phase: Epic Beatings.

The beatings you survive at BUD/S will become some of your best stories and, oddly, some of your most treasured memories. The beatings truly are the things that will separate you from other men. These (and the extended beating known as Hell Week) will harden you to physical pain. You will learn to endure misery that would cripple a regular man. Their violence will temper you and the world will never look the same.

Beatings occur on a regular basis, but they vary in severity. The most severe are referred to as a "Level 3" beating, or getting "jocked up" if you're in Second Phase. There was apparently a period of time where Instructors were required to get approval from the Commanding Officer of BUD/S in order to administer the fabled "Level 3" beating and this legend continues to this day. When you get to BUD/S it may or may not be the case - the rules that govern the Instructor Staff change every few years with each new Commanding Officer. But regardless of the rules the essence of BUD/S and the constituent parts of a beating have remained essentially consistent from Class 1 to Class 301.

In First Phase your physical evolutions are interspersed with academic courses involving everything from basic first aid, tide charts, and hydrographic reconnaissance to NSW History and camouflage techniques. The classes are always a tense affair because the instructors are constantly looking for a sign of weakness. You know that you'll do at least a hundred pushups each class and that it's likely as not that your class will end up hitting the surf. That means your whole class is put on a time limit to stream out one classroom door, hit the surf, and return to the seats. You rarely "make" the time limit even when you actually do, so hitting the surf usually involves a few trips. You expect this flavor of harassment from most every classroom instruction period, but sometimes things go way, way wrong.

During a class on NSW History a classmate of mine fell asleep sitting in his seat. It had been a long day, we'd had a long night the night before, the class was warm and the single instructor present had the lights low to use a Powerpoint presentation. He saw the student's head bob, stopped in his tracks, and screamed "EVERYBODY HIT THE FUCKING SURF! WET AND SANDY."

My class squeezed out the door and sprinted toward the ocean. We dove and flipped into the surf and, just as quickly, rolled to our feet and sprinted up and over the berm. From the top of the berm we dove down the side and rolled, scooping handfuls of sand onto our heads and into our faces to make sure there were no wet spots showing. Missing a single spot is an unforgivable transgression against the instructors at BUD/S. If you get sandy, you get all the way sandy. We screamed back into the class. The projector was off, there were four more instructors present, and the lights were all the way up. Two of the instructors were infamous for their violent beatings, Instructors Benjamin and Reyes. They were both there. That was not a good sign.

They were an effective team. Instructor Benjamin had a quiet, confident, calculating, evil way of never raising his voice. He practically whispered as he beat you. But he was without mercy. He was also the most widely respected of all the First Phase Instructors because he was hard, but not vindictive. He did his job with pride and excellence. Today his job was to hurt us. He proudly and calmly excelled at hurting us. Instructor Reyes was almost the polar opposite of Instructor Benjamin. Reyes was the most feared of all the Instructors because he had a short fuse and did everything violently. He was a tall, powerfully-framed terror. He screamed so hard that veins in his forehead bulged and sweat ran down his face. When he yelled at you he was so close and so forceful that the sweat would fly off his head and snap as it hit your face. This man was no joke. Between them, Benjamin and Reyes made a terrible combination of calculation and malice.

When we returned to the classroom covered in sand and everyone was standing at attention behind his chair, Instructor Benjamin whispered "drop." We dropped into pushup formation, someone counted the 20 pushups, the class called out Instructor Benjamin, and waited to be recovered.

"Gents, this is going to hurt. Some of you are going to break today. Within the hour, in fact," began Benjamin, "I'm afraid we've been too lax with you, too relaxed. You're not showing the proper sense of urgency. You lack attention to detail. You are disrespectful. We are going to cure you of these weaknesses. Recover. Move all the tables and chairs to the edges of the room."

Oh my god. I could see it in the eyes of the guys around me. Fear. Shell-shock. Anticipation. What were we about to do? Like cattle to the slaughter, we quickly cleared the room so we would have enough space to die. The tables and chairs were stacked along one side now and we began to line up to begin our beating. I swam through the mass of sandy bodies to take my place at the front. I wanted my boat crew to see that I was still there and doing whatever they told us to.

"WHAT THE FUCK IS THIS!?" screamed Instructor Reyes as he picked up a student by the shoulders of his blouse. "This motherfucker isn't properly sandy! Hit the fucking surf. You have 60 seconds. Don't be late."

And so it began. The beating continued for over two hours. We got wet, did 8-count body-builders for 10 minutes, got wet and sandy, did Egyptian pushups for 15 minutes, got wet, did pushups for 15 minutes, got wet and sandy, did mountain climbers, and carried on in that fashion for what felt an eternity. We tracked in water from the surf and sweat so profusely that the tile floor of the classroom grew a layer of slime on it. Instructor Reyes plugged up the sink in the classroom and overflowed the sink, adding to the pandemonium by further flooding the classroom. The air was so humid from our concerted efforts that it was raining from the ceiling tiles as men all around me yelled and gasped and collapsed. The overflowing floors began to smell of urine as guys lost control of their bladders and pissed in their pants as they collapsed. Students passed out and shit their pants. My hands were bleeding from the sand rubbing away skin on the backs of my hands where my head hit them during Egyptian pushups. Somebody was crying. More were whimpering. People were quitting - the bell was ringing right outside the door. The room was no longer a classroom. It was hell. Truly. But there were moments of clarity through the suck, there always are, where your consciousness ignores the pain for a moment and sees everything happening around you. There was a beauty of sorts in the professionally orchestrated chaos.

My buddy Jack, with whom I'd completed OCS, was next to me at one point. We looked at each other's misery and just laughed. There was nothing left to do. Then it struck me - we were at BUD/S. Finally. We were getting our asses beat in Navy SEAL training. So I turned back to him and said "Hey Jack, at least we're not at OCS right now!" And we both laughed because, despite the insanity and the pain, we wouldn't give up our spaces for the world. We had arrived.

And the Instructors could focus all our pain and frustration on whichever guy they wanted singled out by simply saying "we're starting over for Smith, now, because he can't do a single fucking pushup right." Instantly the beating seemed to be his fault. If only that guy would put out, the beating would stop! They could have named a guy who wasn't even in the class ("Starting over for Franklin Delano Roosevelt") and we would have hated him and wished he'd quit. We knew it wasn't true, but we were so beaten down that we had to believe in something and the world the instructors created seemed like the thing to believe in. So we hated that guy's guts until someone else got called out for being a pussy. "Same names" the Instructors would say, and teach us that we should fear the negative attention of our peers even more than the beating itself. Guys who got called out multiple times, "same names," were not long for our class. The class simply could not afford to extend every beating because that guy refused to simply put out. It didn't matter whether he was putting out or not. We still hated him.

The beating ended as all do, but I still wear the scars of that beating on the backs of my hands. I expect I'll wear those scars proudly until the day I die. Get some scars of your own and you'll know exactly what I mean and why I like to look at them from time to time.

Not all beatings, even bad ones, are created equal. The first day of Second Phase my class got a solid beating, but it didn't make us better. It simply made us hate the Instructors. The problem was that compared to the incredibly professional, well-oiled machine of the First Phase Instructor Staff, the Second Phase Instructors at that time were a joke. They were out of shape, all, and they accidentally showed their cards on the first day of Second Phase. We were on a run down the beach, an easy run because the Instructor was out of shape. He recognized that we were breezing while he was gasping, so he started to beat us. We crushed the beating. Nobody even looked tired after it. So, when we got back to the Second Phase grinder, he recruited the rest of the staff to show us we still weren't shit. He ran us back out to the beach, where we got another hour-long beating. But during the beating they would call out someone for the first time and yell "same names." They screamed at us and told us that our proctor had been working his ass off to help us figure out how to be a good BUD/S class, but that we were disrespectful and chose to ignore his advice. The thing was that our proctor hadn't even spoken to us yet. We didn't know his name or which one he was.

So we endured a beating of a different sort. The beatings in First Phase were BUD/S. This beating, where we ran footraces with our pants full (to bursting) with dozens of pounds of sand and our mouths, burning, full of seawater, just made us mad. They didn't even have the common courtesy to make up a semi-believable reason to beat us. They just beat us to beat us. And, though we simultaneously learned to hate them, we learned a lesson of BUD/S. Beatings happen. They're going to happen. Sometimes you cause them. In First Phase you always feel like you caused the beating by fucking up. But sometimes you, in reality, didn't. They're fucking scheduled. This beating, the first one of Second Phase, was scheduled. It wasn't the first scheduled beating we endured, but it was the first one that was obviously not caused by a fuck-up on our part.

But these 'bullshit' beatings teach the other side of the same coin: BUD/S is not fair. Suck it up anyways. It took me until my first deployment to really see that this is true, but BUD/S is intended to temper you for combat. And combat isn't fucking fair.

Sometimes beatings just happen. They may happen on the day before you graduate from BUD/S, even after you're back from San Clemente Island and you're just waiting to graduate the next morning. It happens. It's just BUD/S; beatings will continue until morale improves.

First Phase: Hell Week.

Hell Week is a 5 1/2 day man-maker evolution. The vast majority, but not all, of those who complete Hell Week will become Navy SEALs. Hell Week is also the most famous, well-known evolution in BUD/S. Your friends who don't understand what you've been through in First Phase will understand Hell Week. When you finish it, your family will know they underestimated you to some extent. Doesn't matter how highly they thought of you beforehand - there was always at least a sliver of doubt that you would be able to complete it.

The perception of Hell Week is that it's impossible. Only super-humans could do such a thing. 5 1/2 days of beatings with little-to-no sleep and a boat constantly on your head? Not possible. Hell Week is truly your opportunity to show the world, and yourself, that you're that superhuman who's capable of doing the impossible.

To introduce Hell Week I want to share something with you out of my personal collection. This is an email a buddy wrote to friends and family a few days after Hell Week. The moment he was secured he called his girlfriend (now wife) and parents, or so he's told told. He had no recollection of those phone calls just a few days later. And he didn't have the energy to have the same phone conversation with each and every one of his friends and cousins who wanted to hear about Hell Week. So he wrote this email for them. And now you can get an honest assessment of Hell Week from the freshly-brown-shirted now-SEAL who completed it a few days ago.

Hey guys,

I've had a lot of short-breathed conversations with you over the past few days about Hell Week, but I've just been too messed up to give any of you a decent picture of what it was really like. I'm going to be completely forthcoming about everything that happened last week, so prepare yourself for some pretty human details. There are plenty, and the story couldn't be honestly told without including them.

Also, know I'm not looking for sympathy or praise. I chose to do this knowing full well what it would/could entail, so don't feel like I'm looking for pity or applause. I'm sharing this with you only because you're the few of my friends who I think can genuinely appreciate this ridiculousness :-)

So I successfully finished Hell Week last Friday with my BUD/S class. We started with 134 and secured 42 - it was a strong class. I've heard from many seasoned bystanders that they really hammered us, so there won't be any controversies about having an 'easy' Hell Week (these questions have been raised a few times in the past). I'm glad there's no question there. But what does this mean to me now? Well, we've completed the "Selection" phase of the hardest training in the US military (arguably in the world.) We are all now overwhelmingly likely to become SEALs. Which is awesome.

So how do I feel? Like shit, really. You see, after being savagely abused for 5 1/2 days straight (no sleep, constant heinous beatings) your body is in such a state of disarray that it's hard to feel good. About anything. They call it Post-Hell-Week-Depression. It's not like you want to kill yourself, it's just that you're so messed up your body has higher priorities than to create any emotion-controlling hormones. You're mostly a zombie. And I'm just now coming out of zombieness.

By Wednesday my feet were so swollen I couldn't fit my boots on again (and yet, had no choice) and so I don't have feeling in any of my toes (or the outsides of my feet). The nerve damage takes anywhere from 2 weeks to 2 years to fully repair itself, but whatever. I'm definitely going to lose a good handful of my toenails. I've lost 15 pounds of muscle. I've got the skin of an AIDS patient. My legs and back burn when I stand for more than a minute or two. I shuffle like an 80-year-old when I walk. And I have no appetite: the only way I know I need to eat is when I start getting really cold for no reason.

I also contracted VGE (Viral gastroenteritis) - which is a blanket term around here for "massive, horrible stomach bug." Likely it's a vicious strain of E. Coli contracted during our second "surf immersion." (These sessions students call "surf torture.") I called this particular one "sewage immersion" because it happened to take place in a frigid plume of Tijuana sewage so thick (I'm not making this up) there were schools of fish flopping on the beach trying to get out of the water. The water literally smelled and tasted like an outhouse. And we were submerged there, with suppressed immune systems, for an hour.

And so I've been shitting myself a couple dozen times a day since Thursday night. Awesome. But more on that when I come to it. Let's start at the beginning of the week: Breakout.

Breakout is the start of Hell Week. It's engineered to create havoc, to simulate the chaos of a firefight. You start Hell Week sleeping on cots in these nasty-smelling, ill-ventilated tents outside the grinder (the main cement courtyard of the BUD/S Compound). They put you in when it's light out and you wait. And wait. And wait. This is the single worst part of Hell Week. The waiting. You never know when they're actually going to start breakout. Then, all of a sudden, a mortar goes off right outside your tent. The tent fills with smoke from the explosion. 50-cal machine guns start firing off into the night sky all around you and you're quite awake. This is breakout. Guys firing machine guns from the roof, smoke grenades, mortar simulators, flares, screaming, some guy with a fire hose aimed on you. It's something else. The chaos is such that they actually pad all vertical surfaces in/around the grinder with old life-vests, caution tape, and chemlites because people, in the confusion, will simply run into the walls. Yes, it really is that insane.

The moment I heard the mortar go off I rolled off my cot and under the side of the tent. Doors are for suckers I figured. I ducked outside and waited for my swim buddy. We ran outside and melded into the chaos of hitting the surf and running to the grinder to get beat. We, however, quickly realized that the instructors couldn't see anything through the chaos any better than we could, so we got our whole boat crew together and began running back and forth between the edge of the surf zone (not actually getting wet) and the edge of the grinder. We were always on our way to somewhere, but never quite got there. It worked out quite well for the 40-minutes breakout lasted.

Log PTs, beatings, surf tortures, and Boats-on-heads followed. Boats on heads is perhaps the single defining activity of Hell Week: you never go anywhere without an IBS (Inflatable Boat, Small) on your head. And it's not fun. You get hammered into the cement as the instructors push the pace constantly. If you fall back, you get lunges (knees all the way to the cement) and then the instructors push the boat until your neck breaks or someone collapses under the boat, causing it to capsize on your entire crew. One evolution, the "base tour," is nothing but a 6-hour, epic boat-on-heads trip. My boat crew, due to having 2 entirely pathetic members, got dead last in every leg of this evolution. No exaggeration. We were completely last every time. And each time meant hundreds of lunges. And each lunge meant a knee to the pavement with a 200 lb boat on my head pressing down. Let's just say we became pretty hardened to pain that night.

You even have a boat on your head going back and forth to meals - and if you don't put out you get beat pretty ridiculously. These beatings also take time you could've spent eating, so they're doubly cruel.

The week just keeps going on. And as you reach each meal, you're confronted with two opposing, but undeniable facts: one, you're one meal closer to finishing, and two, this shit keeps getting worse.

Thursday night was certainly my low point. You're going to love this.

The evolution is called the "Around the World Paddle." Essentially, you and your boat crew paddle your boat around the entire perimeter of Coronado Island in the middle of the night. It's cold, but you're away from the instructors. All sorts of people

associated with the program (SEALs themselves even) will swim
Ziploc bags of candy, Ensure, and even pizza (on surfboards) out
to your boat as you're paddling. Once you reach this evolution, it's
supposed to be downhill from there.

It was most certainly not the case for me.

The meal before Around-The-World I'd been unable to eat. I
simply couldn't get anything down. I forced down some rice and a
roll. Then we went boats-on-heads (for a change) to the launch
point and began paddling. Due to my (comparatively) sizable
whitewater rafting experience, I always took the coxswain's
position in the boat. The other six guys paddled and I used my
paddle as a rudder to steer and navigate. The moment we got
going I could feel it was going to be a long, long evolution. I
started throwing up violently off the back of the boat as I tried to
steer. Half the boat crew was falling asleep every 15-20 seconds
(we kept having to hit one dude with a paddle to wake him up). It
was freezing and the wind was picking up. It was dark, we were
delirious and disoriented, and the lights reflecting on the water
played with our heads.   Within the first hour we all had begun
hallucinating. I saw mermaids, swimmers who disappeared into
nothing, walls in the water. At one point I thought we were
paddling through a highway tunnel, and I swear we almost got hit
by a train once. Other boat crews thought they were being
pursued by Darth Vader, that their crew had all been replaced by
fat black ladies, or that there were midgets on a party-boat next to
them. By the time we reached the first checkpoint, a rock jetty, I
was seeing dismembered body parts mixed in with the rocks (300-
style)and I couldn't stand up. I was vomiting constantly and my
hip-flexors were so locked-up from shivering I couldn't stand. I
stumbled over to the medic, who promptly decided to probe me.

Yes. So I'm freezing my ass off, enduring phantasmagoric
hallucinations, vomiting my living guts out, with my hands and
forehead on the rear bumper of a god-damn chevy SUV while the
medic is violating my nether-regions as never before with a long,
long wire and metal probe. I'm getting the "silver bullet." He's
laughing at me and the other two medics there are drinking
steaming-hot beverages while telling jokes at my expense. I'm too
messed-up to care. I let my eyes focus once to my right, and what

do I see? The god-damn bell is no more than 4 feet from me, tethered to the back of a pickup. I looked at it and thought "now that's just messed up" and then looked back down and bit the bumper while I continued to be raped.

The night went on for much, much longer than makes a good telling, but you'll be amused to know that for whatever reason, likely his own entertainment, the medic decided to LEAVE the probe in my ass for the next few evolutions. So stay in my ass it did, collecting sand and creating a rather unfortunate chaffing situation. And, if that's not funny enough already, when it was removed, I discovered that the gentlemanly medic's installation of my beloved probe had been just rough enough to give me a large, prolapsing hemorrhoid. Good God I love Hell Week.

The last few meals I was in such a sorry state that they had to give me this "GI Cocktail" that paralyzes your throat muscles to prevent me from throwing up everything I put in me. And all I could get down was Boost (a version of Ensure), so I lived on a liquid diet the remainder of Hell Week. And then the other side of the VGE reared its ugly head early Friday morning: shitting like a faucet being turned on every 30 minutes. It's more than a full-time job to simply keep hydrated in pace with this sort of output. Throw in a touch of sleep and you lose the battle.

So this is the reason I've been so behind in responding to voicemails and texts: I've been pretty messed up and recovery is a full-time job :-)

I'm starting to feel almost human again today, but only because I had a 4L Saline drip this morning at medical... thank god for IVs.

That's not the entirety of the week... not in the slightest. But it should give you all a taste of how savage and miserable Hell Week actually is.

I tell you what though... I have never appreciated dry clothes, a warm bed, or decent food more in my life. Last week just made the rest of my weeks that much sweeter.

-Mark

Now I need you to know that, in many ways, Hell Week sounds worse than it is. There's a real exhilaration to being in Hell Week. Yes, it hurts. Yes, it sucks. But it's fucking Hell Week. If it hurts, the world is as it should be. And if you're in Hell Week, you've made it. There are a thousand ways you can be waylaid on your journey to this point, and if you're starting Hell Week you've doubtless made sacrifices and fought your way there. Now the only thing that can stop you is you. People complete Hell Week on stress fractures, with full-blown pneumonia, with broken ribs, pinched nerves, and concussions. If you want it badly enough you'll finish Hell Week, too. Regardless of what you have to fight through. When you get to Hell Week there is no going back. You have nothing to lose by giving it your everything.

And there's freedom in Hell Week in that you don't think much, not even about basics like self-preservation or physical stimuli. In that way Hell Week offers you more freedom than you've ever had. You're free from care about everything. You eat what you eat. You feel what you feel. You have no options to avoid pain. You have no option to choose how to save yourself. And because these things are inevitable they cease to matter.

When a man is contemplating suicide he may have a lot of cares and distractions. When he decides, finally, that he's going to do it and that he's dead already, he experiences a lightness of being - a freedom from the most basic cares. Psychologically, beginning Hell Week is similar to committing suicide, because the choosing has been done and all that remains is the act of Hell Week. And all you have to do is buckle down, do it, and not quit. And what other chance will you ever have to compete, balls-to-the-wall, for a week straight? I'm excited just thinking about it. You should be too.

Hell Week: Breakout.

Hell Week truly begins prior to Breakout. The week before Hell Week your class receives instructions to bring an extra pair of boots, an extra set of cammies, and an extra set of tri-shorts (black tights you wear under your cammies. These will be put in a plastic bucket with your name on it to change into after your regular medical check. Don't worry though, the clothes aren't often dry when you get to them. The instructors sometimes like to fill the buckets with water while you're getting dressed. But at least they won't be covered in sand. If they don't hose the clothes down in the bucket, you're sure to end up hitting the surf as you wait for the rest of your class to finish med checks anyways. You're never dry or warm for any length of time during Hell Week.

In addition to your extra clothes, you're required to bring a change of clothes (civilian clothes) and put it in a bag with your name to store in the classroom. When guys quit during Hell Week, they're required to spend 24 hours under watch to ensure they recover from their sleep deprivation, have access to medical care, and don't kill themselves. Quitting is an extremely emotional experience, as one can imagine, and it's common for quitters to experience strong, desperate feelings of regret within an hour of ringing out. When you put your bag with the rest of your class's bags and you realize that half the guys around you will be opening them before Hell Week is secured, the evolution very suddenly becomes real.

Breakout usually happens sometime Sunday night but varies from class to class in order to prevent any sort of predictability. The start times range from around 5pm Sunday to 5am Monday. But Hell Week starts, for you, Sunday at noon (or eleven), when your class enters lockdown. Before lockdown you are instructed to make your final phone call and get yourself ready. Once your class is locked down, you wait in the First Phase classroom. There's a DVD player hooked up to the projector. Guys bring movies and put them on. Blackhawk Down, Braveheart, 300: these are probably played during every lockdown. Guys are looking for courage and fire. Some people watch. Others play with handheld videogame systems. I'm sure iPads have taken over lockdown by now. Some guys try to sleep. Most are unsuccessful. I just felt like throwing up the entire time. I was gagging on my heart as it tried to throw itself out of my throat. I tried to read, but couldn't. I could see the words, but they never made it from my eyes to my brain.

Your lockdown time is spent trying to enjoy the movie but having, instead, to focus on your four-four-for-four breathing techniques. Remember arousal control? That's what you'll be doing. But you'll never master it because every SEAL over O-4 and every regular Navy officer over O-5 will want to talk to you. They try to impart some sort of knowledge. They try to pump you up. They try to encourage and cajole and inspire, but, in the end, only annoy.

By the time you've gotten yourself to the threshold of Hell Week, there's nothing anyone can say to help you. It's inside you now or it's not. You just have to harness it. And all these old windbags who come to talk to you are nothing but detrimental. So don't listen to them. Just concentrate on your breathing and visualizations and you'll find your time was much better spent.

Then the time comes to jock up. Really, this just means changing out of sweat pants, but it feels like more. It feels like you're preparing for war, like you're putting on your gear for an op. And you are.

Some guys coat their bodies in Vaseline in an attempt to protect their skin and minimize chafing. I did it. I honestly couldn't tell you if it helped. By the end of Hell Week I was so chaffed around my waist that every step burned as the sand and saltwater were ground deeper in the raw skin. But many, many guys were worse. The real downside to Vaseline, though, is that sand sticks to it. And you immediately feel gross. If you feel so inclined to use Vaseline before Hell Week, use it in moderation. I don't think I'd do it again.

The single best thing you can do before Hell Week is to buy longer tri-shorts. The tri-shorts (also called compression shorts) aren't allowed to go below your knee and they have to be solid black. These are the only rules. The more of your legs you can have covered by a solid, thick pair of tri-shorts, the better. The ones they issue are thin and only cover half your quad. Spend some money and buy two pairs of longer tri-shorts - ones that go right to your knee. The amount of chafing you can save yourself from sand-and-salt-infused cammie pants can really make a world of difference. The more skin you get to keep, the better, right?

After you're dressed you'll sit through some more briefs and words of wisdom from people who either did Hell Week 20 years ago or have never done it and just want to tell you how much they admire you. Either way, keep your mind on your breathing and visualization.

After your honored guests leave, the last thing before you head to the tents is a religious service. This, thank god, is optional. Skip it. The last thing you need is a distraction you're programmed to be open to. Save your praying, if you must pray, for after Hell Week. There's only one person who can get you through Hell Week. That's you. If you open yourself up for someone else, your dubious deity included, to affect your focus and internal dialogue, you're introducing another variable you can't control. Moreover, the supplication and surrender required for any honest prayer puts you in the wrong mindset. Hell Week requires aggression and fire and swagger and ego, not servility and humility.

If you want to be standing tall at the end of Hell Week, you let no one in. You have full control the entire time or you end up quitting.

Your wait in the tent will be the worst part of Hell Week unless you quit. The cots are uncomfortable and dirty. Mostly, though, you know that sooner or later you'll get the rudest wake-up of your life.

You'll hear footsteps outside, jump out of your cot, and poke your head out only to find it was somebody going to the bathroom or it was one of the brownshirt rollbacks (guys who will join your class immediately following Hell Week, used by instructors to do the majority of the grunt labor during Hell Week). I laid there trying to get a little rest but couldn't stop myself from shaking - my nerves were firing out of control. Some guys were snoring. Some guys were sitting up sharing hushed conversations. I imagine the majority were laying on the cots staring at the ceiling and hoping they would perform when the moment came.

In an instant the world crashed down. There was machine-gun fire. There were explosions and the sounds of artillery. The tent was full of smoke and instructors were swarming and screaming. Anticipation gave way to chaos and I understood why they had wrapped all the cement pillars around the grinder in old life-jackets. You really *could* run right into one of those things in the mayhem.

The rest of breakout went just like I wrote in my email home. The chaos is a double-edged blade and the instructors have no way of keeping track of one boat crew. You can't even see well enough through all the smoke and the flash of explosions and the firehouses and the dark of night to recognize faces. If you run to the edge of the water but don't go in and an instructor calls you on it, how does he know another instructor didn't tell you to go "touch the surf, but do not get wet"? He doesn't.

Some guys might call this cheating, they might tell you that you're not getting the "full benefit" of BUD/S. Fuck that. BUD/S is war. Win every small battle you can because, after all, you lose most of them. And what are they going to do to you? Make you stay up 5 1/2 days and beat you the whole time? Oh. Wait. You're already doing that.

After breakout usually comes a Log PT and a surf torture. The rest of the Hell Week schedule varies widely from class to class and year to year, so the remainder of this Hell Week section will mention some of the more prominent evolutions you'll likely experience during the week.

Hell Week: Base Tour.

Base Tour is the first really painful Hell-Week-only evolution. Breakout is more fun than painful and you've done both Log PT and surf torture before. What you haven't done is race, with boats-on-heads (as always in Hell Week), around the entire bay-side base of NAB Coronado, for hours upon hours.

Base Tour is a simple evolution, but epic in length and heavy on pain. The race is broken up into countless legs or sections where you sprint after the instructors with the boat on your head. The last few boat crews get beat. The first-place boat crew sometimes gets to sit down. Often the last boat crew is the same one repeatedly.

During my base tour my boat crew had one guy with stress fractures, a brain-dead faggot who was performance-dropped immediately after Hell Week, and a foreign officer. We lost every single leg of Base Tour. The last half of the evolution we were falling so far back from the rest of the class (because we'd gotten beat at every stop up to that point) that they started making us lunge to the end. We did thousands upon thousands of lunges that night. Our knees were raw and bloody and holes wore through our cammie pants. My kneecaps felt like someone had taken a sledgehammer to them.

At various points during the evolution - which quickly became a blur - the entire class ended up at a boat ramp into the San Diego Bay. We left our boats, a momentary relief before the suck of the next thing registered, and entered the water. One good thing about Base Tour is that you aren't cold - you're putting out too hard. These boat-ramp stops are the instructors' answer to your single comfort.

When the whole class was in the water, an instructor came down and, as he spit his Copenhagen into an empty Red Bull can, yell at the class to "Hide the Grape!" Where that phrase came from, I'll never know. What it meant, however, was that on his count the entire class was to submerge for a set period of time. If we all stayed under, we would be relieved from the water. That never happened though, because you are required to wear bright orange K-pac life-vests that keep you on the surface. To make matters worse, you have to fall backwards into the water with your nose being the last body part to go under and the first to come up after the time limit. The life vest holds you above the water, keeping your nose right around the surface forcing bay water down your nose and throat and into your lungs as you struggle in vain to stay under. When you finally give up and surface guys all around you will be vomiting up seawater and the instructors laughing.

"Well, that wasn't good enough. Again. Hide the grape."

Eventually you get pulled out of the water, put back under the boats, and it's races again. Hour upon endless hour sees you under that god damned boat, racing until daylight comes and you find yourself on Turner Field, the grassy field in the middle of NAB Coronado, where you do boat crew relay races until breakfast. Relays include low-crawling with your boat around an instructor and back. Losers pay, winners are secured, and cheaters get to do the next race with a person in their boat. Amusingly enough, the brain-dead strap-hanger I mentioned above fell asleep during a low-crawl race. We were crawling and heaving the boat on my count and suddenly the boat wouldn't budge. I crawled to the back, where I found him fast asleep holding the rope. Not only was he not contributing, but he was so bad he was *literally* holding us back. Needless to say we're all glad he got dropped, but we would've had an easier time in Hell Week if he'd been dropped sooner.

Hell Week: Chow.

If you're smart you'll use chow as your only metric for how far you are in Hell Week. You'll eat four meals a day and nothing else matters. If you're smart your energy will be focused on no more than getting to your next meal. Looking further than a single meal has broken countless spirits. Meals are your time to refuel, regroup, and sit. From the moment you step out that door into the cold night (it's nighttime all day in Hell Week, it seems) your focus is on getting to your next meal.

You won't know when your next meal is due because you can't wear a watch in Hell Week. Not that you'd want to. Not only would a watch hold sand against your skin and grind your skin away, but the constant reminder of how much time you have left would be impossibly demoralizing. It would be doubly hard to endure the suffering of Hell Week if you had a concept of time after Tuesday.

The only way you know a meal is coming is that you begin a long boats-on-heads trip toward the chow hall. After you've done it a few times you'll begin to pick up on the route the instructors like to lead the boat crews through. The trip quickly becomes desperate as the instructor out front breaks into a shuffle (though it feels like an all-out sprint) and begins to gap the train of boats. You know that if there's a space between you and the crew in front of you you're going to spend extra time getting your dicks kicked in while they eat. This is the way every evolution goes, but the fact that it involves as primal a need as food, and as valuable a commodity as an opportunity to sit unmolested for 30 minutes makes whole boat crews throw themselves across the finish line without regard for the painful crash into the parking lot asphalt.

After the sprint to the chow hall come more games. Sometimes these involve 1-on-1 boat races in impossibly small circles - guaranteeing collisions. Sometimes these involve pushup form. Sometimes these involve trivia, the neatness of your IBS, or whose boat crew can yell the loudest. They are contested with clenched fists and blood pounding. It fucking pays to be a winner. Especially when it comes to eating.

One boat crew is sent into the chow hall at a time. As they run in (anything other than a dead sprint will get a boat crew called back out to keep playing games), they scrub the sand off their hands in a hose held by a brownshirt and run inside. The rest of the class waits until the hose is free, then another boat crew is relieved. Waiting means getting beat. The best case scenario is waiting in the leaning rest with your feet on the boat, the wooden oars on top of your hands, and the constant jostling of your boat crew members grinding asphalt into your water-softened hands.

It has been observed in book after book that those who eat more tend to perform better throughout the week, whereas the guys who just pick at their food tend to taper off toward the end of the week.

It's true, so eat a lot. You often won't be hungry, despite the number of calories you're burning. At first you won't eat because of your nerves. Then you won't eat because you're tired. Then you won't eat because your mind is no longer listening to your body's needs (food, sleep, and safety are out of your control during Hell Week). Then you won't eat because you're getting ill and it's hard to keep your food down.

In each of these situations it's important to ignore your desires and shovel as much food down as you can possibly hold. Eating substantial amounts of food is the best way to stay healthy and strong and warm (relatively). Without calories to burn your body will be unable to stave off the constant cold (or heat, depending). If you can't make yourself care about strong or healthy in Hell Week, I guarantee you'll still care about being warm(er). So eat as much as you can. It's the best thing you can do for yourself.

Avoid spicy foods. This seems like a common-sense idea, but sometimes the galley will give you food with too much spice in it. Your hell-ridden body can't handle it and you'll just get sick to your stomach.

The best standby for a calorie-rich food that you should eat in large quantities all week is peanut butter. For some reason our class wasn't allowed to eat peanut butter for the first three days because they instructors were worried it might make us sick - that it's too rich. Yet they thought cayenne pepper-sprinkled fish was an acceptable menu item. Fuck that. Get that peanut butter as soon as you can get away with it.

Throughout your Hell Week meals brownshirts will be circulating to check on you. They'll refill your water and urge you to drink as much of it as you can: "drink up...it'll keep you warm." Somehow these words change water to magically-imbued wine, and you believe and chug and ask for another until you feel yourself filling up into your throat.

By this time the final minutes of your lunch approach and spirits waver. One minute you might be congratulating yourself for making it to yet another chow, the next you might be fighting off anxious nerves. Take a moment to breathe and reset your goal-clock to the next meal before you push yourself out that door to take up your boat again.

Look around and see how many other guys have quit.

And you're still there.

If you're frogman material, that alone will help you get to the next chow.

Hell Week: Two-Mile Repeats.

Hell Week's two-mile repeats are yet another example of why a solid base of running mileage is so important to have under your shoe before BUD/S. The evolution is simple: run a mile down the beach and back under a time limit. If you make it, you stand. If you don't, you get beat. Repeat.

This evolution generated the most DORs of any in my Hell Week. The class lost close to 20 in a few hours. The part that got me was that, though this evolution was rigged, it was probably one of the easiest, most comfortable evolutions the entire week.

On the first iteration we were given what I thought was a pretty reasonable time limit, and, having run track in college I knew I could beat the time and I knew the pace to run. When I completed the two miles, I got my ass handed to me for missing the time limit. I can tell what pace I'm running to within 5 seconds over a mile. I came in over 60 seconds under the time limit. That moment I realized the evolution was rigged. It's BUD/S, so you expect that sort of mind game. It's Hell Week, so you expect they're going to pull out all the stops to fuck you up in the head. They were. Everybody was a loser even if they weren't.

Knowing the evolution was a farce, I took a decidedly different tack on the second leg. I was going to shuffle just out of range of the regular good squad. If they had a goon squad this leg, I'd be out of it. But I didn't go any faster than I had to to avoid being in that last group. I shuffled (almost walked) and got a little rest. By the time I finished this second leg I was feeling decently rested and ready for the beating. Then I realized another benefit of being slow here: all the guys who finished before me (except the top three finishers) were waiting in the leaning rest (pushup position) or getting beat already. Not only was I resting on my feet, but I was avoiding extra beatings. Sure, I could all-out sprint and try to be in the top three (who got to sit down and relax), but BUD/S and Hell Week are not sprints, they're marathons. I would be better off in the scheme of things not grinding myself into the ground for a few minutes' rest.

Winning wasn't worth it. And coming close was worse than coming close to last. So I subdued the competitive urges years of footraces had taught me and I sandbagged. It seemed cheap, but it was too smart not to do. Why be harder than you have to? Be hard when you must, be smart when you can.

Apparently 20-odd guys in my class let this fixed race beat them. The house always wins. Know that the fix is in, that you have no chance of winning, and play the game. It does not last forever.

Hell Week: Wetsuit Appreciation.

BUD/S Instructors have a cruel sense of humor. If you recall the sadistically-named Mask Appreciation, you might guess that Wetsuit Appreciation is a euphemism in a similar vein. You'd be right.

Wetsuit Appreciation is a game-changer for a lot of guys. The moments before this evolution mark the last time I felt warm for the entirety of Hell Week (and the following weeks, for that matter). The evolution, like most every BUD/S evolution, is simple. Take off your cammies on the beach. Wearing only your UDT shorts (short khaki swim-trunks), a t-shirt, fins, a mask, and your inflatable UDT life vest, you will swim out through the surf zone to an instructor on a jet ski. When you reach him, you'll tread water and "hide the grape" some more before swimming back to the shore. On the shore the instructors pretend like you're about to be secured before sending you back out to the jet ski (which has changed position). When you reach the jet ski you'll tread more water until you're sent back to the shore.

This all seems simple until you realize that your already-weakened body has lost a great deal of its power to regulate temperatures and the water is often in the low 50s. Extended exposure to water this cold in the best of circumstances is bad enough. By the time we were swimming back my body was entirely numb and unresponsive below the waist. My hip flexors were so smoked from days of constant strain and shivering that the effort of kicking combined with the freezing water was the end of them. I swam back to shore the final time using only my arms. When I reached the sand my swim buddy had to help me to my feet. Every single man was so numb and frozen that his buddy had to undo his UDT vest for him - we simply lacked the dexterity to take our own gear off. And we each had to take off our swim buddy's belt for him too, too. It looked gay, almost certainly. But it was the only way. BUD/S feels gay sometimes. Get used to the idea.

Hell Week: Naptime.

There are a few opportunities in every Hell Week to catch a few minutes of sleep. Sometimes these moments are under an overturned IBS, with a spot dug into the sand. Most Hell Weeks give you at least one opportunity to sleep in the same tents you waited for Break Out in. The sum total of all the sleep you'll be able to get in the 5 1/2 days usually hovers between 1 and 3 hours.

During my Hell Week the nap-under-the-boat time turned, within a matter of minutes, into a sadistic relay race. One person at a time from each boat crew would have to run to the surf, get wet and sandy, and then dive back under the boat. Then the next guy would go. Between your turns, you were "free to sleep as much as you want." A fucking joke that was. I honestly can't say whether we thought it was funny at the time - I'm not sure that, at the point, any of us were 'with it' enough to think about anything other than following the instructions. We definitely didn't sleep though. That much I know.

The only true sleep period we got was in the tents. They wouldn't tell us how long we had. It could be 20 minutes or 5 hours they said. Essentially we were going to go through Break Out again. But the sleep we were going to be woken from was going to be so much deeper that the wakeup would feel catastrophic.

I decided not to sleep. I was just going to sit on my cot and wait. I was numb. If I could hold onto the numbness I knew it would be notably easier to deal with whatever sick wakeup call they had waiting for us. If I fell asleep the shock of the wakeup would be more damaging than not sleeping at all.

So I sat. After an hour or so I decided to lay down to relax my back. I hovered on the edge of relaxation, but was resolved not to let down my guard. After another hour I took four deep breaths and let myself begin to drift off. Not two minutes later Instructors burst into the tent blowing whistles, playing the siren on the bullhorn, and screaming. Everyone shot straight up, white-faced and confused. I had fallen asleep - just for a few minutes - but the damage was done. I was groggy. I was disoriented. I felt sick to my stomach. I had a headache. I was dizzy. I couldn't figure out what was going on. Fuck my life.

They made us low-crawl - that's bellies on the ground, dragging your body across the cement - to the berm, over the top, and right into the surf zone. Then we did whistle drills (crawl toward the double whistle blasts, walk toward the triple whistle blasts), which means the instructors walked up and down the surf zone and we low-crawled in the water for over an hour.

That wakeup was so traumatic that just thinking about it still causes my blood pressure to rise and my pulse to quicken. If only I'd held out for a few more minutes. That wakeup wasn't worth two hours of sleep. There's plenty of time to sleep after Hell Week's over. If I could do it again, I'd try harder to stay up the whole time.

Sleep if you must, but be aware that you're giving the instructors an opportunity to prey on you while you're on your heels. By the time your sleep period comes around your body will need sleep so badly that you can't help but fall into a coma-like stupor if you actually fall asleep. Being woken from so deep a sleep is, by nature, disorienting. Being woken Hell Week-style from so deep a sleep is a horrendous experience.

The other fact to consider is that, despite your having been up for days on end, it may be extremely difficult to actually FALL asleep. It seems ridiculous, but you've not allowed yourself to sleep for days. And your subconscious mind knows it's not out of danger - you're still in Hell Week - so sometimes guys will spend the entire rest period trying to sleep, unable to get any rest until the last few minutes. This changes the cost-benefit equation drastically in favor of the Instructors.

The deck's loaded in their favor. Simply not sleeping will help you keep what edge you have remaining. If you're awake, you cannot be surprised. Always expect the worst. Always. But if you're asleep, everything is a surprise.

Hell Week: Drag Races.

Despite the appearance of chaos, Hell Week is surprisingly choreographed. Before you and your class break out, every minute of every evolution for every day of Hell Week has been planned and briefed. There are safety briefs with the instructor staff (that the Hell Week class is, of course neither privy to nor aware of). Your Hell Week is predetermined and stringently controlled.

Sometimes a class ends up ahead of schedule. Sometimes the Instructor staff is behind schedule. Gaps form in the schedule and the Instructors have to fill them. There's a certain point after a day or two of Hell Week where they really have to be careful because, after that point, students no longer think about their physical state. It would be easy for an Instructor to beat a class unconscious; the class would do what it was told until told not to. An instructor could easily tell a student to do something suicidal and he would do it.

On the other hand, there can't be any real rest periods in Hell Week because guys would fall asleep immediately and Hell Week wouldn't be Hell Week without the constant motion and physical exertion.

A favorite filler that strikes the balance between killing a class and allowing them to rest is the drag race. Drag races are exactly what you think they are: a short, straight footrace with, naturally, boats on heads. The races are rarely longer than 50 m, take place on the beach, and involve 2-4 boat crews running at once.

The boats line up and the impatient crews start to jostle each other and prance sideways like racehorses jockeying for position. The instructors scream "bust 'em!" and the boat crews churn up the sand and bounce off one another and swear and sweat and strain as they sprint across the finish line. The moment they finish they line up again and try to strategically position themselves to either maximize rest time or match up against a weaker boat crew.

Winning boat crews often find it's easiest to go out hard and cut other boat crews off. There's no rule against it and it pays to be a winner. The races aren't long enough for a boat crew to go around another boat and win, so cutting your opponents off is a good strategy. Often the class will do a few iterations of the drag races where it doesn't "pay to be a winner," and then boat crews will either get a rest period off to the side or be allowed to leave the beach and move on to the next evolution.

During long bouts of drag races winning boat crews will be rotated in and out of rest. Instructors will send good crews to sit on the sidelines and then, when they remember they're there, pull them back into the fray.

When your class is doing night drag races, particularly during the chaos of Hell Week, you can take advantage of this. When there's nobody really paying attention, just move your boat crew to the rest area. If an instructor asks why you're going there, imply that you were told to go there.

"Who told you you could join the winners?"

"I don't know Instructor Smith, we're supposed to go over here, so we did."

"You don't know who it was?"

"I think it was...shit, who was it? I'm not sure. He yelled that the winners of that race should go take a break."

"Just fucking go before I change my mind."

"Hooyah."

In the grand scheme of BUD/S evolutions, Drag Races aren't very hard and they can be pretty fun. Races are races, and these aren't that long or complicated. They also afford a decent opportunity to get a little rest, both between races and if you win a few.

They also tend to have hilarious-looking boat-crashes where guys trip over the legs of their teammates, fall, and the boat takes a spectacular rolling dive, flattening the entire crew and - if you're lucky - another boat too. These crashes rarely result in injuries, but never fail to amuse.

All told, drag races will be a welcome diversion from the rest of Hell Week.

Hell Week: Med Checks.

Despite their insistence that they hate you and feel you're entirely unworthy to be a SEAL, the instructors care a great deal about your wellbeing. Not only are they constantly taking notes on your performance and health, but they require you to be checked out at BUD/S medical every day during Hell Week to ensure you're not concealing a serious injury, that you're still mentally aware, and to give you an opportunity to clean out chafing and wounds to prevent staph infections/MRSA.

Med Checks are usually conducted after a meal. The class runs, like usual, from chow to the sand berm outside the grinder. This is one of the boats-on-heads runs that it really, really pays to be a winner. So if you think you might be headed to Med Checks, fucking book it. If you're one of the first few boat crews, you get to immediately down your boat and head in. If you're not, you get to do extended arm boat lunges and other lovely exercises. Then you'll probably get to set your boat down and hit the surf repeatedly until it's your turn to go in.

When you leave the berm, you strip down to your tri-shorts and put your uniform, shirt, and socks into a 5-gallon bucket with your name on it. Then you grab a pre-soaped scrub brush and get into the decontamination shower. The water in the decon shower is cold, but by the end of Hell Week you're so cold that it feels amazingly warm. You have a few seconds to a minute to scrub up and clean yourself. Take advantage of the time and clean out all of your open wounds. It hurts to scrub out your chafing, but if you don't get the sand and bacteria out you'll end up getting rolled for a staph infection or worse.

After your shower you'll run over to the medical building and stand in line shivering - but happy because you're not getting beat - as you wait to get checked by the doctors. The doctors ask you a few questions and do a cursory check to make sure there's nothing terribly wrong with you. They also watch you walk to make sure you're not guarding an injury. Then you head outside to a picnic table where corpsmen patch up any hotspots and coat your feet in anti-fungal/anti-bacterial goo - just enjoy the 3-second foot massages - before you put your socks on.

It's an odd experience talking to the doctors and corpsmen during Hell Week because you forget that you're a human and forget that people don't always want to kill you. Their civility combined with the fact that you've dried off and you're not getting beat makes Med Checks feel awesome.

After you're done you've got to run down to the instructors and get a new (clean) uniform on. If you're lucky, your uniform is dry. If you're really lucky, some brown shirt rollback has stuffed a Snickers bar in your pocket. You'll get changed quickly because there is an instructor right there with a hose that he turns on anyone he's displeased with. If you take too long or look stupid, you'll probably end up getting hosed down while you dress. If the instructor doesn't like you, your bucket of clothes was already filled with water before you got there.

Once you're dressed, you check in and get inspected by the instructor with the hose. If your uniform and boots are wrong, you get soaked before you head back to your boat. When you get back to your boat, you get to stand next to it. This is an unbelievable luxury - to be dry and still - but it comes with teeth: your whole boat crew has to stay awake. You'll stand there shaking your head and punching your forehead and you'll still fall asleep. Or, more likely, somebody else in your boat crew will fall asleep. His head will dip, his chin will hit his chest, and the instructor watching you will 'help' by sending you to take an 'invigorating dip' in the ocean. You've done well if you're dry for five minutes, but just standing by your boat dripping wet is still pretty nice.

After the entire class is done, you'll all go hit the surf, fall in on your boats, and run to the next evolution. This is another reason why it's good to be in the first boat crews to get Med Checks. Not only will you not get beat, but you get a longer rest AFTER the fact. And PART of that rest is even dry. That is not a reward to snub.

Despite the relative pleasantness of the medical check evolution, it results in a lot of rolls and drops. In fact a great number of guys use the medical check as a reason to quit without technically 'quitting.' The stark contrast between the violence of Hell Week and womb-like warmth and peace of Med Checks makes guys reconsider their commitment to completing training. There's a certain point in Hell Week where you are so messed up that you could easily get medically rolled. Everyone is messed up. By Wednesday night I could not keep any food down, I was shitting my pants, and I even shat out part of my intestines. There is no question that, had I complained, I could have gotten medically pulled from training. If I didn't have the balls to quit but didn't want to be there anymore, all I had to do was say something.

By the end of Hell Week every man is hiding something worthy of a roll. The difference between the guys who make it and the guys who get perpetually rolled is what we say, not how 'broken' we are. The guys who genuinely want to stay don't say anything about their problems. Eventually the medical staff realized I couldn't keep any food down and they gave me a "GI Cocktail," which paralyzed my peristaltic muscles - preventing me from being ABLE to throw up. My stomach constantly churned like I was throwing up. I felt like I was. But nothing ever made it up. My throat wouldn't allow it. And they fed me with Boost, which is like an off-brand formula of Ensure. I never asked for this; they saw my condition and helped.

Had I gone to the medical staff and complained of all my problems, I guarantee I could've gotten rolled. Other guys had pneumonia (to the point that they had to be hospitalized after Hell Week) but they never said a thing. They dealt with the problem because they wanted to finish Hell Week. When the medical staff asked how they were feeling, they'd say "I'm fucking great."

Other guys were different. When the medical staff asked them, they'd respond with a list of complaints. Once these guys allowed themselves one small complaint, it was only a matter of time before they were listing everything not quite right. And this acknowledgment that they were hurting made everything seem worse to them, which made them increasingly more likely to notice all the little things. This takes you out of the game. Don't be that guy unless you want to quit, because they'll offer you a roll if your list gets long enough. Shin splints/stress fractures are an extremely common complaint and there's no real way to verify them with certainty. So if you complain about your leg pain enough, they'll assume you've got them and roll you. And you will have done that to yourself.

The longer you stay at BUD/S, the lower the likelihood you'll complete it. A good number of guys in every class will use medical rolls and medical drops to get themselves out of BUD/S for good. Some of them, I'm sure, realize they're quitting without "quitting." Others might not realize this is what they're doing. A 'voluntary' or 'assisted' med drop shows up on FaceBook as a Med Drop ("I can't believe I broke my legs and now I can't be a Navy SEAL.") The FaceBook posts often fail to mention that there were two dozen guys worse off who managed to stay in the program. It's a large grey area that you can, consciously or subconsciously, influence the result of.

There are hundreds of ailments I know guys have covered up in order to complete Hell Week. Here's a small list:
- Pneumonia
- E. Coli
- Viral Gastroenteritis (VGE)
- Prolapsed Rectum
- Fever
- Diarrhea
- Concussion
- Broken Fingers
- Stress Fractures

- Shin Splints
- Broken toes
- Sprains (ankles, wrists, knees)
- Broken Ribs
- Influenza (including the Bird Flu)

There are very few things (compound fractures, broken backs) that you cannot complete Hell Week with. That being said, I'm not recommending you don't seek medical attention if you need it.

I am, however, saying that you might want to reexamine your personal definition of the word "need."

Hell Week: Camp Surf.

Camp Surf, a hallmark evolution of Hell Week, usually takes place on Wednesday night. It begins with a long southward paddle in the Pacific as the sun sets to the right and the beach on the left disappears in the dark. By the time the boat crews reach the instructor staff's trucks, they're only recognizable as headlights on the shore. The boat crews paddle in and, depending on what order they arrived in, sit, stand, or get beat until the entire class gets there.

Next, the class forms up on the top of the berm with paddles in hand and either digs a hole or builds a mountain depending on what the previous Hell Week class did. If the class before you dug a huge hole, you might have to fill in the huge hole and build a mountain. If the previous class built a mountain - you guessed it - you'll likely have to dig out the mountain and replace it with a large hole.

The evolution is not results-based. If your class digs a hole to the required specifications with hours and hours remaining in the evolution, you'll probably end up building a mountain inside the hole. Then you'll build a flat path up the hill. Then you'll make the moat deeper.

At random the instructors will remark that the class looks hot from working so hard. Because they care too much about you to let you suffer a heat casualty, they're going to let you take a dip in the ocean. They signal their concern for you by sounding the alarm on their bullhorn and then yelling a time limit. If the entire class doesn't make it back in time, you get to do it again. The bullhorn sounds right when the class starts to relax and get dry. It breaks your heart every time. Even now, half a decade later, the sound of a bullhorn alarm still gives me that sinking feeling of impending doom. It's that bad.

After you've dug sufficiently, it might be time for dinner. Dinner here (and a few other times during Hell Week when you don't go to the chow hall) is a cold MRE entree. There is no meal more truly disheartening than a cold, slimy MRE. A cold cheese and veggie omelet can steal your soul, especially when you're expected to eat it out of the bag like a huge chunk of congealed snot encrusted with sand (because you're completely sandy). But you'll eat. Not because you're hungry - you probably aren't. By this point you probably have to force down every meal. And you will, because you remember what you've been told (and what you've read) about the importance of eating as much as you can at every opportunity. You know that even though the thought of food is nauseating, you're going to eat and continue to eat until they make you stop. Because you want to finish; you want to be a Navy SEAL.

So you choke down an MRE entree or two and you drink water until you feel like you're going to pop, and then it's back to digging. Occasionally the instructors will reward hard work with a few minutes standing by the fire. When you get up to their bonfire, you'll see that they're all drinking Sugar-Free Monster energy drinks (SEALs should be sponsored by the blue Monsters), eating, and telling stories around the fire. There may or may not be a few beers passed around. The instructors are having such a good time with their bonfire on the beach that you just wish you could be invisible and stay next to the fire for the rest of the night. Despite wishful thinking, you'll stand by the fire for only a few minutes (if that) before you head back to digging.

Once the instructors are satisfied with the digging (and maybe a little liquored up) the class begins to perform for them. They move their chairs to the edge of the pit and students climb to the top of the mountain one-by-one to tell jokes. If the instructors like the joke, you get to stay dry. If the instructors don't like your joke, you hit the surf.

Jokes range from:

Q: What's brown and sticky?
A: A stick
Instructors: Hit the surf. You're a faggot.

to

Student: I just got back from leave and found out that my roommate is mad at me for having sex with his mom. I don't get it, I'm a good looking guy and his mom was lonely.
Instructors: What?
Student: My roommate's right over there (as he points to his identical twin, also in the class)
Instructors: Disgusting. Hit the surf.

Most jokes end with the teller hitting the surf, but at this point you don't care too much about getting wet. You've been wet since Sunday. Fuck it.

But one student in my class decided not to hit the surf. Instead, he went down to the water, looked up and thought nobody was watching, and turned around. Unfortunately he missed the instructor who was on the western side of the berm on his cell phone, who watched the entire thing.

The instructors caught on fire and made the entire class run back and forth from the surf for a while before they realized hitting the surf wasn't enough to make them feel better. No, what they wanted was for us to die. So they gave us an extra, unscheduled surf torture. And this was the surf torture to end all surf tortures because it was in a huge plume of Tijuana sewage just then washing ashore. The water was so bad that the waves crashing over us held a school of fish that chose death on the shore over swimming in the shitwater. This was the beginning of the end for me and a large number of guys in my class.

The sewage immersion caused a number of us to become

violently ill. We began by throwing up and shitting uncontrollably. One guy went from 175 lbs to 135 lbs before he fully recovered a few weeks later. The BUD/S doctors called it VGE (Viral Gastroenteritis), but it was more likely E. Coli poisoning.

The point of the Camp Surf evolution isn't to give you E. Coli poisoning though. It's a relatively low-impact way to keep you and your class moving while minimizing the chances of real injury. It's also an easy to way for the instructors to make note of who's eating, who's hiding injuries, and who's putting out despite poor physical condition. In the scheme of Hell Week it's a nice break from the violence. As long as you hit the surf when you're told to and don't have the bad luck to soak in frigid sewage for 15 minutes.

Hell Week: Around The World Paddle.

I always looked forward to the Around the World Paddle on Thursday night because I knew that the worst of Hell Week would be over by that point. I knew that if I made it that far, I would make it. I knew that if I got injured I would probably be rolled forward and not have to redo Hell Week. I felt that I would be safe once I got to it. I also eagerly anticipated the evolution because of its notable lack of instructor involvement - it's hours and hours paddling your IBS from the Pacific Ocean deep into San Diego Bay at night.

Around-the-World begins directly in front of the BUD/S compound, where the boats all launch as the sun sets. As the sun goes down students lose their grip on reality and they begin to hallucinate. The lights undulating on the waves start to look like a traffic jam to some, like a railroad tunnel to others. Guys drift and out of consciousness and row in their sleep. Some guys stop paddling every 10 seconds and their boat crews have to wake them up by hitting them. Some slump over the side and into the water. The water wakes them up and their boat crew pulls them back in.

They paddle northwest along the coastline until they run into a stone jetty at the westernmost tip of Coronado. They pull out of the water there so the instructors can get a headcount, get beat a bit, they eat some cold MREs, and get back into the water.

Before the boats get to leave, however, the instructors put the whole class in the water and make the crews dump boat (just in case you thought you were going to be dry on Around-the-World: you're not). The fastest crew to dump boat gets to go. Then the class dumps boat again. The fastest crew gets to go again. And this continues until there are no more boats left to torture.

The boat crews continue to skirt the northern shoreline of Coronado as the Instructors told them to, but sleep deprivation takes over their senses and they have an extremely hard time figuring out where they are and where they have to go. So they paddle on unsure of themselves until they reach a boat ramp with a bunch of headlights indicating another stop. This stop is more of the same: a water break, some hazing, a headcount, and a bunch of boat-dumping before the class continues on.

The class's next destination is on the southern end of NAB Coronado. The route takes them past a number of marinas and mooring areas where Team Guys and SQT students wait on surf boards or in kayaks to deliver bags of candy or pizzas to the ravenous, delirious students. As the boats pass their hideouts, they paddle out and make their deliveries. Often the whole boat crew is so unaware of its surroundings that they don't notice the deliverymen approaching until a pizza lands in their laps. And they're gone before the stunned boat crew has time to cough out a "thank you."

The students have been given explicit instructions not to eat anything they're given until the instructors examine it and make sure it's not going to upset their weary, disease-addled bodies. But the smarter students know this is a load of shit. Boat crews that turn in their pizzas and candy won't get it back, regardless of what the instructors told them. The instructors will eat it. And any students who ask for their snacks back will be rewarded with a very special trip to the surf to cool off because "stupid questions like those can only be symptoms of heat stroke."

The next stop is the final destination: Crown Cove, by the Leows Coronado Bay Resort. This leg is a race. It pays to be a winner. The first few boat crews wait for the rest of the class by the fire. The next get to sit on their boat. The next get to stand by their boat. The next stand under the boat. If you're after that, the majority of your time until sunrise will be spent getting wet and playing "fuck-fuck" games with the Instructors.

Even the winners don't escape the games though. Before too long everyone gets to play. Some are drag races around the perimeter of the bay and back. Other games are races around the flag in the middle of the bay. Sometimes your boat is upside-down. Sometimes you have to paddle with the handles of the oars and hold onto the paddle side. But it always pays to be a winner.

The Around-the-World Paddle post-evolution fuck-fuck games last until the sun rises. Everyone knows this and the instructors will use it to play with your head. They'll look up at the sky as it lightens (excruciatingly) slowly as ask "hey, sir, do you think it's morning yet?"

"Hooyah Instructor Smith. It's definitely morning."

"Nice try, sir. Go hit the fucking surf. Actually, why don't you take your whole class with you for being so stupid."

Eventually, despite the Instructors' best efforts to convince you otherwise, the sun rises and the evolution ends.

And then you know you have only a few hours remaining in Hell Week.

Hell Week: So Solly Day.

The final evolution of Hell Week is So Solly Day, a final "hooyah" evolution to cement the violence of the week in the collective memory of the class. Because it's the final real evolution and it resembles a combat-simulation obstacle course you might think So Solly Day would be fun on some level. You would be wrong.

So Solly Day takes place inside a fenced-off area south of the BUD/S Obstacle Course called "the demo pits." A big, muddy, sandy pit is filled with rancid water and various areas of the pit are separated from one another by cement pipes. When the class gets there they submerge in the water as smoke grenades and blank-firing machine guns go off around them. Artillery simulators ("arti sims") shriek and explode and the instructors yell orders through a megaphone and give commands with whistles while the class drags itself through the mud.

The water gradually goes from gross to borderline toxic waste as the class drags itself back and forth in the pits. Guys have shit their pants - either during this evolution or prior to it - and their feces are marinating in the water with you. And nobody cares enough not to piss in the water. The longer you stay in the water, the more it smells and tastes like the raw sewage it's becoming.

The smoke and explosions and gunfire and yelling and whistles make chaos in the pits. And students slog through the mud on their stomachs. The brass casings left over from dozens of So

Solly Days are still in the mud and as the students drag themselves back and forth the casings cut into their elbows and stomach and legs. And you can't help but think how the sewage water from the pits is soaking into these freshly-opened wounds and realize that this is not healthy.

To make matters more frustrating still: every man there knows he's going to finish Hell Week. If he was going to quit, he'd have quit already. If he was to get medically-rolled, he would be a Brown Shirt Rollback and not have to go through Hell Week again. For each man bleeding in the mud and screaming responses to the instructors' orders, Hell Week is more or less over. They've made it and they know it. So, in the moment, this evolution feels unnecessary. And it pisses you off because you've come this far and now you're crawling through metal shards for no reason. You know you're not going to quit. You know nobody else is. In retrospect you'll realize that there HAS to be a last evolution and whatever it was, you'd feel the same way.

After you've been sliced up and soaked in shit for an hour or so (timelines vary from class to class to ensure unpredictability - every evolution varies from class to class), So Solly Day ends. The instructors are out of smoke grenades and blanks and arti sims and order the class back to the boats.

Lightheaded and dizzy with anticipation that Hell Week is nearly over, the class falls in on its boats.

"Prepare to up boat."
"PREPARE TO UP BOAT!"
"Up boat."
"UP BOAT!"
"Moving."

The instructor takes off running toward the BUD/S Compound. The boats feel light at first, but quickly regain their weight as the instructor leading the run slows down at the BUD/S Compound, but then turns and laughs as he takes off again past it. All the instructors laugh as they see the class almost collapse with disappointment.

* * *

"You guys didn't think it was over, did you? We've got ALL DAY! In fact, why don't we start the day off by cleaning that shit-water off of you? Down boats."

"DOWN BOATS!"

"Hit the surf."

"Hooyah!" and the class slumps into the water and shuffles back to the boats.

"Not fast enough fuckers. Do it again."

"Hooyah!" and the class again stumbles into the surf zone.

"Fuck you guys. You think you deserve to finish Hell Week today? You're fucking pathetic. In fact we asked the CO to give us another 18 hours with you because you were so pathetic. Face the water. Lock arms."

Fuck. Surf torture. Again. Students steel their faces as they prepare for yet more handfuls of sand in their eyes and mouths. Their hip flexors are stiff and brittle - each shiver and each step hurts. But they'll do everything they're told. They've already come this far.

The threat that there could be another 18 hours to go barely registers. They know it's probably bullshit, but they don't think about it. All they think about is putting one foot in front of the other as they wade into the surf again.

"Forward march." The command to move deeper into the surf.

"FORWARD MARCH!" The class echoes and begins to move forward.

"Stop." The command to stop is usually given much deeper. Odd. The class is to tired to take much note.

"STOP." They prepare to turn around when commanded to, to take seats, and to endure the bitter lonely cold again.

"About face." Turn around.

"ABOUT FACE." The class turns and immediately some drop to their knees. Others stand tall, proud. While they were walking out into the surf, a crowd appeared over the top of the sand berm. A flag waves. Instructors are smiling. They have Gatorade in their hands. Old frogmen have come to see them secured - some of the only men in the world who knows what this moment feels like.

* * *

An old man, the CO or distinguished guest: "Class 264: Hell Week is secured."

Students wear stupid grins and help the injured among them to walk out of the surf. The adrenaline that had kept men on their broken legs is replaced by relief. They don't care how much their legs hurt. They can't feel them. But some of them can't walk. These are details to be worked out later. Right now, they're securing Hell Week - something nobody can ever take from them.

Gatorades are passed around as a few words of praise are given to the delirious students. Next students go through the decon station and, an unheard of luxury, those who are waiting can sit/slump and close their eyes without reproof. After cleaning up the students are taken through a final medical check and then allowed to put on the post-Hell-Week clothes that had been standing by in the quitter's room. They had been there for use in shameful sleep if they'd quit. Now they're put on in victory. Most choose sweat pants and fleece sweaters. After being cold all week, there's nothing better.

But the most important clothing item - the warmest clothing article these young men have ever worn - is not the fleece. The brown shirt is the symbol of victory. They are nothing without one - there is nothing lower than a "white shirt". Once you get one you've earned your spot in training. You're not a SEAL - not even close - but you've earned the right to train. The t-shirt is so iconic in BUD/S that you are your shirt. If you have not completed Hell Week, you are a "white shirt." If you've completed Hell Week, you are a "brown shirt."

The new brownshirt is helped to his box of pizza, another Gatorade, and his brown t-shirt stenciled front and back with his name. Forgetting the pizza and Gatorade, each man will pick his shirt up in disbelief. He'll hold it to his face to soak in the warmth and smell the newness. Then it goes on and will not leave his body for days. He eats a little pizza and staggers to his room to sleep.

His barracks room has been rearranged from before Hell Week. The mattresses have been moved from the bunks to the ground.

Hell Week survivors can barely climb into the lower bunk and would certainly fall if they tried to get off it. The top bunk would be an absurdity - an impossible goal at this point. So the mattresses of the new brownshirts have been moved onto the floor. But most mattresses are still on the bunks - these belong to the quitters. Walking into your room can be shocking because you've lost track of all who quit and when. You might have heard mutterings about this guy or that, but you might not have. The shock of finding out you've lost a roommate (or two or three) is easy to get over, though, as the rollbacks help you to your mattress on the floor. They put your pizza in the refrigerator for when you wake up starving, make sure you're okay, and leave you in peace. This is the first time you've been alone in a week. It's quiet. It's warm. You can sit. You can sleep. Most students will text a picture and/or make a quick call to loved ones and then climb into bed.

The feeling of release that accompanies the first time you lay down is euphoria, quickly giving way to drooling stupor and sleep. Victory.

Hell Week: Post-Hell-Week Depression.

In the few days following Hell Week your body goes through a reasonably predictable progression. The first few times you wake up after going to sleep for the first time in 5 ½ days your faces is so puffy it's hard to see. A number of guys will have urinated in their sleep (who can really blame them?) Feet are swollen, knees and hips are stiff to the point of immobility, and stamina is absurdly low. As time progresses, the swelling subsides and joints begin to loosen, but stamina drops even more as your body spends its energy on repairs.

If you have loved ones or friends in the San Diego area, it's a good idea to have them come down and stay with you over that first weekend. Some families come in from other parts of the country and put their enfeebled graduate up in a nice hotel room to recover over the weekend. Your family should know you're going to want to sleep and eat and will have very little energy for anything else. After Hell Week you're going to feel cold constantly. It might be 90-degrees out and you could be wearing sweatpants and a fleece and you would still be shivering. No amount of blankets will stop you from feeling cold for a few weeks. Even if you sit in a hot tub and you can recognize signs that your body is overheating, you will often still feel chilled. This goes away as your body recovers, but can be disconcerting.

My friends asked me if Hell Week made me immune to

discomfort or pain. I told them it was the opposite: that Hell Week turned me into a pussy who's always cold and doesn't want to get his ass out of bed. I was only half-joking.

The most notable effect of completing Hell Week, however, was also the most unexpected: depression. A friend who graduated a few classes ahead of me warned me about Post Hell Week Depression - he said it was real and happened to him. But I never really gave it much weight. I never thought that completing the biggest accomplishment imaginable would depress me. I assumed that pride and exhilaration would displace everything else. The thought of Post Hell Week Depression just seemed silly.

Until the Monday after I completed Hell Week.

My personality began to flatline. I was completely numb. I had an emotional stroke and I felt nothing. I was underwhelmed by life. It was an effort to pretend to feel something. When I spoke with my parents or girlfriend (now my wife) I was robotic. Just carrying on a conversation was difficult. It was hard to convince my girlfriend that I didn't hate her because I couldn't smile unless I strained my face - and that smile, as you can imagine, didn't look remotely natural or sincere. It wasn't. I was simply not happy. Nothing could make me happy.

I remember talking to my parents on the phone:

"Hi mom, hi dad."
"Hi! How are you? You sound better."
"Fine."
"What have you been doing?"
"Stuff."
"How's Sabine?" (That's my then-girlfriend-now-wife.)
"Fine."
"Well we..."
"I'm gonna go. Bye." And I hung up.

I simply couldn't hold a conversation. I couldn't even pretend to be present. It was like I was holding my breath and I could only last so long until I was going to pass out from socialization. I never intended to be rude. The only reason I endured conversation for as long as I did was to be polite. I never wanted to hurt anyone's feelings or make anyone worry about me, but there was only so much I could take. And, for a time, that amount was very little. According to my wife, who is the best resource for what I was like during this time, it took me about two months to begin climbing out of the fog and start acting like my normal, natural self again.

While I was probably depressed longer than most guys, I was not the only one who dealt with this problem. A large proportion of students deal with a level of depression after completing Hell Week. Most guys won't admit it. It's not a macho thing to talk about. But they feel it. And most SEALs won't admit they dealt with similar feelings either, mostly because they've forgotten and/or blocked it out. The SEAL Teams are a testosterone-fueled community and no weakness is tolerated, so any thoughts of emotional disturbance are, for better or worse, put out of mind and never spoken of.

But you'll find that a lot of older, more mature/humble SEALs will remember. Even the retired Master Chief who taught us stoic philosophy and mental toughness techniques also spoke about the seemingly inexplicable onset of depression following Hell Week.

This depression is caused by two factors. One is psychological and one is physical.

The physical factor is cause by extreme exhaustion and a substantial amount of physical damage. Your body gets wrecked by Hell Week. Muscles are destroyed as they work for 132 hours straight without an opportunity to repair. Ligaments and tendons suffer thousands of micro-fissures from constant stress and strain under heavy load while cold. Your skin is shredded from chafing, your hands and feet are swollen, you can't stop shivering. Your body is in the worst shape it's ever been unless you've been through chemotherapy. There's a lot of damage that needs to be repaired and it takes your body all the energy and resources it has to fix itself up. There's no free energy for hormones that create joy. There's no energy for facial expressions. Your body is in survival mode - and it will be until the damage done by Hell Week (and exacerbated by the following weeks and months of continual abuse) is repaired.

The psychological factor plays a larger, more insidious role. By the time the average student has reached Hell Week, it's been a dream and a goal of his for years. He's been fixated on making to Hell Week. Finishing Hell Week has been the center of his dreams, thoughts, and prayers. And then he finished it for real.

Everything after Hell Week had been the stuff of fantasy which he's kept to a minimum in order to keep his focus on Hell Week. He knows that Hell Week is really only the beginning, but deep in his subconscious Hell Week was the end. It was the goal. Completing Hell Week was so statistically unlikely that focusing on goals beyond it seemed foolish. So he concentrated on Hell Week alone for months and years.

Then Hell Week was behind him. Immediately it felt good to have accomplished his goal. But now what? He knows he's got a lot more to go, but deep inside the fire has calmed. His goal, the one he thought of every night and every day, is finished. After years of conditioning himself to look at Hell Week and not beyond, it takes some serious time to ingrain a new forward-looking mindset. Thousands of hours of mental training are not undone in a day or a week.

And when he completes Hell Week and finds that, aside from no more boats-on-heads, very little has changed, it can cause some serious internal conflict. Then the fact that he's only 3 weeks into a 21-week nut-kick sets in and he feels like he's actually accomplished very little. In the scheme of things, he's right. Hell Week is the beginning. The magnitude of his undertaking sets in and he realizes, for the first time, how much BUD/S is going to suck.

These two mental incongruities combine: the goal he's been sizing up for years is not only complete, but it turns out to be only the beginning. It's like a runner sizing up a huge hill, only to run up it and find that he's in the foothills of Mt. Everest. And now he has to climb Everest in running shorts and those gay toe-shoes everybody wears. The result: mental exhaustion.

Another effect of his years-long focus is that Hell Week gets built up in his head. There's already a mythos surrounding it: that it forges boys into impervious killing machines, that only olympic-calibre athletes complete it, that it's the ultimate crucible. Then, when he completes it and looks at himself, he still sees the same guy who got cut from his high school sports team, who blew it with that girl that one time, or who didn't get recruited to play football in the NCAA. He sees that he's not dramatically changed. In fact, he's weaker now because he hasn't yet recovered. He feels like he must've missed the transmutation evolution where everyone else got their bones replaced with titanium alloy and their eyes replaced with lasers.

What's more, he knows he could have handled more. This was his one chance to be born again in the crucible and he could have endured more. They should have made it harder. He was never close to quitting. He could have handled more pain. He might even feel shame that it wasn't as hard as he thought it would be. He had been cheated out of his modern-day agoge.

Eventually he'll look at the fact that his class started First Phase with over 300 people and finished Hell Week with 43. He'll realize that his Hell Week was as hard as any other had been. If they had made it half-again as hard it wouldn't have done anything but cause more permanent harm. He'll realize that he only feels this way because in his years of work toward this goal, Hell Week loomed large and impossible on his horizon. It was the test. He was resigned to die before he quit and he half-expected to actually die before he finished it. He knew in his head it wasn't impossible, but in his heart he was prepared to march all the way to the black to finish. No real hardship, Hell Week included, can match these fantastical expectations. And nothing in life is ever so bad in the doing as it is in the anticipation. Hell Week is hard and unforgiving, but it is entirely doable.

When you combine these inconceivably high levels of mental and physical exhaustion with disappointment that the week wasn't actually impossible, experiencing depression in the wake of Hell Week is almost understandable.

If you complete Hell Week it will probably happen to you on some level. Maybe it won't. But if it does remember that it's natural, that it makes sense, that a large majority of your class shares your dilemma in some way, and that you'll get over it as you refocus on both short- and long-term goals (the beginning of Second Phase, Pool Comp, the Island, graduating BUD/S, SQT,

SQT graduation, etc.) Unfortunately, the lingering depression makes the remainder of First Phase and the beginning of Second Phase that much worse.

Guess what? Hell Week is over but Hell has just begun.

First Phase: As A Brownshirt Now.

Though Hell Week is First Phase's most visible evolution, completing Hell Week does not complete First Phase. The first week after Hell Week is low on intensity. The days include stretch-heavy physical training. Trust me when I say this hurts. This week you'll find it's impossible to complete 20 pushups or touch your toes. It's an effort to walk: sitting down and standing up are a workout. The majority of the week, however, is spent in class. Instructors provide lectures on subjects like the History of NSW, camouflage and concealment techniques, hydrographic reconnaissance, and over-the-beach (OTB) insertions.

The week following the week of recovery was the worst week of BUD/S for me. Not Hell Week. Not Pool Week. Chart week.

At the time I'm writing this, Chart Week no longer exists. As I understand it, it has been replaced by a lengthier OTB curriculum - a more worthwhile use of your time. But BUD/S is a fluid course and changes with the personality of its Commanding Officer and Command Master Chief. By the time you get there, Chart Week may be back.

Chart Week involves doing a hydrographic reconnaissance during the morning. A hydrographic reconnaissance requires the entire class to pair up. The pairs enter the water and space out 20m between each pair in a line perpendicular to the shore. They stretch out about 500m into the water. When the OIC on the beach gives the signal, each pair drops a lead weight to the bottom and records the depth on a board with a grease pencil. Then the OIC on the beach moves 20m to one side or another, the pairs shift over to line up with him, and they do it again. It takes hours and it's cold and it's boring. Because you're barely moving - only treading water - the cold gets to you pretty quickly. Your hands get so frozen numb that it becomes almost impossible to write; some pairs have to record in tally marks once they lose fine motor function.

When the class comes in all the data has to be transcribed and ordered. Then the real fun begins. Each member of the class is required to stay after dinner and complete an intricate chart detailing the contour lines of the shallow seabed. The charts are roughly 30"x30", require perfection, and are judged with violent scrutiny. If there is one visible eraser-mark, if one line is off by ⅛", if the bubble letters of the title don't look perfectly formed, if the edge of the paper is wrinkled - if the chart is anything less than perfect, you fail. If you fail, you have to come back the next night, after another full day of training, and do it again. This is particularly crushing because it often takes until 4 or 5 in the morning to complete a chart. Some guys will be working up to morning muster at 0530. Some don't finish and have to turn in an incomplete chart that they will have to start over the next night. It is not unusual for it to take 3-4 submissions to receive a PASS. That's 3-4 nights in a row of painstaking drafting, bent over a table with pencil in hand for hours each night, with little to no sleep. Chart Week was more miserable than Hell Week.

In more recent classes Chart Week has been replaced by more extensive over-the-beach (OTB) insertion training. OTB training is significantly more applicable to being a Navy SEAL. It's still not fun.

OTBs start out with planning. The instructors designate a target from overhead imagery (ie Google Maps). The target is usually somewhere on North Island Air Station (the northern part of Coronado Island). From there, you are to plan an operation coming from the ocean, inserting over the beach, sneaking up to the target in order to provide detailed sketches and descriptions, getting off the beach without detection, and linking up with the extract package. In practice it's much more complicated than this.

The majority of the time practicing OTBs will only involve parts of the whole process. It's not until the OTB Final Training Exercise (FTX) that you and your class put the whole thing together. The FTX is fun and is an excellent learning experience. The training prior to the FTX is just another opportunity for the instructors to make your question your commitment.

The worst part of the OTB is the dreaded "change out" from soaking wetsuit to cammies. It seems like it would be simple and painless, but it is not. The changeout has to be done silently, with low profile, in the sand dunes, and in such a manner that it can be done blind. This last part is not to be understated. If, at any point, the instructors tell you to close your eyes and keep going, you have to know where everything is. You have to be able to finish changing, pack everything up without leaving a single item behind, and maintain control of your weapon at all times. Instructors are not beyond stealing weapons out from under less-than-vigilant students. I always kept a knee or foot on my rifle so they had no chance of stealing it. The instructors will set absurdly low time requirements and scream as you don't meet them. Once you're changed into your cammies, you do a quick 'notional patrol' and come back to get back into your wetsuit. The notional patrol is just long enough to make sure your wetsuit is cold all the way through, and the location the instructors chose to have you change out is probably sand, which means you're going to get a lovely amount of sand between your cold skin and your cold wet neoprene. Then you do it again and again and again. Then you do it some more. Change outs are never fun, but you'll do them throughout your training. You'll do them in Third Phase on San Clemente Island as a means of inserting for your full mission-profile (FMP) FTXs. You'll do them in black of night in the icy waters off Kodiak Island in Alaska during SQT and you'll do them during your first platoon's pre-deployment workup.

The OTB FTXs are the first things you'll do in BUD/S that resemble a real mission. The instructors will deliver a FRAGO, which stands for 'fragmentary order,' or mission-assignment.

They'll give a location and mission and it will be up to the class to plan and execute. One of my class's FTX targets was the MWR/ Family Recreation Center on the beach of North Island Air Station. Our insert platform was to be RHIBs (Rigid Hull Inflatable Boats) piloted by the Boat Support unit for the Naval Special Warfare Center (NSWC) that usually act as safety boats during ocean swims.

The class determined the ideal insert point on the beach, calculated the projected currents at the time of insert, and located the optimal drop-off point for the swimmers from the boats. It had to be far enough out to avoid visibility from the land, but near enough to preserve energy for the mission. This was no joke: the instructors would be on shore watching for us. They would have night vision, flashlights, trucks, and probably beer. The beer wasn't really for catching us so much as it was for drinking. But the rest of the stuff was to catch us with. If your understanding of a BUD/S Instructor's job is clear, you'll know why it would be a bad idea to get caught.

While we were planning the class was also preparing mission gear. We were testing drybags, getting garbage bags (to change out on and to keep gear dry when the old drybags leaked), and ensuring all "shapes" (the term for a fake, realistically-weighted, rubber weapon) had bungie cord straps on them to be tied to our bodies on insert. We cut nylon rope loops to tie the drybags to our belts and found carabiners to clip all this shit to us.

When we had completed our planning we briefed to the Instructors. When I briefed that the water temperature was going to be 46-degrees Fahrenheit that night, one of the instructors scoffed and said "Maybe 56 degrees. Definitely not 46." So I erased the "4" from the whiteboard and wrote a "5" in its place. Nobody ever bothered to check whether I was right. I just assumed I'd been wrong and moved on.

Dressed in our wetsuits with our faces painted black, the class ran from the First Phase grinder across the street to a dock near the SQT building where the Boat Support RHIBs bobbed along the dock waiting for us. We got a muster, loaded the boats, unloaded the boats, got beat on the dock for a while, did swimmer-checks, got beat a little more, and then reloaded the boats. The OIC (call sign "meat snorkel") did last-minute radio checks with the Instructor staff (call sign "pole smoker") and I gave the insert/ extract coordinates and timelines to the Boat Support drivers, who plugged them into their GPS units. The instructors gave us a final bit of advice: "If you fuck this up you're going to pay," and we were on our way.

The ride to the insert point was longer than we thought it would be, but it was a welcome break from having to do anything. Most of us slumped onto the rear deck of the RHIB and slept in a big pile. The big waves of the Pacific woke me from my half-sleep as we rounded the jetty and moved into the Pacific. I was in charge of navigating so I stood up next to the pilot as we approached the waypoint on the GPS. We arrived at the drop-off location, but something was wrong. We weren't in the right place.

I looked at the GPS unit and saw that the Boat Support guy had put our coordinates in completely wrong. We were almost 3km from our intended drop-off point. What's more, he hadn't even noticed that the coordinate formats required by the boat's GPS and the ones I'd give him were different. I learned an extremely valuable lesson right there on that boat: don't trust your insert platform. Verify repeatedly and invasively. This lesson paid off in SQT, in training, and in combat Afghanistan. These sorts of things get messed up constantly in real-life scenarios even when the assets care deeply about the mission. Boat Support really didn't care - half of them were made of BUD/S drop-outs anyways - so I would be sure to put the grids in myself from then on.

Fortunately I remembered how to convert between different coordinate formats and did it right there on the fly as I re-entered a new insert point. The boats started moving again (with the class registering confusion as to why we stopped but resignation that things were working out) and got us to our real insert-point. It looked right, but I verified it anyways. I pulled out a map and compass I'd brought in case the boat GPS died altogether and shot resections to notable landmarks to triple-verify we were where we wanted to be. A resection is looking at a landmark and finding what bearing it is on a compass. Then you can take that bearing and draw a line on the map from that landmark: you are somewhere on that line. Then you take a bearing on a second landmark and draw a second line. The two lines will cross at your exact location.

The lines crossed right where we wanted to be, so we launched our swimmer scouts. They gasped loudly as they hit the water and began swimming frantically toward the shore. Swimmer scouts are usually two swim-pairs who swim in initially to verify the area is safe, determine the best location to come ashore at, and lead the main body to a concealed change-out area. When the scouts have determined the coast is clear, they'll signal to the main body (still in the boats). Tonight they signaled with red chemlites moving up and down. They also could have signaled with buzz-saws. A buzz-saw is a chemlite attached to a 2-3 foot length of 550 cord (also known as para-cord). When you crack the light and spin the buzz-saw it looks like a circle of light from the water. It's an easily-recognizable signal and tonight would have indicated the beach was safe. If they had instead signaled with red chemlites moving horizontally back and forth, we would have known to abort. But they signaled with red chemlites moving up and down repeatedly, indicating that we should approach with caution: there was danger nearby.

Swim pairs slipped into the water as the boats slowly backed away from the shore. They were making a lot of noise tonight. This wasn't our first OTB and things were usually much quieter. The moment I hit the water my lungs seized and I let out an uncontrollable gasp. The water was so cold I could not breath in. I was instantly numb and shortly I was in significant pain. The faces around me told similar stories. The water was a full 10 degrees colder than the instructors thought. I had been right in the brief. This was going to be a miserable and dangerous night.

During a tactical insert the boats never face away from the beach because the noise of the engines will travel to the shore. And most of their guns are on the front, too. So the boats back, slowly, allowing swimmer pairs to slip into the water. The dry-bags attached to our web belts floated and the nylon lines tangled in our fins and threatened to drown us before we even started as we gasped through the cold. Gradually everybody got control of their lines and pushed the bags in front of them to use as a weapon rest as they swam slowly toward shore shoulder-to-shoulder.

Approaching the beach this way ensured that if we were contacted in the water from the shore, every man would have a field of fire and we would be able to bring a maximum amount of firepower to bear.

We angled against the current and slowly crept in on the chemlite markers of the swimmer scouts. As we approached the breaking waves, the chemlites disappeared. 15 seconds later a bright spotlight shined out into the water. We froze, knowing that the human eye is attracted to unnatural movement, and laid low floating in the surging waves as they looked for us. We felt exposed. We shivered in place and moved with the ocean. We were fucked. We were 50ft offshore. No way they couldn't see us. But the light turned off and the truck it was mounted on started up and drove away. A moment later the swimmer scouts again displayed the "approach with caution" signal and we continued in.

To avoid silhouetting ourselves against the white surf and foam we dove under the crashing waves until we were waist-deep. I took a knee between my swim buddy and the beach and scanned the dunes for hostiles while he took his fins off and strung them over his wrist for safekeeping in the surf. Every few seconds he'd whisper "water" in my ear and we would brace for the impact of a wave crashing over our heads. When he was done with his fins, we switched.

Within a few minutes everyone was ready and the class left the safety of the surf for the sand. The very center swim pair started in and every pair shifted towards the center like a zipper and awaited their turn to cross the beach in the same footsteps. This way the size of the landing force couldn't be judged by counting footprints. When we reached the safety of tactical terrain we split into boat crews and went to find suitable change-out locations. Half of the boat crew held security while the other half changed, we switched, and then we began progressing toward our boat crew's target.

My boat crew's job was to sketch and observe an outdoor gazebo. There just so happened to be four BUD/S Instructors sitting at the picnic tables with a fire in the barrel they were gathered around. We set up an Observation Point on a sand dune about 50m from the gazebo and drew our sketches. I wanted to have more to fill out our report with - something that might get my boat crew out of a beating at some point - so we didn't stop there.

I took a swim buddy and we low-crawled down the berm. We stayed behind the low-lying shrubbery and slowly crept up to the gazebo. We were counting on the fact that the fire would blind the instructors to everything in the dark outside the gazebo. My swim buddy and I slithered to within 15 or 20 feet of the Instructors as they traded war stories. I wrote the stories down while my swim buddy noted everything each Instructor was wearing, what he was drinking, and his facial expressions during the stories.

During this time a few "lane grader" instructors came around to make sure everyone was performing adequately. They found two guys in ENS Armando's boat crew asleep on the backside of the berm. What's more, some of the guys had decided not to 'change out' according to the standards and still had their wetsuits on under their cammies. The instructors made the entire boat crew strip down and give up their wetsuits. The whole boat crew would be required to swim back out to the boats without wetsuits to keep them warm.

When it was time to meet up with the rest of the class we made our way back, changed out, and pushed out through the surf. The cold felt like it was ripping at my skin. The guys without wetsuits were writhing in pain as they began to swim. We were at the pickup point five minutes early so I was continually shooting resections to keep us from drifting from the designated point. The pickup time came and went with no boat support. I checked again. We were in the right place. So we waited. Maybe they were behind schedule. Wait, no. One of them turned its lights on for a moment and then turned them right back off. They were about 1500m to our southwest. Sitting there. Smoking and relaxing. While we froze our asses off. We huddled around the guys without wetsuits, hoping we could help keep them warm. They weren't in great shape.

Those lazy boat support assholes had dropped us and simply turned their boats off. They had been drifting with the tides and current for the last two hours. And because their boats were off, so were their GPS units. We sent the two fastest swimmers in the class to get the boats and bring them to us. By this point the guys without wetsuits were too frozen to swim (or talk), so this was our only option.

When the boats finally got to us we clambered in and the boats took off. We took off the cammies of the guys without wetsuits and laid in a pile on top of them to warm them up. A few of the guys were almost unconscious from hypothermia. We rubbed their arms and chest and legs and piled ourselves on top of them and they slowly began to come around. When the boats finally delivered us to the docks nobody said anything to the instructors about the guys who had hyped-out. To say something would be to get a beating and we just wanted to sleep. As far as I know the instructors never found out they almost killed a boat crew that night. But we learned a great deal from the close call.

After the final First Phase FTX you'll turn your green helmet in (or, if you're me, turn in one you stole and keep your own helmet) and get the blue helmet of Second Phase. With First Phase and Hell Week behind you you wouldn't think it, but it won't be long before you're wishing you could just go back to First Phase where things were physical, but simple. The long hours, demanding evolutions, and ambiguous environment of Second Phase will have you wishing for Surf Passage in no time. But you won't quit because you've come too far already.

First Phase: TTPs.

Have a Good Cartoonist. Every morning of First Phase your class will be required to provide a cartoon for the instructors. The cartoon is placed in the First Phase office at the start of every day, before the instructors arrive. It's the first thing the instructors see when they get to work. A good, funny cartoon can start your day off on a good note. A poor cartoon is likely to piss the staff off.

The cartoon is important because it's the single acknowledgement that BUD/S is a game and that students and instructors alike are playing their roles. It's a chance to make fun of the instructors without fear of real reprisal.

An instructor took the class on a conditioning run on the beach one day. On conditioning runs the class runs in formation four wide and as many deep as necessary. If the instructor runs along the edge of the water, two of the columns following him will be running in the water. On this particular run the instructor was constantly weaving along the waterline and running away from waves as they approached. Since we were required to run in the water "because men don't give a fuck if their socks get wet" we all thought it was hilarious he *did* give a fuck. Either he was a hypocrite or a woman. So the next morning's cartoon featured the instructor in a skirt and high-heels squealing "eeek!" as he lifted his skirt and pirouetted away from the water. The rest of the staff thought the cartoon was so funny that we could hear them laughing at him through the closed door of the First Phase Office.

* * *

"Cartoonist!" the instructor yelled when he finally got there and found the entire staff laughing at him.

"Hooyah" said our cartoonist when he sprinted to the office.

"Did you fucking draw this shit?" The rest of the staff can't contain their laughter from inside the office, completely undermining his scolding.

"Hooyah."

"It's fucking gay."

"Hooyah."

"Hit the surf." The staff erupted in even more raucous laughter at the instructor's expense.

"Hooyah." And the cartoonist hit the surf.

If you don't think starting the staff off with a good laugh makes the rest of your day go smoother, you're nuts. Other cartoons made fun of instructors taking their shirts off on runs for the civilian women sunbathing but getting distracted by how attractive their fellow instructors are. Still other cartoonists feature very penis-heavy themes, with instructors constantly choking on, being slapped by, or dreaming about cocks.

If the instructors think it's funny, you win. If they don't, you're screwed that day. So choose a good cartoonist. They don't' necessarily have to be the ones coming up with the jokes, but they *do* need to be able to make jokes work on paper. Artistic ability helps a great deal. My class had a phenomenal artist/cartoonist (the guy who drew the cartoon of the instructor in a skirt and high-heels), but when he quit we had nobody left. Our cartoons went from phenomenal to pathetic. The tone of the mornings changed dramatically from that day on.

Don't underestimate the power of a good cartoonist.

Weekly Massage. There is nothing better for physical (and mental) recovery during BUD/S than getting a massage every weekend. There are a number of massage parlors that offer memberships and discounted rates on massages in the area. Join one and go every weekend. Get a 90-minute or 2-hour massage. It might seem wasteful, but think of it as an investment in your future career.

370

Getting a massage can increase recovery, help flexibility, and relieve muscle tension. Each of these things will help you remain healthy and fit and better able to endure the hardship and rigors of BUD/S.

Nightly hot tub and stretch. In addition to regular weekend massages, be sure to stretch every night. But don't stretch cold muscles. Find a hot tub. Someone in your class has an apartment in a complex with a hot tub. Find one and go there every night to limber up. Get in and warm up and then begin stretching *in* the hot tub. The warm water will help relax your muscles and allow you to stretch without worsening micro-tears in your muscle fibers. And the whole process will dramatically improve your flexibility. Flexibility is one of the major keys in remaining injury-free at BUD/S.

The only downside of the hot tub is that it will tend to dehydrate you, so bring a jug of water with you and you'll be golden. It might seem like a waste of time (or an unnecessary luxury), but if you want to give your body every advantage in recovery and injury-prevention, you'll take this advice and make it a habit to stretch out in a hot tub every night of First Phase.

Take Care of Yourself. Take time to maintain your body every night. Wash well to prevent infections. Use hot water and hydrogen peroxide in your ears to prevent ear infections. Get a callus scraper from the store and shave your hand-calluses down so they don't get torn off when you do the O-course (or a pull-up pyramid) with wet hands. Keep your fingernails and toenails trimmed and clean to prevent ingrown or ripped-out nails. Pay attention to your feet. Wear flip-flops when not training to give them sufficient chance to dry out. Use anti-fungal cream and powder when you need them.

If your knees and ankles are swelling (not unlikely), invest in some compression socks. You can get the expensive athletic versions from Under Armor or Reebok etc or you can go to a Walgreens and look in the old-lady department for "support hosiery." The kind old people use for varicose veins. They cost dramatically less than the athletic versions and do the same thing. They keep slight pressure on your lower extremities (get ones that go from your toes all the way to your hips for best results), which prevents your joints from swelling and becoming increasingly inflamed. Combine this with a dose of an anti-inflammatory (like Aleve or Ibuprofen) and your legs will feel fresher and newer every morning. That can make all the difference in how you approach your day of training.

One Evolution at a Time. The single best - though generic - piece of advice for completing BUD/S is to live one evolution at a time. Remember "segmenting" from the mental toughness techniques? That's the key here. It's really the key to everything at BUD/S (and every really daunting task ever undertaken).

Eat Big. During First Phase you will be incredibly active all day. And you will be cold. And you will be injured in some way or another. All of these will increase your appetite. Make sure you're eating enough. I averaged over 7000 calories every day in First Phase.

You'll eat "Dinner Chow" at BUD/S, but that won't be your dinner. You're done for the day at 5 or 6pm most days of First Phase (when there's not a night evolution), so you'll need at least one more solid meal before you go to sleep. During First Phase a "solid meal" will be a large supreme pizza, two hamburgers, and a liter of Gatorade. Or two breakfast burritos from Clayton's diner, a milkshake, and a homemade cinnamon roll - which was my meal three times a week throughout BUD/S.

Really though, don't go to bed hungry. Go to bed stuffed. You need every calorie you can possibly consume.

Sleep Big. In addition to an increased appetite, First Phase brings an increased need for sleep. When you sleep your muscles rebuild themselves. Without sufficient sleep you'll always be a step slow and an injury closer to failure.

It is entirely plausible to get 8 or 9 hours of sleep most nights of First Phase. Not so with Second or Third Phase, but entirely possible in First Phase. Make every effort to do this. Take care of your gear quickly and efficiently. Don't worry overly much about inspections. Sleep is more important. And if you front-loaded your gear prep like I've suggested, you won't have more than 30 minutes of work to do on any given night.

If you have a family with you in San Diego, ensure they understand the importance of this during training. You should not be expected to babysit or get up with an infant in the middle of the night. These things can quickly take you out of the game. If your wife will not understand this, then you're either going to quit or get a divorce before your first platoon is done.

Find Inspiration on the weekends. Watch badass macho movies on the weekends. Gladiator. 300. Black Hawk Down. Constantly help yourself maintain motivation by revisiting the things that made you want to go to BUD/S in the first place.

Read *Gates of Fire*. Not only will you be able to identify with it better than most people who read about the Spartans, but the book will fire you up and encourage you not to be a pussy.

First Phase: Don't Be That Guy.

Don't Do Extra BUD/S. The first advice my SEAL Mentor gave me when I learned I'd been accepted was to finish training as fast as I can. Having been there, I understand why he told me this. It was excellent advice.

There are countless opportunities to, essentially, roll yourself. If you're hurt you can choose to report some or all of your issues to BUD/S medical and take a roll. Or you can deal with it and carry on in the program. For example, when I broke three ribs during PTRR (doing the obstacle course) I told no one. I worked out a way to convince the doctor to give me a "No O-Course" chit for the three weeks before we went to Great Lakes. I figured that three weeks easy on the ribs plus a few weeks in Great Lakes would be enough time for the ribs to mend. I was right and it worked out. But I could have (maybe should have) gotten rolled to the next class.

The more BUD/S you expose yourself to, the higher your chances of getting hurt are. On an infinite curve everyone gets hurt. So get in and get out and get on with it. You're not going to BUD/S to **be** at BUD/S, you're going to become a Navy SEAL. Extra BUD/S does not make you a better SEAL. It just makes you less likely to become one. Finish training as fast as you can. Don't stay a second longer than is absolutely necessary.

Don't Be Negative. There is an important difference between acknowledging that BUD/S sucks and having a bad attitude about it. Some guys become extremely negative and take out their frustrations on their boat crews. A lot of the time if you don't keep honest track of your perspective, you'll find that the stress and pain will begin to get to you and you'll start thinking that your boat crew is not putting out as hard as you are. If you have a foreign officer in your crew, you're probably right. Otherwise it's just likely that you're grumpy and tired. So keep yourself honest and stay positive. Everything in BUD/S ends, so suck it up.

Don't Be Dramatic. Always remember that you're not the only one in pain or the only one who's putting out under your boat or log. Then look around and notice that nobody worthwhile is complaining. So don't be the one to make dramatic noises or painful faces. The idea is to suffer in silence.

Other than making you look like a bitch, being dramatic also makes you worse. The moment you begin to acknowledge your own misery is the moment that misery grows dramatically. And the more you pay attention to it, the worse you're going to feel. You'll put out less and feel worse. So don't give in. Be stoic, be strong.

Don't get psyched out. Your mental state is your greatest ally and most formidable enemy in BUD/S. Keep your thoughts under control. Students quit all the time because they can't handle the training mentally. And a few minutes after they quit, the 'intolerable' evolution is over. They could have handled it, clearly. They just let their minds get away from them. Remember the story about the two BUD/S-returnees who quit Monday morning before PT? They got psyched out. They lost the game. Keep control of your mind. Keep your thoughts disciplined and your resolve strong and you'll have little trouble with most of BUD/S.

Don't lie if you quit. Be a man regardless of whether you make it. If you make it, it's easy to be a man. If you quit, it's much harder. The temptation to lie or exaggerate the circumstances of you quitting is huge. There's a lot of ego to overcome. But if you quit, be respectful of the program and the occupation. Don't lie about it.

The number of people who quit and then claim it was a medical problem is insane. In fact when I hear that somebody got med-dropped, I almost automatically assume he quit. Sure, you may have quit because you were in physical pain from one injury or another, but for every person who quits because of his shin-splints or stress fractures, there's another guy hard enough to continue training *despite* the pain from the same injuries.

But quitters tend to quit because they're immature, and one of the greatest indicators of immaturity is a selfish mindset. So a great deal of quitters assume that because they couldn't handle the pain and others *could*, it's because their own pain was so much worse. Which is not true. These are the same people with so little self-realization that they quit because they think "nobody else in my boat crew is a team player. I'm the only team player there." By definition, if you're on a team by yourself, you're not a team player.

And you weren't the only person putting out. And everyone else was hurting too. They just sucked it up and you didn't and you owe them the proper amount of respect for sticking it out. So don't lie and blame the program or the instructors or a medical condition if you quit. If you quit, the least you can do is be a man about it.

First Phase: Mark's Parting Words of Wisdom.

BUD/S is a tremendous opportunity to prove and improve yourself. It forces you to be hard. It forces you to confront your own mental and physical weaknesses and best them.

And it dramatically alters the way you look at the world. The hardest times, in Hell Week, in First Phase, on The Island, these are what truly separate you from lesser men. You may finish Hell Week and not feel any different, but think of the number of people you know who could've done that. Then you'll start to do this all the time: you'll size people up differently than you used to. And you'll find that you're the exception.

And what's more: other people will acknowledge your achievements with awe. BUD/S simply forces you to pay (in pain) up front for a lifetime of respect.

So don't squander the opportunity. If you get to BUD/S, make the most of it. Take the hardest times and put them in your mental 'kit bag' or 'tool box' or whatever metaphor you want. But look at the program as an opportunity to truly test your mettle and temper your mind and body. Because it will do all these things and more. All you have to do is give it your all.

Chapter 11

Second Phase: It's Not Over?

"Such as are your habitual thoughts,
such also will be the character of your mind;
for the soul is dyed by the thoughts."

- Mark Aurelius

Second Phase: Key Tasks.

The Tread. The Tread is one of the most widely feared evolutions in Second Phase, second only to Pool Comp. Students don the twin-80 dive tanks and fins and enter the water. During the tread the students waiting to go will be sitting on the pool deck facing away from the pool. On command the participants raise their hands out of the water. When every man in the group has his hands out of the water, the timer starts. Students will tread water with their hands out of the water for 5 minutes. If their hands dip under, they fail. Some students try to keep their heads out of the water the entire time, too. This is not required. Students are allowed to have their heads underwater and their arms fully extended over their heads. The sound of the test heard from the pool deck is silence punctuated with semi-rhythmic, powerful exhalations and inhalations and the occasional panicked splash when a student starts to drown and puts his hands in the water. Anticipation of The Tread is worse than the actual evolution.

Dive Physics Test. The Second Phase Dive Physics test is the most academically-challenging test in BUD/S and SQT. That does not mean it's hard. Everybody will pass this test. If you can memorize one formula and perform basic algebra you're set. If the word "algebra" scares you, then you can memorize six easy formulas instead. Either way, the test is a joke. And they give a

"BUD/S-style review" before the test (usually consisting of reading every question on the test and providing the answers). The review is immediately followed by the actual test, making passing all but certain.

Jock Up Drills. When Pool Week evolutions begin students will be required to put on gear underwater when they can't see. This requires the utmost attention to detail and an intimate familiarity with all the dive gear required in Second Phase. In order to make gear procedures automatic, BUD/S Instructors will conduct "Jock Up" drills.

Jocking up is a term for getting your gear on. Before an op, you jock up by putting on your op uniform, getting your plates and kit on, and ensuring you have all your additional gear ready and on. In Second Phase, this means getting all of your dive gear on. The instructor staff hold the students to an exacting standard of detailed requirements and will enforce a strict (often shrinking) timeline.

Jock Up drills usually start with all your dive gear arranged on the Second Phase grinder in a manner similar to how it would be secured underwater in the event you had to ditch gear on the bottom. When the instructors whistle "go," you'll run out to your dive gear with your dive buddy and will both *don*, or put on, your gear. Some parts require a buddy's helping hands to get it done in the required time. After the time limit is up, you will be inspected by the instructors to determine whether you completed the task properly and completely. This inspection is called a *dive supe* (pronounced "soup") check, which is short for "dive supervisor." Things like a twisted strap, wrong gear order or orientation, or sloppy appearance are all possible grounds for failure.

There is also an evolution that involves having all the class's dive gear tossed into a dip tank (used for checking gear for leaks - or for getting wet when the instructors don't want to send you all the way to the ocean). The class has to retrieve and sort all the gear before donning, making it imperative that all your dive gear is labelled clearly. This evolution is sometimes referred to as "Dive Soup," a play on words from *dive supe*.

* * *

Pool Deck Beatings. Just as a great majority of beatings in First Phase involve either logs or IBS, a majority of Second Phase beatings involve either wetsuits, dive gear, or both. The awkward and heavy twin 80 open-circuit rigs used in Pool Week make little things like leg lifts and pushups difficult. It's hard to even maintain a proper leaning rest with a dive rig on. Add a wetsuit to the mix, often put on after you've gotten wet and sandy, makes for a hot, chafing, terrible beating.

Pool Week. Pool week is when BUD/S students progressively prove themselves capable of performing underwater in stressful situations. It is made up of a series of increasingly-complicated tasks to be performed underwater. Most of them involve working with a dive buddy. Dive evolutions are detailed below:

- **FSA (Free-Swimming Ascent).** The FSA evolution begins with a dive rig on the bottom of the pool. The instructor signals for the student to enter the water. The student steps into the water and swims down to the dive rig. He takes a few breaths off the rig (in order to fill his lungs with high-pressured air), turns the rig off and secures it properly, and signals that he's prepared to surface (thumb up). When the instructor checks the rig and finds it's properly stowed, the student kisses the pool deck and slowly rises to the surface while constantly exhaling, ensuring that he rises slower than the ascent rate of the bubbles he's exhaled. Rising too quickly can cause the pressurized air in his lungs to expand the lungs beyond their normal capacity, so instructors are unforgiving in their grading. He breaks the surface of the water with a hand raised over his head. When he is fully surfaced, he makes the "okay" sign with his hand and loudly says "I feel fine."

- **Ditch and Don (Day/Night).** Ditch and Don builds on the FSA. A jocked-up student enters the water, descends to the bottom of the pool, and takes off his dive gear. He stows it correctly on the bottom of the pool, the standards for which are precise and the evaluation exacting, and conducts an FSA. Upon successful completion of the FSA, the student descends to his dive rig, puts it on in the correct manner, and breathes his way to the surface.

After completing Ditch and Don with a normal mask on, the student is then expected to complete the evolution again with a blacked-out mask. He cannot see anything the entire time - the dive is conducted by touch alone. When it comes time for the student to descend back to his ditched rig, the instructor guides him down to it and he is expected to put it on perfectly and conduct a safe FSA while still in the dark.

- **Gear Exchange (Day/Night).** Gear exchange is conducted with your dive buddy and one dive rig between you. One buddy is wearing the rig as you descend, and the other is diving along with him and breathing off the rig when he needs to. When the buddy without a dive rig is running short on air he taps the regulator twice and the guy breathing takes a deep breath before releasing the regulator to his buddy. This is called *buddy breathing* and is done throughout this dive. When the dive pair reaches the bottom of the pool, they begin to take the dive gear off the first student and put it onto the second. When the transition is complete, the student who no longer has a dive rig conducts an FSA. After this the student descends to his buddy and they exchange gear again, buddy breathing the entire dive, until all gear has been exchanged. Then

- **Pool Comp.**

Pool Comp. Pool Comp (short for "Pool Competency") is the last major evolution between a BUD/S student and a statistical likelihood of becoming a Team Guy. That is, the moment a student passes Pool Comp, he's overwhelmingly likely to complete the rest of training. Statistically, the only bigger hurdle to becoming a SEAL is Hell Week.

Pool Comp is the culminating dive of Pool Week, but in character is dramatically different. At its most basic level, Pool Comp involves a student crawling back and forth underwater. Instructors will administer increasingly difficult "surf hits," where they simultaneously deliver physical abuse and cause malfunctions in the student's dive rig. At the conclusion of each "hit" the student is expected to right himself and follow a rigid series of procedures in order to resolve all equipment malfunctions. The slightest deviation from the rigid procedures can constitute a failure for the evolution. Some students will even fail without having made a mistake because they performed the procedures too slowly or too quickly or looked uncomfortable when the instructor didn't think it was appropriate.

"Surf hits" are violent. It's more common than not to see students exit the water with torn shirts and bloody faces from having their heads stomped (sometimes literally) into the bottom of the pool. And surf hits are long. Some last over a minute. Combine that length with the violence and the requirement that procedures are done slowly and without the appearance of panic and you can see how things can go very badly very quickly in this evolution. Ultimately the evolution ends with the "whammy knot," which is physically impossible to remove from the breathing hoses. The tricky part is figuring out whether a knot is removable or whether it's the whammy knot. If you assume a regular knot is the whammy knot, you will fail for inadequate attempts. If you assume the whammy knot is a solvable knot, you may run out of breath before you realize your mistake and panic as you ditch your gear and ascent. Panic = failure.

You have two chances to pass on the initial test day and two additional chances to pass on the retest day.

Draeger Hell Week. Draeger Hell Week is called "Hell Week" because of the amazingly small amount of sleep students will get as they dive twice a day. It takes its first name from the oxygen-rebreather rig we dive in combat diving situations. The Draeger allows nearly four hours of "time on bag" and produces no bubbles to indicate the presence of a diver in hostile waters. Draeger dives are more generically called *closed-circuit* because nothing leaves the dive rig and your lungs, whereas the regular dive gear used in Pool Week is called *open-circuit* because the air you exhale is released into the water as bubbles.

During Draeger Hell Week, the class will still muster every morning before it's light out, PT, and run to breakfast as usual. Then they will prepare their dive rigs (a sometimes lengthy process) and plan their dives. Next come ROC (rehearsal of concept) drills, known as dirt dives, where students walk through their legs and bearings over and over until the dive is memorized and feels second-nature. When you're 16 feet underwater and it's pitch black it's a bad time to realize you've forgotten your dive plan. After the dirt dives, you and your buddy get jocked up and get a dive supervisor check. If you or your buddy fail the check, you both get beat. Getting beat with a dive rig on is less comfortable than it sounds. Then the whole class is driven across the street to the insert point in the bay and the dive is conducted. Dives start simple and quickly ramp up. Students learn techniques such as contour dives (where you follow the contour of a coastline by staying at a given depth and following the terrain), offset navigation (where you ensure you hit the correct target by aiming off it slightly), and box searches. Dives quickly get longer and more difficult and require greater precision with more techniques. Dives begin to account for tidal flow and probable enemy activity.

During Draeger Hell Week you'll dive once in the morning and once at night. Each dive is harder than the last. You eat MREs and get beat regularly. The whole ordeal is exhausting, but instructive: it might be the first time you'll feel you're actually learning something in BUD/S. Student tempers run short on account of the poor food (MREs do not make happy students), the lack of sleep (sometimes only 3 or 4 hours a night), and the increased irritability caused by breathing pure oxygen for hours each day. Draeger Hell Week is a good foundation for combat diving, but the real-world dives don't come until SQT.

Emergency Descents. An emergency descent is required when a turtle-backing dive pair needs to get underwater immediately. The term turtle-backing refers to a dive pair swimming on the surface in order to preserve the oxygen in their dive rigs for when being underwater is entirely necessary. The emergency descent is dangerous because it dramatically increases a diver's risk of "flooding his dive rig," or introducing enough water into the rebreather to cause a chemical reaction with the CO_2-scrubbing chemicals (generically termed soda lime). Soda lime is toxic, and introducing too much water to the rebreather can create a caustic cocktail, where you breathe in soda lime water. Caustic cocktails produce violent chemical burns in the mouth, throat, and stomach/lungs. During the emergency descent, divers immediately submerge. Underwater they put their masks on and mouthpieces in, and forcefully blow all their air into the closed mouthpiece to expel water. Then they open the breathing valve on the mouthpiece while inhaling in order to prevent any excess water from entering the system. While they're doing this, the divers are simultaneously using the bubbles from their mouthpiece clearance to clear their masks of water. The whole process should take no more than five seconds.

Students will practice these techniques endlessly until the descents become second nature. Initially, however, each student will again confront his fear of drowning as he gets tangled in the buddy-line while his buddy dives to the bottom as he's simultaneously being pulled to the service by an over-inflated buoyancy-control vest and is unable to breathe because his valve is stuck closed. All the while he realizes that if he pulls too hard on the wrong thing, his rig might flood and his huge panicked breath might be toxic soup instead of life-giving air. It's during these moments that each student realizes why he was put through the terror of Pool Comp. Because the real thing is sometimes even worse than getting roughed up in a warm swimming pool.

Second Phase: TTPs.

The Tread is easy when done correctly. I could have gone for 10 minutes with the following knowledge and technique. The twin-80 dive tanks you wear during The Tread are neutrally-buoyant (even a little positive) when they're fully submerged. And the deeper underwater they are, the more buoyant they become. While you're doing the tread, you want your entire head underwater. Your arms should be extended comfortably above your head so that your hands and wrists stay out of the water. Since you're wearing fins there's only one option for the kick - you'll be doing a regular freestyle-technique kick. Make your kicks long and slow. Fight the temptation to kick fast with a limited range of motion. This will tire you out faster and ultimately require more oxygen. Long, slow kicks will be enough to keep your hands out of the water. Every 3-5 kicks you'll need to breathe. Do this by kicking only slightly harder to get your upward-looking face out of the water. Exhale by blowing in a short burst (to get the water out of your mouth) and breathe in deeply and quickly. The air in your lungs had been keeping you afloat just under the surface, so it's important to keep the time your lungs are empty to a minimum. Any more than half-a-second without air in your lungs will put undue stress on your legs. The breath almost sounds like a lamaze-breath: a powerful and rapid out-and-in. And then you slide back underwater and kick in relaxed silence until your next breath.

The Dive Physics exam is really a joke. Don't bother trying to study before you get the classes because you'll stress yourself out and you won't learn exactly what they want you to learn. The class is easy. The test is easy. Don't make it harder than it is. If you're at all algebraically inclined you can save yourself even more time by memorizing the Ideal Gas Law:

$PV = nRT$

Pressure x Volume = amount of gas x (the gas constant) x temperature

This is the equation from which all the other gas law equations are derived. Memorize this and, ignoring the gas constant, solve for the variable not given.

Again, if algebra is scary to you, don't worry: you can just memorize the 5 or 6 equations over the week and be just fine. Nobody fails this test. Nobody. The BUD/S-style test-prep right before the test is administered will help catch everyone up. If you fail you simply retake the test until you pass it.

Have a Good Dive Buddy. One of the keys to having a successful Pool Week is having a good dive buddy. A good dive buddy is calm, confident, and easy to work with. Most classes are allowed to choose their own dive buddies. Make sure you get your choice set and agreed upon before the melee starts.

Practice, Bitches. Another key to success in Pool Week is practice. Do dry runs with your buddy. You should know it cold. You should be able to do it in your living room blindfolded with your buddy. Some of the Pool Week dives seem simple, but have small steps that are easy to forget. When you practice, both you and your buddy should say the steps out loud. It might feel gay, but when you're underwater and things are harder/more complicated, you'll be glad for that voice track playing in the back of your head telling you what to do.

Be Overweight. Having an overly-heavy weight belt in Pool

Week is an awesome advantage. You are going to be asked to do a number of procedures underwater that require concentration and a solid breath hold. There is nothing more distracting than having to spend half of your time and effort pushing yourself back down to the bottom of the pool. It wastes time and energy and looks bad to the instructors. Spend some extra money and buy yourself extra dive weights for your belt. I wore a 21 lb belt. Most guys wore between 10 and 15 lbs. During every dive in Pool Week your weight belt will either be around your waist or across the back of your knees. The weight belt is your anchor. Why not invest a little extra money in a stronger anchor for a more solid foundation?

Smooth FSAs.

Move Slowly. Pool Comp is not like the other Pool Week dives - the instructors see it as a last chance to cull the herd, and so there is a lot more subjectivity in Pool Comp. Move slowly. I was failed for my first two Pool Comps not because I messed up the procedures - I did everything right. They failed me within 5 minutes (a typical Pool Comp takes around 20 minutes) because I was moving too fast. They said I looked "panicky" or "uncomfortable in the water." I was not the only one who failed for this. It turned out that I was tracing my hoses and performing my procedures too fast for their comfort. So I slowed down. Way down. Almost too slow. And they were much happier.

Know Procedures Cold. During Pool Comp you will be drowning. You will probably bleed. Your shirt will be torn off you as the instructors grind your face against the pool bottom. Your air hoses will be tied in knots and sometimes ripped off the dive rig. And you will be without air for minutes. And you will have to move slowly to avoid the appearance of discomfort. Through all this, you will be required to perform the procedures perfectly. If you even start to do the wrong procedure, you will fail immediately. Twenty years ago Pool Comp was more violent, but the only way to fail was to surface before it was time. All you had to do was stay underwater and not drown. Times have changed. Know your procedures cold. Know them backwards. Know them forwards. Most importantly: know you know them. Be confident in your knowledge and you'll do just fine.

MRE Advice. You'll be living on MREs for weeks during Second Phase. Get good at them. Try emptying out the big bag and putting all the different parts of the meal into that bag and mashing them to a goo. It sounds gross, but it usually works. Plus, it's faster and easier to eat - saving you time that you can otherwise use for taking a short nap.

Blow it Up. When you're turtle-backing before being told to do your emergency descent, cheat. Inflate your BC (buoyancy control vest) a bit so you don't kill yourself finning. This is what you're going to do at night anyways. Just keep your hand on the release valve, so when you have to go under you can empty it.

Take Your Time. When you're conducting your emergency descent, don't feel the need to get-under-water-right-now-or-you're-gonna-die. Take a second. Get a good deep breath. It'll pay off when shit goes sour underwater.

The Thing in Your Mouth. There is valve on the mouthpiece of the Draeger. When it's closed it prevents water from flooding the rig when the mouthpiece is submerged. When it's open it allows you to breathe on the rig. During a turtleback the valve stays closed as the mouthpiece is hanging around the diver's neck. When the diver conducts an emergency descent, he submerges, puts the mouthpiece in, exhales forcefully to clear the mouthpiece of water, and then opens the valve to breathe. Often the diver is in extreme need of air by the time he opens the valve and it is a terrible stress when the valve requires the full strength of two arms to free it open. Some valves are easy to open and close. Others are hard. Some are broken and thus impossible to use. Sometimes a hard valve can be lubricated and made to be workable. Sometimes students simply trade out valves. The smart student will ensure he and his dive buddy both end up with smooth, easy-operating mouthpiece valves.

* * *

Stay Positive. Breathing Oxygen can cause pronounced irritability. Most BUD/S students are miserable to start with. They're cold, tired, and pissed off. Increasing their tendency to snap at one another can result in some explosive situations. When you're diving twice a day, be prepared to be irrationally short-tempered. Counteract your natural tendency to hate everyone (especially your dive buddy, who will invariably fuck up) by punctuating your dives with jokes. There are a lot of official hand signals for "surface," "descend," and "I'm Okay." There are hand signals for numbers which can be used to remind your dive buddy of distances and bearings for different legs of the dive. My dive buddy and I created a signal that indicated "BIG ASS TITTIES!" to be used as a sign of success. When we hit the right pier, when we placed the "limpet" on the right boat, and when we successfully evaded enemy contact we would stop, face each other, and vigorously fondle our enormous imaginary tits. The "Big Ass Titties" dance always lightened the mood on a dive, no matter how cold or tired we were, and helped us complete the mission in the top few pairs every single dive.

Protect Dive Pair Lists. For each dive the instructor staff requires a dive pair list similar to the swim pair lists required for ocean swims. Medical emergencies and other problems will require the lists prepared from the previous night to be modified only a few minutes before the dive. These changes need to be made in a way that cannot be imitated or denied by any instructor. For example: do not cross a name out in pencil. They will erase it and feign ignorance. If you cross names out, do it in a color you do not provide the instructors on their clipboards. That way you can say, without a doubt, that they fucked with the list. For example, provide a red and a black sharpie for each clipboard, but cross out/write in names in a blue or green pen. If it's not in blue or green, the Instructors made those changes. This is important to remember because my class caught an epic beating for a "fucked up dive pair list that endangered the lives of students while they dove." The real story? An instructor crossed a name out and wrote another name in - making the list wrong. He did it just to beat us.

And so we got wet and sandy in our wetsuits. Then we took off our wetsuits. Then we got wet and sandy in our UDT shorts. Then we put our sandy wetsuits on over our sandy bodies. Then we got beat on the Second Phase Grinder, doing duck-walks and circle pushups on the blistering (literally) hot blacktop. The blacktop was so hot our hands started to burn. It wasn't until 20 minutes into the beating that an instructor got a hose to cool the cement. By that time a majority of us had blistering burns on our hands that took weeks to heal - which was not helped by the fact that we were diving in the extremely-polluted San Diego Bay twice a day. Prevent your instructors from being able to change the dive pair lists and save your class the pain.

Get Good Pornography. Yes, pornography. Your class will be responsible for maintaining the Second Phase Binders. These contain student records, dive sheets, evolution results, and all sorts of documents required for evolutions. It is the responsibility of the class to fill these binders with a rotating selection of pornographic images - amateur photography, of ex-girlfriends and local San Diego girls, is considered top-notch. There is, I guarantee it, at least one porn-fiend in your class. Make him the "Porn Petty Officer" and have him refresh the porn in the binders weekly. The instructors will notice and will spend their spare time "working on the binders" instead of looking for reasons to beat you. Fresh porn = excellent distraction = less beatings.

Second Phase: Don't Be That Guy.

Don't freak out on The Tread. It's easy. If it's not easy, you're doing it wrong. Most of your class will do it right. If you're the one freaking out like a little bitch, they'll remember that. Little bitches don't have good luck getting good dive buddies for Draeger Hell Week.

Don't study for Dive Physics before you're given the classes. They give you all you need to know and nothing you don't. If you study the Navy Dive Manual on your own, you're wasting time you should be using to work out or sleep. Don't be dumb. They give you a BUD/S-style test prep before you take the test and, if you fail, they'll let you retake the test with no consequences.

Don't stress out if you fail a dive evolution or two. Some guys are fixated on being "First Time, Every Time." The guys who actually do this are as lucky as they are good. A lot of the tests are subjective. One tester might pass with one instructor on a worse performance than he failed for on another. You're probably going to fail some evolutions. Take it on the chin, learn what you need to improve, and crush it the next time. Stressing over the almost-inevitable failures is a sure way to increase your chances of failing again. Chill out. You'll be fine.

* * *

Don't fuck your buddy over. This applies to every evolution and to real life, but in this context I mean in Pool Week and on Draeger Dives. During Pool Week practicing with your buddy can make all the difference, but some buddies refuse to practice. Don't do that. Practice until you both feel confident. During Draeger Hell Week a dive pair wins or loses as a pair. Both of you should know every leg and every distance, regardless of who's driving. You never know when the primary navigator's mask might break and the secondary navigator might have to navigate the entire mission. Be prepared. Act as though you're going to be diving alone, so you can take the reins if necessary. And when your buddy is driving, ensure he doesn't have to worry about you. Don't lose focus and start pulling him off course. Your only job is to swim above and beside him. Don't fuck that up and distract him from his job.

Don't take too much time preparing your dive rig. But don't do it so fast you miss a seal and have to do it again.

Don't take out frustrations on your dive buddy. Whatever his mistake, just know that you could be the next one to do it. Don't be ruled by your Oxygen-fueled short temper. Don't make him feel any worse for his fuckups (they will happen) - he already feels bad. If you treat him well during these times, he'll do the same for you when you fuck up.

There is an Irish proverb that says:

"If you dig a grave for others, you might fall into it yourself."

Keep that in mind and you'll be alright.

The primary thing to remember when entering Second Phase is that it's still BUD/S. You may feel on some level that since you've come through First Phase and completed Hell Week, you're going to be treated more humanely. That's a pipe-dream and you'd best kill it now. You may also, in some small corner of your mind, harbor hope that since Second Phase is diving, it might be fun sometimes. Kill that hope.

You will be miserable in Second Phase. You will hate your life.

You see, BUD/S has a magical way of taking all things enjoyable - diving, shooting, working out on the beach - and making them miserable. Try to enjoy what you can when you can, but anticipate being cold, tired, and demoralized the entire time.

Thinking things are going to be fun, or that you're going to enjoy diving in BUD/S, can only get you into trouble. One of my best friends in BUD/S quit during Draeger Hell Week. He crushed First Phase. He passed Pool Comp. But on some level he thought the rest of training would be fun. It was not. He couldn't handle it. He surfaced in the middle of a Draeger Hell Week dive, waved down a safety boat, and quit. He's in the fleet now. Working with computers or something.

Set your expectations appropriately and you won't find yourself maintaining generators deep inside a destroyer someday.

Chapter 12

Third Phase: The Best/Worst Phase Yet.

"Man is disturbed not by things, but by the views he takes of them."

- Mark Aurelius

Third Phase: Key Tasks.

Land Navigation. Land Navigation, or "land nav" as it's referred to, is widely considered to be the best two weeks of BUD/S. The first week takes place at the BUD/S compound in Coronado where the class is taught the fundamentals of map-reading and land navigation. Students are taught how to shoot resections, how to read maps, and how to navigate using the terrain. The classroom instruction usually involves plotting points on a map and making bets among the class to see who's closest. Bets have involved anything from having to eat only wheat bread and cheese the following week to a slap in the face to getting wet and sandy. At the end of the week there's a test. Everyone passes.

After the week of classroom instruction, the class takes off for the Laguna Mountain Recreation Area for a week of practical land navigation. Each day starts with every student being given a set of grid coordinates and being dropped off at one of four starting points. After being dropped off, students plot their points on their maps and head off into the mountains to find them. Each point is marked by a 3-foot tall blue metal post with a dog-tag hanging from it. When a student finds his point, he is to create a pencil-rubbing from the tag to show he was actually there. Having found all his points, he moves to the designated extract area and sets up, hidden from view, to make radio contact with base and wait for extract. Students are usually so well-hidden that female runners have been known to unwittingly change in front of waiting BUD/S students. It's not all fun though. One of my friends had an old lady on a walk drop her shorts right in front of him and take a huge steaming dump not 10 feet from where he was waiting for pickup.

Some nights in Laguna the class will sleep in a "layup position" - an ostensible tactical position with security awake all night. Other nights the class will sleep in camp and eat MREs while the instructors watch movies, BBQ, and drink beer inside their tent. Regardless, Laguna is pleasant. You walk through the mountains by yourself all day long. You rest when you want, you eat when you want. It's quiet and peaceful. Even back at camp the instructors are so happy to be camping out and drinking beer that they fuck with the class very little. Enjoy it. It's the best part of BUD/S and it's followed by the worst part: The Island.

The Island. There is a BUD/S-specific compound on San Clemente Island (also known as "The Island," "The Rock," or "SCI") where BUD/S classes spend their last month of training. While on The Island there are no weekends. Every day is a full training day. There's nobody around to save you and nobody around to temper the instructors.

Pistol Week. Pistol week begins with weapons safety, the disassembly and cleaning of the Sig Sauer P226 handgun, and classes on marksmanship principles. Throughout the week the class will go to the range and engage in a large number of live-fire marksmanship drills, firing hundreds of rounds every day. At the end of the week students will take the Pistol Qualification Test, which is different (and substantially harder) than the standard Navy Pistol Qual. Failures will be given remedial training and re-tested the following day. Failing the re-test results in a roll.

You will be wet the entire week, as any mistake, no matter how small, is punished by a trip to the dip tank just outside the pistol range. The worst part is that guys will be hitting that same small tank all week long. It's the same water - never changed - so by the end of the week the water is foul, like tea steeped from hundreds of sweaty, dirty bodies. And it only gets worse as your month on the Island goes on.

* * *

Rifle Week. Rifle Week is exactly like Pistol Week, except for the M-4 replaces the P226. The M-4s used are equipped only with iron sights - students aren't introduced to optics until SQT. At the end of rifle week students take the Rifle Qualification Test - again harder than the standard Navy equivalent.

Demo Week. Demo Week is the most tense week on The Island because standards are so rigorous. Here students learn the difference between det cord and time trains. They learn how to handle blasting caps, how to use non-electric ("none") leads, how to use claymores and satchel charges, how to build SEAL Standard Charges, cratering charges, shaped charges, cutting charges, and sniper mouse-hole charges.

At the end of Demo Week a BUD/S student will be safe and competent in the handling and use of all basic military-grade explosives. The end of the week is punctuated by a full demo-shot, where students are given free-reign to build whatever types of charges they want and test them. Some students choose to cut down telephone poles, others blast holes in 4" steel with explosively-fired projectiles (EFPs), while others use damping techniques to launch tanks of diesel into the air before detonating them mid-air with a delayed charge.

The final "hooyah" activity of the week is the single instance of underwater demolition in Basic Underwater Demolition/SEAL (BUD/S) training. Classes are directed offshore to a number of underwater obstacles 13-17 feet deep and given 40 lb satchel-charges with which to blow the obstacles. The catch is that these satchel charges have to be in 'intimate contact' with the obstacles. If they are not tied tight enough the charge's energy will not transfer to the obstacle. In order to achieve the required level of contact a rough windlass needs to be created and spun tight. This process take a while, but the satchel charge cannot be left underwater unattended or it will quickly come loose and ride the tides away, so someone always has to be working on it. You dive down, tap out your buddy who surfaces for a breath, and start working. Once your buddy thinks you need relief, he'll swim down and take over so you can surface. This goes on until the satchel is sufficiently tight to guarantee destruction of the obstacle. It can be quite the athletic event, and it's important not to fuck your buddy over by leaving him down there too long without a breath. The resulting explosions shoot plumes of water 30-40m into the air and are permanently etching in the mind of every BUD/S graduate.

Tactics. While on SCI you will also learn the basic tactics of Immediate Action Drills (IADs) and assaults. Immediate Action Drills are how a squad or platoon will react to enemy contact, with multiple units moving in choreographed ways to gain the tactical upper-hand on the enemy. Assaults involve well-controlled target assaults of compounds and buildings. Close-Quarters Combat (CQC) and Urban Combat (SOUC) don't come until SQT or your first workup, respectively.

Combat Conditioning Course. The CCC is a combination of running, swimming, shooting, and obstacle courses done in full combat gear with a full rucksack. The events move from a swim to a run to shooting to a run to an obstacle course (sometimes with CS gas) to a run to a swim to a run to a pull-up finisher. All of these things are done in full combat load. The winners receive prizes like not having to do chow PT. Some losers (and if you're not in the top-5 pairs, you're a loser) have to get wet and sandy. The last losers get to be wet for days at a time: wet on the hour every hour. These guys end up sleeping in the showers to stay warm.

FTX Week. FTX Week begins with FTX Breakout. The instructors sneak up on the class in the early morning, throw smoke grenades and flash-bangs into the barracks rooms, and the class enacts its "respond to contact" drill - a pre-planned defensive posture in the barracks. The goal of the instructors is to shock and scare students into forgetting their rifle shapes in their rooms. After the initial shock and headcount, the class is forced to run to various parts of the camp to get beat. The ultimate line of retreat is the ocean, the path to which is often obscured by a cloud of CS gas. After reaching the ocean and enjoying a little taste of the cold, the class is congratulated and "secured" into FTX Week.

During each day of FTX Week the class is assigned a mission in the morning, plans during the day, briefs the plan in the evening, and executes the mission that night. Missions include rescuing down pilots, killing a high-value individual (HVI), or intercepting a weapons shipment. Some missions insert by boat/OTB while others use simulated helicopters (flatbed trucks). The target areas are populated by role-players (usually white shirts) and instructors there to grade your performance. These missions are mostly fun and are the first taste of what life in the SEAL Teams can be like.

After FTX Week is completed the class has a party with awesome BBQ and, depending on how cool the BUD/S CO is that year, a keg or four of beer. The party is held in the instructors' lounge, called the "Hell Box" that had been strictly off-limits up to that point. This party is the first occasion that instructors and students can socialize without the constant threat of violence.

Graduation. Once the class gets back to The Strand (which is what Team Guys call Coronado), all that remains is gear turn-in and a small graduation ceremony. BUD/S graduation is not open to the public. Your parents (unless one of them is a Team Guy) will not be there. You will stand in formation in your cammies with your class on the grinder, the BUD/S Commanding Officer will speak to you, the instructors will award the Honor Man plaque (your BUD/S valedictorian), you'll receive your BUD/S certificate, shake hands with the instructors who are there, and you're done.

Third Phase: TTPs.

Terrain Navigation. Ensure that you have a good grasp of terrain navigation before you head to Laguna. If you can easily reconcile contour lines on a map with actual terrain, you will do just fine in Laguna. If you have a difficult time, get as much extra time with a map as you can until you intuitively see the terrain as it's drawn on a map. Once you grasp the idea, you'll be able to see the terrain by looking at a map. Then you can look up and see what matches what and be able to walk right up to your points.

Pacing Your Points. At Laguna you have 8 hours to get 7 points and reach your extract site. This means that you have 1 hour to find each point and an hour to reach your pickup location. You can easily walk from one point to another in 45 minutes. If you hustle, it's usually around 30 minutes. Don't run, walk. If you regularly take 45 minutes to find your point you'll be able to spare an extra 30 minutes to find a difficult point. Keep track of the times, however, and be prepared to skip a point if you spend too much time on it. You don't need 100% of the points to pass. You can get 4 of 7 on the first day, 5 of 7 on the second day, and 6 of 7 on the third day and still pass. Obviously you don't want to get near those numbers: it's best to get all your points. But you can absolutely afford to skip one point if you're spending too much time on it and it's proving impossible.

* * *

Walking Snacks. At Laguna I found I never wanted to stop and eat a full MRE meal. I would stop and sit down for 5 minutes after every point I found. That was enough. I could drop my ruck and give my shoulders and legs a rest while I downed some water and replaced snacks I'd eaten on that last walk. I sustained myself through the day by eating granola bars, drinking water, and savoring rehydration snacks like Sharkies or GU Chomps. These snacks help your body stay hydrated and I would ration them out during the day and suck on them (instead of chewing) to make them last. I strongly recommend a supply of these to keep your energy up in Laguna.

Extra Supplies. Bring Chapstick (with SPF), sunscreen, and bug spray to Laguna. A small thing of sunscreen and a small thing of bug spray will suffice - you have to carry them so keep your weight down. These will make your life walking through the woods that much better. And some of your boys will forget them, so you can share with them too.

Island Wakeup. Bring a watch whose alarm is guaranteed to wake you up. Oversleeping is bad news on The Island. Test it before you bring it, because you'll be sleeping heavily and making sure your fire-team is up on time could well fall to your responsibility.

Warmies. Bring as many poly-pro warmies, both tops and bottoms, as you can. If you don't need them, someone else will. These will keep you warm even when you're soaking wet and are the single most important piece of gear you have with you. I'm going to repeat this: your poly-pro warms are the single most important piece of optional gear you're going to have on The Island. You can even wear them under your cammies and nobody will know. If you ever have to spend the night on Camp Stupid, you'll find that you'll even be able to sleep if you wear poly-pros under your cammies. I feel like they saved my life. They certainly let me sleep when sleep would have been otherwise impossible. And sleep is gold in BUD/S.

* * *

Don't Forget Shit. Other necessary items students often forget to bring to the island are toothbrush, toothpaste, towel, soap, flip-flops, and Chapstick. A sleeping bag is also highly recommended, as is a pillow. Otherwise you'll be sleeping under piled-up clothes on a bare mattress. If you can get ahold of a poncho-liner or two you can tie these down over your bed and add to your warmth and cleanliness. You will not have the option of going to the store to buy these things, so don't forget them. The instructors - probably just your proctor - will occasionally collect money to get needed items from the one store on the other side of the island, but this is rare and should not be counted on.

Bring Cash. I would recommend bringing $40-$100 in cash to give to your proctor for if (when) you or one of your guys needs something. Some proctors will even bring cans of dip for guys who ask, so you know you'll be popular if you can buy a log of dip to share with the boys.

Use Your Time Well. There will be times when you're locked in a classroom and told to dry-fire your pistol. These times can last for hours. Dry-firing gets boring after 10 minutes. Be disciplined and continue to practice. This work pays off. You will not enjoy it, but you'll enjoy the results. Just remember that "smooth is fast." Focus on building muscle memory.

Take Care of Your Boys. Look out for your classmates. If one of your guys is forced to sleep on the beach or get wet every hour on the hour, look out for him. Make sure he's got enough warmies. Bring him some food and water. Take care of him.

Clean Your Guns Quickly. There is no need to spend 2 hours cleaning your weapons every night. Take them apart. Wipe them down. Get the bolt clean. Light lube. Back together. Anything more than this is masturbatory and wastes valuable time you could be sleeping.

Check the Frog. There is a large bronze frog on top of "Frog

Hill." You'll know it well because you have to put it up there when you get to The Island and chow PT is often running up Frog Hill. Have someone get up an hour early every day to ensure it's still there. There is a Team Guy compound on SCI and Team Guys love to fuck with BUD/S Students. It's not an uncommon thing for them to kidnap the Frog and move it somewhere or rearrange the white rocks that spell out your class number into a choice four-letter word. Your class will get beat for such antics, as is the BUD/S way. So have someone get up every morning early enough to check the Frog and the class number. That way you'll have enough time to fix things before the instructors wake up. If all is well, then they can go right back to sleep.

Make Crazy Fucking Bets. Instructors will often give the class an opportunity to get out of a beating or a Chow PT by winning a bet. The bets are always tilted in the Instructors' favor, but they're often still winnable. Sometimes these bets involve doing a certain task quickly after eating a can of dip, or after taking a shot of tabasco, or naked. The more ridiculous the bet, the better off you are. You see, the instructors are bored as fuck. If you do something hilarious or impressive, they're much more likely to take it easy on you because you've eased their boredom - even if you ultimately lose. If you bet like a little bitch, they'll just want to crush you. So bet big and bold and win. Running Frog Hill naked for time after eating a can of dip and doing a shot of Tabasco can get you some serious credit. I know because I've seen it and it worked.

Third Phase: Don't Be That Guy.

Don't set your bag down in Laguna. Your ruck is heavy. It holds a huge HF radio, MREs, and a good amount of water. It's tempting to set it down in order to climb a hill or descend a ravine to a point and then come back to it.

Do not do this.

It happens every other class: someone does this and finds that he can't locate his bag again because all the terrain looks the same. Beyond this, though, there are Instructors out there. You won't see them, but they'll see you. They'll set up on hilltops with spotting scopes and wait to see you drop your ruck against a tree and run to a point and back. You'll think you got away with it until you get back and the hammer drops. Trust me when I tell you it's not worth it.

Not only is an unnecessary luxury - which is a sin in BUD/S - but it also has real-life implications. Overseas you cannot leave a radio out of your sight for a moment. Radios are more closely guarded than are weapons. They always have a watch on them. If someone loses one overseas, the entire COUNTRY has to reset its crypto. This is a huge deal. So learn right from the start: don't ever leave your radio unattended.

Don't leave your life on the mainland a mess. When you go to The Island, you will be 100% out of communication with your life back home for a month. Do not leave your life at home a mess or in question. The Island is stressful enough without worrying about whether your girlfriend maxed out your credit card while getting the train run on her by a platoon of Marines.

Don't get too negative. It's easy to get bitter by Third Phase. You're obviously not going to quit, so why are the Instructors still assholes? Why are they still beating you? You want to learn these skills. You want to master your rifle and your pistol and explosives. You don't need them making things dumber by sending you to the dip tank. You wish these sadistic faggot instructors would just leave you in peace to work on your skills. In fact the beatings and dip-tank trips directly take away from your range time - effectively making you worse. It's easy to hate them and to be miserable. Don't let them get to you. It's just BUD/S. Do some ridiculous bets. Get what laughs you can. You're almost done with BUD/S, so fuck it. You'll learn still. And you're not even close to done with your professional training.

Don't let your guard down. Classes regularly get beat after they get back from SCI but before they graduate. Don't think that because you're back from The Island you're safe. Oftentimes instructors will look to it as a last chance to teach you humility. You're never safe. On the bus-ride back from Laguna the Instructors decided we had too much energy, and scheduled a 4-mile timed beach run for 15 minutes after we got back. It was night and the tide was in, making the beach terrible to run on. We did it anyways. We had thought we were done for the weekend, but we had been wrong. You're not safe from capricious instructors until you walk off the Grinder at Graduation.

Third Phase: Mark's Parting Words of Wisdom.

Third Phase is a mixture of the best and worst of BUD/S. You get to shoot guns and blow shit up, but you have to live on a small, secluded island with a bunch of sadistic and violent instructors. But if you made it that far, you know how to deal with adversity and you can endure any level of hardship. The only thing about Third Phase that will truly strike you to the bone is that, after the graduation ceremony, you can walk off the Grinder.

Throughout BUD/S you've been conditioned to run everywhere. You never walk. Ever. If an Instructor can see you, he'd better see you sprinting.

The moment you graduate, however, you can walk across the grinder without fear of repercussion. You haven't earned much yet. You're not a SEAL by any means. But you have earned the right to walk and to look SEAL Instructors in the eye and talk to them without fearing them anymore.

After 6 months of Hell, that's good enough for now. In fact, it's everything.

Additional Content

Appendices, Lists, etc.

"The connecting is the thinking."
- William James

Additional Content: On SQT.

I'm not going to go into depth on SEAL Qualification Training (SQT) because this book is about BUD/S. Besides, there are a number of classified techniques taught in SQT; nothing in BUD/S is classified.

SQT is also called "The Finishing School" because it's the real Navy SEAL training. BUD/S is a 6-month gut-check to make sure you want to be there. SQT turns you into a SEAL and awards you the Trident on completion. But don't think the gut-checks are over. SQT Students often call SQT "Fourth Phase" for a reason. Training blocks in SQT include:

- Cold Weather Training in Kodiak, AK.
- Land Warfare in Niland, CA
- CQC in La Posta, CA
- Maritime Operations (MAROPS) and Combat Diving in San Diego, CA
- Close-Quarters Defense (hand-to-hand) and NSW SERE in Imperial Beach, CA
- Static Line, HALO, and HAHO Freefall Jumping in Jamul, CA

After SQT graduation students will attend language training before reporting to their first command.

Additional Content: Reading List.

Required Reading.
The Warrior Elite - Dick Couch.
The Finishing School - Dick Couch.
Warrior Soul - Chuck Pfarrer
Men in Green Faces - Gene Wentz and B. Abell Jurus
Gates Of Fire - Stephen Pressfield
Man's Search For Meaning - Victor Frankyl

Optional Reading.
No Easy Day - Mark Owen
Suffer In Silence - David Reid
Navy SEALs: The Complete History - Kevin Dockery
Death in the Jungle - Gary Smith and Alan Maki
The Element of Surprise - Darryl Young
Rogue Warrior - Richard Marcinko
American Sniper - Chris Kyle
The Only Easy Day Was Yesterday - Richard Schoenberg
Catch-22 - Joseph Heller
The Naked and the Dead - Norman Mailer

The General Orders of a Sentry:

1. To take charge of this post and all government property in view.

2. To walk my post in a military manner, keeping always on the alert, and observing everything that takes place within sight or hearing.

3. To report all violations of orders I am instructed to enforce.

4. To repeat all calls from posts more distant from the guard house than my own.

5. To quit my post only when properly relieved.

6. To receive, obey and pass on to the sentry who relieves me, all orders from the Commanding Officer, Command Duty Officer, Officer of the Deck, and Officers and Petty Officers of the Watch only.

7. To talk to no one except in the line of duty.

8. To give the alarm in case of fire or disorder.

9. To call the Officer of the Deck in any case not covered by instructions.

10. To salute all officers and all colors and standards not cased.

11. To be especially watchful at night, and, during the time for challenging, to challenge all persons on or near my post and to allow no one to pass without proper authority.

The Code of Conduct.

(1) I am an American, fighting in the forces which guard my country and our way of life. I am prepared to give my life in their defense.

(2) I will never surrender of my own free will. If in command, I will never surrender the members of my command while they still have the means to resist.

(3) If I am captured, I will continue to resist by all means available. I will make every effort to escape and aid others to escape. I will accept neither parole nor special favors from the enemy.

(4) If I become a prisoner of war, I will keep faith with my fellow prisoners. I will give no information or take part in any action which might be harmful to my comrades. If I am senior, I will take command. If not, I will obey the lawful orders of those appointed over me, and will back them up in every way.

(5) When questioned, should I become a prisoner of war, I am required to give only my name, rank, service number, and date of birth. I will evade answering further questions to the utmost of my ability. I will make no oral or written statements disloyal to my country and its allies or harmful to their cause.

(6) I will never forget that I am an American, fighting for freedom, responsible for my actions, and dedicated to the principles which made my country free. I will trust in my God and in the United States of America.

Additional Content: 10 Commandments For BUD/S.

1. Thou shalt never quit.
2. Thou shalt never feel sorry for thyself.
3. Thou shalt carry thine own weight.
4. Thou shalt never be a buddy-fucker.
5. Thou shalt put out.
6. Thou shalt put team before self.
7. Thou shalt not be a pussy.
8. Thou shalt never be late.
9. Thou shalt always have the right gear.
10. Thou shalt not get into any trouble when alcohol is present.

The SEAL Code

Loyalty to Country, Team and Teammate
Serve with Honor and Integrity On and Off the Battlefield
Ready to Lead, Ready to Follow, Never Quit
Take responsibility for your actions and the actions of your teammates
Excel as Warriors through Discipline and Innovation
Train for War, Fight to Win, Defeat our Nation's Enemies
Earn your Trident everyday

United States Navy SEAL Ethos

1.   In times of war or uncertainty there is a special breed of warrior ready to answer our Nation's call; common men with uncommon desire to succeed.   Forged by adversity, they stand alongside America's finest special operations forces to serve their country, the American people, and protect their way of life. We are those men.

2.   Our Trident is a symbol of honor and heritage.   Bestowed upon us by the heroes that have gone before, it embodies the trust of those we have sworn to protect.   By wearing the Trident we accept the responsibility of our chosen profession and way of life. It is a privilege that we must earn every day.

3.   Our loyalty to Country and Team is beyond reproach.   We humbly serve as a guardian to our fellow Americans always ready to defend those who are unable to defend themselves. We do not advertise the nature of our work, nor seek recognition for our actions.   We voluntarily accept the inherent hazards of our profession, placing the welfare and security of others before our own.

4. We serve with honor on and off the battlefield. The ability to

control our emotions and our actions, regardless of circumstance, sets us apart from other men. Uncompromising integrity is our standard. Our character and honor are steadfast. Our word is our bond.

5. We expect to lead and be led. In the absence of orders we will take charge, lead our teammates and accomplish the mission. We lead by example in all situations.

6. We will never quit. We persevere and thrive on adversity. Our Nation expects us to be physically harder and mentally stronger than our enemies. If knocked down, we will get back up, every time. We will draw on every remaining ounce of strength to protect our teammates and to accomplish our mission. We are never out of the fight.

7. We demand discipline. We expect innovation. The lives of our teammates and the success of our mission depend on us - our technical skill, tactical proficiency, and attention to detail. Our training is never complete.

8. We train for war and fight to win. We stand ready to bring the full spectrum of combat power to bear in order to achieve our mission and the goals established by our country. The execution of our duties will be swift and violent when required yet guided by the very principles that we serve to defend.

9. Brave men have fought and died building the proud tradition and feared reputation that we are bound to uphold. In the worst of conditions, the legacy of our teammates steadies our resolve and silently guides our every deed. **We will not fail.**

CPSIA information can be obtained at www.ICGtesting.com
Printed in the USA
LVOW12s2208120114

369156LV00005B/314/P